Knowledge Communication in Global Organisations

While organisations become more and more global, they also become more and more dispersed and virtual. This challenges the sense of a shared organisational identity and the ability of employees to communicate personally held knowledge. To address these challenges, this book offers an innovative multidisciplinary approach to knowledge communication in global organisations. The book develops a multidisciplinary analytical lens through which to understand employee identity formations and knowledge communication practises. Using detailed analyses of interviews from a real organisation, the book builds an understanding of how 21st-century employees make sense of a virtual organisational reality characterised by multiple simultaneous projects and virtual, dispersed teams. These analyses are conducted using a new discourse analysis method for analysing research interviews, Discursive Sensemaking Analysis. Using these methods and findings, researchers, project managers and HR professionals will be able to analyse their own organisations to discover how employees make sense of the complexity of 21st-century global organisations.

Nils Braad Petersen holds a PhD in Business Communicating from Aarhus University, Denmark. He can be contacted at NilsBraad@gmail.com.

Routledge Studies in Management, Organizations and Society

This series presents innovative work grounded in new realities, addressing issues crucial to an understanding of the contemporary world. This is the world of organized societies, where boundaries between formal and informal, public and private, local and global organizations have been displaced or have vanished, along with other nineteenth century dichotomies and oppositions. Management, apart from becoming a specialized profession for a growing number of people, is an everyday activity for most members of modern societies.

Similarly, at the level of enquiry, culture and technology, and literature and economics, can no longer be conceived as isolated intellectual fields; conventional canons and established mainstreams are contested. *Management, Organizations and Society* addresses these contemporary dynamics of transformation in a manner that transcends disciplinary boundaries, with books that will appeal to researchers, students and practitioners alike.

Recent titles in this series include:

Business Groups and Strategic Coopetition
Edited by Wioletta Mierzejewska and Patryk Dziurski

Flexible Human Resource Management and Vocational Behaviour
The Employability Market Orientation Model
Anna Pawłowska

Knowledge Communication in Global Organisations
Making Sense of Virtual Teams
Nils Braad Petersen

For more information about this series, please visit: https://www.routledge.com/Routledge-Studies-in-Genocide-and-Crimes-against-Humanity/book-series/RSGCH

Knowledge Communication in Global Organisations

Making Sense of Virtual Teams

Nils Braad Petersen

Routledge
Taylor & Francis Group
NEW YORK AND LONDON

First published 2023
by Routledge
605 Third Avenue, New York, NY 10158

and by Routledge
4 Park Square, Milton Park, Abingdon, Oxon, OX14 4RN

Routledge is an imprint of the Taylor & Francis Group, an informa business

Library of Congress Cataloging-in-Publication Data
Names: Petersen, Nils Braad, author.
Title: Knowledge communication in global organisations : making sense of virtual teams / Nils Braad Petersen.
Description: 1 Edition. | New York, NY : Routledge, 2023. | Series: Routledge studies in management, organizations and society | Includes bibliographical references and index.
Identifiers: LCCN 2022035148 | ISBN 9780367857950 (hardback) | ISBN 9781032419701 (paperback) | ISBN 9781003015925 (ebook)
Subjects: LCSH: Virtual work teams—Management. | Telecommunication—Social aspects. | Knowledge, Sociology of. | International business enterprises. | Communication in organizations. | Organizational change.
Classification: LCC HD66 .P4288 2023 | DDC 658.4/022—dc23/eng/20220721
LC record available at https://lccn.loc.gov/2022035148

ISBN: 978-0-367-85795-0 (hbk)
ISBN: 978-1-032-41970-1 (pbk)
ISBN: 978-1-003-01592-5 (ebk)

DOI: 10.4324/9781003015925

Typeset in Bembo
by codeMantra

Contents

Illustrations

Figures

Tables

1 Introduction

Chapter Contents

> Virtual work environments allow organizations to build cross-boundary teams consisting of members located in different countries and allow employees to work out of the office to be closer to clients who are not located near the head office. A survey cited by Gilson et al. (2015) found that approximately 66% of multinational organisations used virtual teams in 2015. Only three years later, Gupta and Pathak (2018) found that the figure for knowledge workers working virtually was nearly 80%. At the same time, employees are often involved in several projects and teams.

But that evolution comes with its challenges; Espinosa et al. (2003) argue that a lack of identification may occur when employee commitment is spread over several teams and projects, and that this challenges commitment to the team and the effectiveness of the team. Furthermore, Spinuzzi (2004) argues that technology not only shapes social structures, but changes mental models. That's nothing new; technologies have always required new mental models and new practices, regardless whether we're talking about the invention of agriculture, the invention of the printing press or the invention of the internet.

But what are the characteristics of the mental models which adapt the easiest to this new virtual, multi-team work environment? And what does it mean for communication of knowledge in global organisations. These are the core questions explored in this book.

According to Espinosa et al. (2003), research on virtual teams (aka 'hybrid', 'dispersed' or 'distributed teams') seems to have overemphasised

DOI: 10.4324/9781003015925-1

the temporal and geographical boundaries while neglecting identity boundaries in virtual organisations. Although almost 20 years have passed since their paper was published, this still seems to hold true.

Furthermore, few studies in the literature on virtual teams look beyond the team to take into account the complexity of this virtual team work environment where multiple team membership and projects compete for employee work attention. Nor does the existing literature identify how the mediation of technology shapes and changes the mental models and the communication practices.

Furthermore, Gilson et al. (2015) found that only 43% of the 441 articles in their literature review used real-life case studies. This challenges the findings making them difficult to apply in real 21st century global organisations. This study therefore uses an organisational case study to focus on how employees in a real organisation communicate knowledge, and how they use online and off-line relationships to build and sustain coherent professional identities in the virtual work environment of a global organisation. I have given this global organisation the alias, 'HR Consult'.

This is but one case, but a rich and detailed one at that. It's also a critical case in that the corporate strategy discourages the kind of virtual knowledge communication practices I found among a handful of employees. If this type of deep, complex knowledge communication occurs in an organisation which discourages it, then it is likely to occur in other organisations with more lenient knowledge management practices (cp. Flyvbjerg, 2006).

Furthermore, this book seeks to fill these gaps in the literature by developing a multidisciplinary analytical lens through which to understand organisational Identity Prototypes[1].

Using detailed analyses of interviews from a real organisation, the book thus offers a new multidisciplinary approach for understanding how 21st-century employees make sense of a virtual organisational reality and how they communicate knowledge across geographical and professional boundaries. The findings in this book identify three Identity Configurations at HR Consult which differed in two key areas:

1 Their perception of organisational knowledge, and
2 The level of autonomy in their approach to organisational strategy.

To analyse these Identity Configurations in depth, three interview participants were selected as prototypical examples. Those interviews were analysed using my multidisciplinary discourse analysis approach, which I term Discursive Sensemaking Analysis (DSA). This should not be confused with Berente's (2011) use of the term Discursive Sensemaking to describe a focus on the structure of arguments in discourse production.

DSA Combines Weick's (1995, 2001) and Weick et al.'s (2005) theories of how people retrospectively make sense of their actions with

Discourse Analysis tools from James Paul Gee's discourse analysis method (2011, 2014) and linguistic level analysis of prosody (Cheng & Lam, 2011; Drew & Heritage, 1992), discourse markers (Schiffrin, 1988) and to a lesser extent grammatical and lexical choices (Halliday & Hasan, 1976/2014).

My findings suggest that employees with professional identities which may be marginalised in co-located organisational contexts, find a social basis for their identity in online, virtual networks of employees with similar professional identities and approaches to organisational knowledge.

These findings impact on virtual knowledge communication practices. Thus awareness among employees and managers of different Identity Configurations may help design better strategies and processes for utilising the strengths of different professional identities when organising and managing virtual teams. A failure by both employees and management to recognise differences in approaches may also present a barrier to the efficiency of knowledge communication at both team and organisational levels. The importance of intra-organisational knowledge communication and creation (i.e. innovation) to ensure competitive advantage in the current economy may be the most oft cited claim in the proliferate knowledge management literature over the past three decades (e.g. Gerard, 2001; Nonaka & Takeuchi, 1995; Virtanen, 2010).

Therefore, organisations need to understand and listen to the shift in professional identities and employee Sensemaking discourse. The shift in professional identity and discourse seems to co-occur with the shift towards a more virtual organisational architecture.

To briefly situate the study within this virtual work environment, the following section outlines three tendencies emerging in current organisational architecture, and the implications for professional identities and the communication of organisational knowledge. This will be followed by the research aims of the study. I then outline the key characteristics of each of the Identity Prototypes which represent the three configurations of professional identities identified at HR Consult.

Three tendencies in the current organisational architecture

The book uses a case study to exemplify the arguments. The case study of HR Consult represents a virtual work environment, which can be seen as an example of a tendency towards an increasingly complex work environment in the organisational architecture of global organisations. This complex work environment entails three tendencies:

1 The tendency for employees to work in multiple teams and on multiple projects simultaneously complicates the maintenance of strong social relations within the individual team (Espinosa et al., 2003).

2 The current ubiquity of Information and Communication Technology (ICT) means that ICT is a mediator of most organisational communication (Al-Ani et al., 2011; Assudani, 2011; Schulze & Krumm, 2017).
3 There seems to be a tendency towards more virtual organisations where some employees are co-located and some are remotely located.

The first tendency towards multi-team, multi-project commitments of employees is evident at the three local offices of HR Consult, and has been identified in other cases from, for example, the IT sector (Daim et al., 2012) and the construction sector (Rezgui, 2007). Mortensen et al. (2007) found that 65% of the 401 respondents in 'junior to middle-level staff members' (p. 218), worked in more than one team at a time, and that a majority of these were cross-functional (67%) and/or inter-organisational (54%), while 34% were also internationally dispersed.

The first tendency implies that the challenge to team identity and the building of team relations needs to be addressed, because strong relations have been identified as a prerequisite for the communication of complex knowledge (Hansen, 1999). The communication of knowledge is a key component of team success, particularly in service sector organisations such as the one examined in this study.

The second tendency, towards technology ubiquity, means that all employees of global organisations are connected through a variety of technologies, including e-mails, intranet and Teams in addition to more conventional forms such as telephones and face-to-face interaction. This tendency can be found in all organisational sectors as evidenced by The Economist Intelligence Unit (2009) who found that 318 out of 407 respondents worked in 'some form of virtual team' (p. 1). This tendency towards ICT as mediator in most organisational communication seems to hold true even for co-located employees. For example, the co-located employees at my Danish case site reported that they often use email or phone when communicating with employees situated on a different floor or in a neighbouring building. Assudani (2011) and Al-Ani et al. (2011) found similar usage of ICT at their case organisations.

The second tendency means that the study of virtual teams is no longer a niche in management, business studies or information systems studies. Spinuzzi's (2004) argument that technology not only shapes social structures, but changes mental models is important, because few studies examine how employees' mental models, including their professional identities and construction of professional relationships, change the way organisational knowledge is communicated in global organisations.

The third tendency towards increased dispersion of organisations can be seen as a consequence of ICT ubiquity: outsourcing. Particularly within the software sector, outsourcing often implies cross-national, cross-cultural knowledge work leading to specific challenges of differences in understandings of shared concepts (Lehtonen & Kampf, 2014) and power hierarchies between co-located and outsourced staff (Nayak & Taylor, 2009).

Nevertheless, the tendency towards increased dispersion can also be seen in other sectors where outsourcing is not involved. For example, business-to-business consultancy services place employees closer to current or potential clients when clients are geographically dispersed. This tendency can both be seen in the literature on virtual teams (e.g. Breu & Hemingway, 2004), and at my case company's offices in Denmark and the UK. At the Danish office, employees are spread across two physical locations, because the main site was too remote for clients in east Denmark area; and at HR Consult UK, individual members of their so-called Direct Channel Team are spread across the UK to be physically closer to their clients.

An implication of the third tendency seems to be a raised level of autonomy and self-management, because unified corporate strategies may be difficult to implement in a virtual organisational architecture and managers are far away physically and mentally. This again requires a different mind-set or mental model. Yet few studies examine what this increased employee autonomy means for knowledge communication in global organisations.

Research aims evolving through iterations between theory and practice

The research aims of the project have evolved as the project progressed. Moving between theory, empirical findings and critical reflection sparked this evolution of the project. This section briefly outlines the trajectory of the research aims, thereby providing justification for the selection of theory in the book.

This project started with a vague notion that some of the most prevalent knowledge management theories building on the seminal works of Nonaka and Takeuchi (1995) and Wenger (1998) seemed to neglect theorising on individual motivations for attempting to communicate knowledge. Within an organisational context, the flow of knowledge between employees and the evolution of that knowledge into new products and services is a key economic success factor as clearly demonstrated by the cases presented by Nonaka and Takeuchi (1995).

However, intuitively I thought trust-based relationships were more important than the knowledge management literature suggested, because trust can function as a screen, or filter, which helps decide whether to accept or reject new knowledge, or whether to attempt to communicate personally held knowledge to others. Trust can therefore be seen as a mediator that helps individuals and groups decide whether to accept a knowledge source as reliable, valid and useful, and whether your own self-interests might be hurt by sharing your own hard won insights with a specific group or person.

As my literature review into interpersonal trust in virtual organisational contexts progressed, this intuition was confirmed. Several sources found covariance between trust and knowledge sharing, e.g. Staples and Webster (2008). Nandhakumar and Baskerville (2006) conclude that trust can be seen as both an antecedent and outcome of knowledge sharing.

A positive outcome of a trusting relationship could be development of knowledge or the receipt of new useful knowledge in return. 'Useful' here is both an individual and a social construct; knowledge perceived as 'useful' by one person or group may be irrelevant to another. Therefore, at this stage my theoretical aims of the project focussed on combining knowledge management theory with relationship theory from applied psychology.

Another research aim from the outset of the project was to build a research design which took into account the current trajectory of organisational contexts towards the three tendencies outlined in the previous section. The selection of HR Consult reflects this aim, because the company is present in 30 countries, and the local offices only had some co-located employees; other employees were dispersed within the individual countries. At the same time, each employee was engaged in several teams and projects simultaneously, again reflecting the tendencies identified in the previous section.

The book therefore aims to examine how this virtual, multi-team organisational work environment affects the knowledge communication between employees. This research aim reflects Spinuzzi's (2004) argument that the mediation of technology in human relations changes mental models. My research aim with regard to technology is not to examine technology explicitly, but to examine how, employees communicate knowledge and build the relationships needed to do so when ICT mediates and supports most organisational relationships.

Alongside my ongoing review of the literature and narrowing of my research aims, I started conducting interviews in the case company. Details about the data collection and analysis can be found in Chapter 4. I mention it here, because the findings from the first few interviews and more informal interactions with employees and managers at HR Consult suggested that professional identities played a much larger role than I had expected. Furthermore, the virtual work environment seemed to be used actively by employees to build networks with colleagues with similar perceptions of organisational knowledge and similar professional identities attached to those perceptions of knowledge. I therefore found a need to review identity theory and to combine this in a multidisciplinary theoretical lens encompassing knowledge theory, identity theory and relationship theory in addition to my ongoing review of literature on case studies of virtual teams.

My research aim with this multidisciplinary theoretical lens is to build a holistic and coherent lens to analyse the cognitive and relational processes that influence knowledge communication in global organisations. The analytical lens therefore spans the humanities (linguistic theories), social sciences (relationships and identity theories), business studies (knowledge management theories) and information systems (virtual team theory).

As participants told about their practices, they also justified these practices with reference to the values and practices they tried to live up to, to be successful. These practices and the values attached to them seemed to form the basis for configurations of professional identities. Identity Configurations emerged as employees identified and justified their practices and values with reference to colleagues who shared similar professional identities. At the same time, they dissociated their own practices and values from the practices and values of other employees. Therefore, as interviews progressed, configurations of professional identities began to emerge.

These configurations went far beyond the set of 21 participants in the project, as participants mentioned other teams, networks and individuals within and beyond the organisation whom they either identified themselves with or distinguished themselves from. For all three Identity Configurations, ICT was used to stay connected to virtual members met at the infrequent global organisational conferences. Often virtual members introduced new members into the virtual community, based on their similar professional identities.

However, employees were not always connected with other members of an Identity Configuration. Instead, the shared identity of an Identity Configuration can be seen as a mental model or 'Prototype' which employees try to adhere to in their practices, and through which they justify and make sense of their past practices.

The research aims therefore changed to reflect these early findings, as well as to reflect the trajectory of the current labour market in the direction of the three tendencies outlined in the previous section. Because the participants in more recent virtual teams studies, such as Al-Ani et al. (2011), Assudani (2011) and Schulze and Krumm (2017) did not problematise technology but saw it as a mediator of all organisational relations, co-located or otherwise, I chose not to focus on technology specifically, but on how employees make sense of the virtual, multi-team environment in which they work. Nonetheless, because the context of the inquiry is virtual, ICTs always play a role.

The research aim can therefore be condensed to:

> Examining how different employee perceptions of organisational knowledge are reflected in different configurations of professional identity in a virtual work environment of a global organisation.

This overall aim can be divided into three parts:

1 Building a multidisciplinary theoretical lens to enable analysis of the interplay of employee perceptions of knowledge, identity and relationships in a global organisation. This allows a holistic approach to analysing the impact of the three tendencies on the knowledge communicating practices.
2 Examine how employees maintain a coherent sense of identity in the organisation in the absence of more clearly defined co-located relationships.
3 Examine what the configurations of professional identity formations mean for the ways organisational knowledge is communicated among employees.

The next section will define what is meant by 'configurations of professional identity', and how such 'Identity Configurations' are linked to identity 'Prototypes'.

A note on terminology: 'Identity Configuration' and 'Identity Prototype'

I will adopt the term 'Identity Configuration' in the book to describe employees with:

- Similar perceptions of knowledge,
- Similar professional identity and
- Similar use of relationships to support their practices and identities.

When employees differ in their perceptions of one of these three aspects, they will, for analytical purposes, be seen as belonging to different professional Identity Configurations. When I use the term 'analytical', I mean that the members of an Identity Configuration do not necessarily know all the other members, but they still share a common professional identity.

Relationships can be seen as fulfilling two purposes both of which impact on virtual knowledge communication: first, they provide a social foundation for employees' perception of knowledge thereby also supporting their professional identity through joint Sensemaking with colleagues. Second, relationships can be seen as supporting similar knowledge communication practices of the Identity Configuration.

The term 'Identity Prototype' will be adopted in the book to describe employees who can be seen as epitomising the key characteristics of a particular Identity Configuration. Providing more detail about what these 'characteristics' consist of, Jansen and Roodt (2014) offer a definition of Identity Prototypes:

> The Prototype is the interrelated set of perceptions, attitudes, feelings, and behaviour that captures similarities among in-group members and differences between in-group members and outgroup members'
> (pp. 118–119)

This definition includes both cognitive aspects, such as 'attitudes and feelings', and social aspects in the form of 'behaviour'. Behaviour, as a reflection of cognitive processes of identity formation, will be theorised further in the presentation of Weick's (1995, 2001) theory of 'Sensemaking' (Chapter 2), while identity theory will be reviewed in Chapter 8.

The book builds on the analysis of research interviews, and I offer analyses of these interviews as examples throughout part II of the book. I see interviews as a dialogue in which employees (re)present themselves and their practices in the light of their preferred Identity Prototype. Research interviews can therefore be seen as idealised, retrospective accounts representing the social contexts described from the perspective of the interview participant's mental model.

Identity Prototypes can be seen as one such mental model (Jansen & Roodt, 2014), while participants' perspective on the organisational contexts described can be seen as another mental model, or more specifically a 'Context Model' (Van Dijk, 2005). Context models can be shared or individually held:

> Indeed we may assume that the more situations are formal, normative and institutional, the more the context models of participants will be similar and overlapping, whereas the more informal situations may be more idosyncratic.
> (van Dijk, 2006, pp. 172–173)

Because the book sees identity as both a cognitive and a social process, distinctly different configurations of identity can be seen as represented by individuals who can be seen as 'Prototypes' of such Identity Configurations. Each Identity Configuration shares similar knowledge communication practices, similar perceptions of organisational knowledge, and similar interpretations of organisational practice and strategy. These shared identities are reflected in the relationships they build and the values they attach to these relationships.

I do not argue that three Identity Configuration which I identified at HR Consult are universal or even that they are the only ones at HR Consult, but rather that they can be used as point of reference for examining configurations of similar and other identities in other organisations.

Brief introduction to the three Identity Prototypes

As the analysis of my data progressed, three distinctly different approaches to the work as consultants at HR Consult emerged. Interview participants' stories about their practices and occasional reflections on those practices could be seen as reflecting the values underlying these approaches to the job.

Similarly, participants often criticised values associated with one or both of the other Identity Configurations. Thus, in telling stories about past and current virtual team projects, employees construct heroes and villains, and often they end their story with a concluding morale. It is these Sensemaking morales, which will take centre stage in the case studies analysed throughout Part 2 of the book.

I've been asked why I rarely quote my question before quoting a participant. The answer is that there was no direct question; I asked participants to tell about virtual team projects, both successful ones and less successful ones. When a story had been told, encouraged by probes from me as researcher, I often stayed silent for a while, and then the Sensemaking reflection, our 'morale' came.

Because each Identity Configuration was both supported by some employees (in-group) and criticised by others (out-group), I analysed them as fairly stable social constructions, even though not all employees seemed consciously aware that there were other approaches than their own.

To allow for a deeper analysis of the characteristics of each Identity Configuration emerging from the coding of the interviews, I selected one participant from each configuration who seemed to represent the prototypical traits of that Identity Configuration. In this analysis of the prototypical characteristics of each Identity Configuration, my selection of theories on knowledge communication (Chapters 6 and 7), identity (Chapter 8) and relationships (Chapter 9) can be seen as ways to describe the formation of professional identities centred on specific perceptions of knowledge. These professional identities can be seen as maintained through global organisational relationships and knowledge communication practices with colleagues sharing that professional identity.

The strategy of the first prototypical identity, the Knowledge Transfer Prototype, seems to be aligned with the strategy of the case company, which entailed reapplication of the existing portfolio of modular solutions for individual, team, leadership and sales training. The strength of this Prototype thus seems to be a focus on implementing organisational strategy, and delivering existing organisational knowledge to clients. Because of this focus on communicating organisational knowledge without transforming it, I termed this professional identity the Knowledge Transfer Prototype. 'Transfer' is used here to denote 1:1 transmission of knowledge from one person or group to another person or group without loss or transformation of knowledge. While this is impossible in practice, it should be seen as an ideal which the knowledge transfer Prototype strives to attain.

For the last two of the three Identity Prototypes, the employee autonomy and management distance characterising virtual work environments seem to be important pre-requisites for maintaining their professional identity. These two Prototypes centred their professional identity on a discourse valuing client satisfaction achieved through time-consuming development of tailored solutions. The tailored solutions were constructed by transforming and adapting organisational knowledge to the client's context. For the two employees representing each of these Prototypes, their approach to knowledge communication resulted in additional, international orders from the client. However, the two differed in the extent to which they undertook this knowledge transformation alone, or made a virtue of using their network to find team members with exactly the right skills and abilities needed for the project. I term the first Prototype the Knowledge Creator, and the second one the Knowledge Broker Prototype (see Table 1.1 for an overview of strengths and weaknesses of each Prototype). The knowledge transformation strategy that these two Prototypes shared stood in opposition to the organisational strategy discourse in the case company. The term 'Knowledge Broker' was coined by Wenger (1998) to describe employees who are part of several networks, thereby communicating knowledge between different locations and communities; I'll return to knowledge brokering in Chapter 7.

Management awareness and support for different needs for leadership and different strategies and practices of the three Prototypes may lead to more effective virtual teams that build on a common ground of identification between the members. This may also help leveraging the fruits of employee knowledge creation thereby driving innovation from below. An overview of the key characteristics of each Prototype is provided in Table 1.1.

The three participants selected as prototypical examples of the three Identity Configurations do have their own idiosyncratic traits. However, because identity, and particular professional identity, is also to a large degree social and situated within communities (Wenger, 1998), they do represent larger Identity Configurations which were identified consistently as in-groups and out-groups by employees from different Identity Configurations. This seems to support the existence of identity 'Prototypes' as Mental Models, which employees associate with or dissociate themselves from.

Please note the following three conventions that are adopted throughout the analyses of the interviews with the latter two Prototypes. First, all capitalised words are defined in the glossary at the back of the book. Second, I systematically use the transcription conventions explained in Chapter 4 for showing prosodic detail in the quoted passages from the interviews. An overview of the transcription codes is provided in Table 4.2, which can also be found in Appendix A for ease of reference. This means that the interview passages quoted do not follow normal orthographic conventions: for example, a full stop may occur in mid-sentence, because the participant used an 'end-of-sentence' intonation contour to put emphasis

Table 1.1 Overview of key characteristics of the three Identity Prototypes found in the study

	Knowledge transfer prototype (Dorthe)	*Community supported knowledge creator prototype (Henrik)*	*Knowledge broker prototype (Linda)*
Perception of knowledge	Near loss-less communication of existing knowledge designed by R&D. Highly codified knowledge as useful.	HR Consult knowledge as inspiration for knowledge creation. Personal knowledge transformation to suit client contexts as useful.	HR Consult knowledge as inspiration for knowledge creation. Focus on who-knows-what (relational knowledge).
Identity	Dedicated to fulfilling the strategies and vision of HR Consult. Aims to fulfil organisational expectations.	Achieving client satisfaction. Ownership and sense of meaning through knowledge transformation.	Achieving client satisfaction Sense of meaning and identity in using network to find the right combination of skills to solve client problem.
Use of relationships	Limited focus on building knowledge communication relations and communities. Relationships mainly emotional, and as approach to new clients.	Finds a foundation for a social identity in a community of like-minded knowledge creators. Community as providing meaning to daily practices.	Finds meaning in creating knowledge with their social network. Creates solutions by building a global virtual team with the right skill set.
Strengths	Ensures that global clients receive same development intervention regardless of local context.	Listens and understands client needs. Builds creative solutions by unifying HR knowledge with client culture and needs.	Addresses specific client needs by finding the right competencies to solve the problem. Builds creative solutions by unifying HR knowledge with client culture and needs.

on a particular phrase or word. In the analyses of these quotes, I refer to words or phrases without the transcription codes, but refer to the line numbers of the full quote.

The third convention adopted is that I refer to the interview quotes using the following format:

([participant's name], 'my translation', [paragraph number of the transcription], [time stamp of the audio])

For example: (Henrik, my translation, 456, 0:34:56). All the quotes have been translated from Danish.

I provide notes beneath the quotes when interviewees used non-verbal semiosis to support their argument (e.g. pointing at something and using the deictic 'that', rather than using a noun phrase to describe what 'that' is).

Structure of the book

The book has been divided into two parts: Part I (Chapters 1–4) constructs the *Discursive Sensemaking Analysis* method. If you're not particularly interested in discourse analysis or in what type of knowledge we are able to construct by using discourse analysis to analyse interviews in global organisations, you might just read Chapter 2, which introduces Karl E. Weick's theory of how we humans make sense of our lives and practices, or, more specifically, how we make sense of our professional lives and of our knowledge communication practices.

Part II (Chapters 5–8) reviews literature, builds theory and provides extensive interview data analysis to illustrate the theories in the light of practice.

The main argument will be that if we want to understand how and why employees in global 21st-century organisations communicate knowledge – or why they choose not to, we need a multidisciplinary approach. In part 2 of the book, I combine theories from research on virtual teams (Chapter 5), knowledge management theory (Chapters 6 and 7), identity theory (Chapter 8), and relationship theory (Chapter 9). The analyses focus on interview participants that could be seen as Prototypes of the three Identity Configurations. The most common of these Prototypes, the Knowledge Transfer Prototype is subjected to a less thorough analysis to form a background against which to analyse the other two. Those latter two are more interesting due to their innovative knowledge creation, their ability to question status quo in the organisation, and their ability to communicate professional knowledge across geographical, vocational and organisational boundaries. These few employees, representing the Knowledge Creator and the Knowledge Broker Prototypes, seem to stand out as rare in the organisation. They can both be seen as potential knowledge leaders driving innovation and knowledge creation from below in the global case organisation. Therefore, I chose to analyse these Prototypes in more depth.

Finally, Chapter 10 draws conclusions on the findings, and discusses the interrelations between the theories. The book finishes with a discussion of the implications of the findings as well as suggestions for future research.

Note

1 I will define this term later in this introduction, and last out my theory of identity in Chapter 7. Furthermore, all capitalised words in the book are defined in the glossary in the back of the book.

References

Al-Ani, B., Horspool, A., & Bligh, M. C. (2011). Collaborating with 'virtual strangers': Towards developing a framework for leadership in distributed teams. *Leadership,* 7(3), 219–249.

Berente, N., Hansen, S., Pike, J. C., & Bateman, P. J. (2011). Arguing the value of virtual worlds: Patterns of discursive sensemaking of an innovative technology. *MIS Quarterly, 3*(3), 685–709.

Breu, K., & Hemingway, C. J. (2004). Making organisations virtual: The hidden cost of distributed teams. *Journal of Information Technology, 19*(3), 191–202.

Cheng, W., & Lam, P. (2011). Prosody in discourse. In J. P. Gee & M. Handford (Eds.), *Routledge handbook of discourse analysis* (pp. 271–284). New York: Routledge.

Daim, T. U., Ha, A., Reutiman, S., Hughes, B., Pathak, U., Bynum, W., & Bhatla, A. (2012). Exploring the communication breakdown in global virtual teams. *International Journal of Project Management, 30*(2), 199–212.

Drew, P., & Heritage, J. (1992). *Talk at work: interaction in institutional settings.* Cambridge: Cambridge University Press.

Espinosa, J. A., Cummings, J. N., Wilson, J. M., & Pearce, B. M. (2003). Team boundary issues across multiple global firms. *Journal of Management Information Systems, 19*(4), 157–190.

Flyvbjerg, B. (2006). From Nobel Prize to project management: Getting risks right. *Project Management Journal, 37*(3), 5–15.

Gee, J. P. (2011). *An introduction to discourse* analysis. London: Routledge.

Gee, J. P. (2014). *How to do discourse analysis: a toolkit.* London: Routledge.

Gerard, J. (2001). The tacit knowing framework: A look at sustained competitive advantage under a unified tacit and Explicit Knowledge. Paper presented at the *Fourth International Conference on Organizational Learning and Knowledge Management,* Ontario, Canada.

Gilson, L. L., Maynard, M. T., Jones Young, N. C., Vartiainen, M., & Hakonen, M. (2015). Virtual teams research: 10 years, 10 themes, and 10 opportunities. *Journal of Management, 41*(5), 1313–1337.

Gupta, S., & Pathak, G. S. (2018). Virtual team experiences in an emerging economy: a qualitative study. *Journal of Organizational Change Management,* 31(4), 778–794.

Halliday, M. A. K., & Hasan, R. (1976/2014). *Cohesion in English.* London: Routledge.

Hansen, M. T. (1999). The search-transfer problem: the role of weak ties in sharing knowledge across organization subunits. *Administrative Science Quarterly, 44*, 82–111.

Jansen, P. G., & Roodt, G. (2014). Conceptualising and measuring work identity. Retrieved from: http://link.springer.com/book/10.1007/978-94-017-9242-4

Lehtonen, M., & Kampf, C. (2014). Virtual teams and knowledge communication: Drawing on semiotics for making knowledge about virtual teams and collaboration visible. *International Journal of Sociotechnology and Knowledge Development (IJSKD), 6*(3), 1–25.

Mortensen, M., Woolley, A. W., & O'Leary, M. (2007). Conditions enabling effective multiple team membership. *Virtuality and virtualization* (pp. 215–228). New York: Springer.

Nandhakumar, J., & Baskerville, R. (2006). Durability of online teamworking: Patterns of trust. *Information Technology and People, 19*(4), 371–389.

Nayak, N. V., & Taylor, J. E. (2009). Offshore outsourcing in global design networks. *Journal of Management in Engineering, 25*(4), 177–184. doi: 10.1061/(asce)0742597x (2009)25:4(177)

Nonaka, I., & Takeuchi, H. (1995). *Knowledge-creating company: How Japanese companies create the dynamics of innovation*. Oxford: Oxford University.

Rezgui, Y. (2007). Exploring virtual team-working effectiveness in the construction sector. *Interacting with Computers, 19*(1), 96–112.

Schiffrin, D. (1988). *Discourse markers*. Cambridge: Cambridge University Press.

Schulze, J., & Krumm, S. (2017). The "virtual team player" A review and initial model of knowledge, skills, abilities, and other characteristics for virtual collaboration. *Organizational Psychology Review,* 7(1), 66–95. doi: 10.1177%2F2041386616675522

Spinuzzi, C. (2004). Describing assemblages: Genre sets, systems, repertoires, and ecologies. *Computer Writing and Research Lab, White paper,* 1–7. Retrieved from *Computer Writing and Research Lab White Paper* website: http://www.cwrl.utexas.edu/files/040505-2.pdf

Staples, D. S., & Webster, J. (2008). Exploring the effects of trust, task interdependence and virtualness on knowledge sharing in teams. *Information Systems Journal, 18*(6), 617–640.

The Economist Intelligence Unit. (2009). Managing virtual teams - Taking a more strategic approach. Retrieved from http://graphics.eiu.com/upload/eb/NEC_Managing_virtual_teams_WEB.pdf

Van Dijk, T. A. (2005). Contextual knowledge management in discourse production. *A new agenda in (critical) discourse analysis* (pp. 71–100). Amsterdam: John Benjamins.

Van Dijk, T. A. (2006). Discourse, context and cognition. *Discourse Studies, 8*(1), 159–177.

Weick, K. E. (1995). *Sensemaking in organizations*. London: Sage

Weick, K. E. (2001). *Making sense of the organization*. Oxford: Blackwell.

Weick, K. E., Sutcliffe, K. M., & Obstfeld, D. (2005). Organizing and the process of sensemaking. *Organization Science, 16*(4), 409–421.

Wenger, E. (1998). *Communities of practice: Learning, meaning, and identity.* New York: Cambridge University Press.

Part 1

Discursive Sensemaking – foundation, theory and method

2 Discursive Sensemaking Analysis – a foundation

Chapter Contents

This chapter introduces Weick's Sensemaking theory (Weick, 1995, 2001) as a lens for understanding how employees build knowledge communication practices. Weick's Sensemaking theory can thus be seen as a scaffold supporting all other chapters in the present volume. Weick has defined Sensemaking as 'the ongoing retrospective development of plausible images that rationalize what people are doing' (Weick, 2008, p. 1403). Weick's theory additionally provides a theory of identity formations and interpretations of (or Sensemaking about) relationships in the virtual work environment at HR Consult, thus making the theory highly relevant for the present volume.

It should be noted that the presentation of Weick's Sensemaking model in this chapter builds on Weick's later works (Weick, 1995, 2001; Weick et al., 2005, the latter co-written with K. M. Sutcliffe & D. Obstfeld), which Sandberg and Tsoukas (2015) identify as having a phenomenological focus not present in Weick's earlier work (all capitalised words, such as 'Sensemaking', are defined in the glossary at the back of the book). This means that Sensemaking theory builds on the assumption that individuals cannot grasp reality as it is but perceive it through a filter of past experiences and the need to maintain a coherent narrative of personal identity. Sensemaking, according to Weick (1995, 2001), is a process through which individuals and groups align experiences and identities with their interpretations of the situation they are in. This Sensemaking is then used as the basis for (re)action ('**Enactment**' in Weick's terminology) to the environment; in this way the Sensemaking perspective is Enacted upon the situation and the outcome becomes the source for a new circle of Sensemaking and Enactment.

DOI: 10.4324/9781003015925-3

Sensemaking in organisations

Although I use Weick's (1995, 2001) theory of Sensemaking to examine employee experience of their virtual work environment, access to individual experience is never straightforward or simple. While providing accounts of specific working life practices in the research interviews conducted, employees engage in a form of Discursive Sensemaking about their experiences of the complex virtual work environment in which they are embedded. Through these Sensemaking perspectives, interviewees construct identities, relations and knowledge communication practices. Despite their nature as 'constructed' in the interview situation, these practices will be assumed to have an affinity with the interviewee's actions and beliefs outside the interview situation (see Chapter 4 for my theory of interview discourse). The operationalisation of Sensemaking as a discursive phenomenon is elaborated in Chapter 3 to argue for Discursive Sensemaking Analysis (DSA) as a lens for understanding how employees build Identity Prototypes and Identity Configurations centred around particular perceptions of knowledge with particular patterns of knowledge communication practices attached to them.

The value of Sensemaking as a theoretical lens for understanding knowledge communication practices arises from its shift in agency and causality from external factors (such as ICT mediation) towards how individuals and groups understand, interpret and make sense of these factors. Therefore, Sensemaking can be used as a lens for understanding how the complex set of factors in a virtual work environment are understood by the actors themselves and how their interpretation of these factors forms the basis for Enactment through knowledge communication practices.

Weick's model of Sensemaking incorporates the Phenomenological insight that people do not have an objective understanding of the contexts in which they are embedded: 'Depending on who I am, my definition of what is out there will also change' (Weick, 1995, p. 20). And because contexts are rarely stable, they occasionally need to be reinterpreted. In place of an objective and complete understanding of contexts, people build on partial and subjective understandings of the contexts they are embedded in. We use existing Mental Models to select and retain interpretations of those aspects of the context which can be aligned with our existing Mental Models. Weick terms changes in the environment 'Ecological Change', while the existing Mental Models are termed 'Retention' (see Figure 2.1).

The Retention aspect of Weick's model consists of past experiences and current identity. Because these two elements form the basis for understanding ecological changes and for selecting responses to those changes, Weick argues that Sensemaking is always retrospective. The emphasis on the impact of Retention on how individuals and groups Enact their interpretations of context on the environment means that identity plays a key role. Thus, identity impacts both on how individuals interpret a situation and on how they react to it. 'Retrospective Sensemaking' means that individuals and groups respond to new or ambiguous situations by drawing on what worked in similar situations in the past.

Because interpretations of ecological changes are based on existing Mental Models, we tend to select the aspects of the context which can be aligned with the existing retention system of identity and past experience. This selection process results in a selection of 'Extracted Cues'. The interpretation of these extracted cues decides the cause for action in response to the Ecological Change. Weick uses the term 'enactment' rather 'action' thereby emphasising that it is the interpretation based on identity values which is enacted on the context.

This process sounds complex and rational when written out into individual steps, but should be seen as an intuitive and ongoing loop between selection, retention and enactment in response to ongoing changes in the ecologies (contexts or social situations) we are embedded in. The three tendencies in the current labour market identified in the introduction to the book, particularly the tendency towards individual participation in multiple projects and teams, suggests that the current virtual work environment represents ecologies of ongoing changes. Tsoukas and Chia (2002) see change rather than stability as the norm in the globalised economy of the 21st century. This increases the need for ongoing Sensemaking cycles. Thus, the current virtual work environment can be seen as sparking a need to make sense of the complexity. Weick (1995) terms this complexity 'Equivocality', or in its adjectival form 'Equivocal'. The term is used to describe ecologies in which there is no single 'correct' interpretation

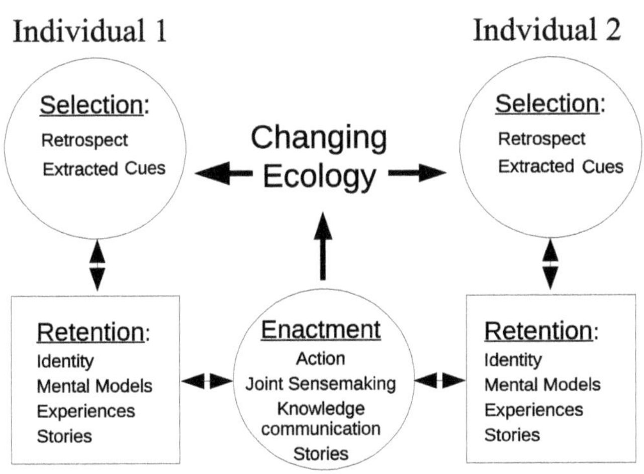

Figure 2.1 The sensemaking process as individual and social construct

or enactment, and in which the current Retention does not necessarily provide an answer.

Enactment in response to Ecological Change again leads to a process of retrospective Sensemaking about the effects of the enactment (visualised by the double arrow between *Ecological Change* and *Enactment* and the arrow from *enactment* to *selection* in Figure 2.1). This leads to an update of the retention system thereby starting a new Sensemaking cycle.

Identity in Weick's theory of Sensemaking

Weick's understanding of identity includes the performative, multiple identity perspective found in Goffman (Goffman, 1967; Weick, 2001) and Harré (2005), but contrary to Goffman and Harré, Weick emphasises the need of the individual to maintain a coherent identity over time and across different social contexts (Weick, 1995). Harré (2005) terms the process of identity formation 'interpellation', meaning that a subject is called into the performance of a certain social identity, e.g., when a teacher takes on the identity role of 'teacher' by standing in front of the black board addressing the students (who are in turn called into the student identity), and taking responsibility for leading the class activities during a lesson. To sum up. the book argues that identity can shift as different social identities are called for in different contexts and situations, yet individuals have a need to maintain a coherent sense of identity across contexts, and this more stable identity forms a background for identity constructions (and thereby for enactment) within a given context. I elaborate on my perspective on identity in Chapter 8.

Sensemaking and the virtual work environment

The present increasingly virtual work environment with multiple team and project commitments arguably increases the need for Sensemaking (Colville et al., 2012). The virtual work environment as a context for ongoing Ecological Change involves maintaining a coherent identity across multiple teams and projects. This identity negotiation also occurs in relation to organisational pushes and pulls through organisational strategies, practices and cultures, thus building expectations for how employees should act. From this perspective, how employees make sense of the work environment is important for understanding why, how and with whom they communicate knowledge.

In terms of virtual work environment, Weick's Sensemaking theory offers a useful lens for examining how individuals make sense of the virtual work environment. This can offer insight into how the context seems to change the Mental Models of individuals, but also how they use that context actively to build a coherent sense of self in the absence of a more predictable co-located work environment.

Sensemaking and storytelling

As part of the Sensemaking process, we build stories around our experiences (Isabella, 1990). As stated by Weick (2012): 'A good story holds elements together, which enables it to serve as a guide for Sensemaking and organising' (p. 149). In fact, it has been argued that the ultimate failure of Sensemaking is when you cannot produce a story which fits the situation (Wallemacq and Sims 1998). Supporting this focus on storytelling, Van Dijk (2003) argues that, 'Personal knowledge is usually represented in episodic memory, as part of our "personal history" of experiences. In discourse processing it is the typical source of personal storytelling, and knowledge that is not presupposed but asserted.' (p. 93).

Boje (1991) also sees storytelling as a key Sensemaking device and argues that stories are rarely told in their entirety; part of the story is presupposed, and the telling changes depending on the audience. The listener thus becomes a co-creator of the story. This results in what Boje (1991) terms 'terse storytelling':

> A terse telling is an abbreviated and succinct simplification of the story in which parts of the plot, some of the characters, and segments of the sequence of events are left to the hearer's imagination. One hypothesis is that the terser the telling, the more shared the understanding of the social context since insiders know what to leave to the imagination.
>
> (pp. 115–116)

Research interviews represent a context in which stories are told more elaborately, due to the lack of pre-existing shared understanding (Boje, 1991). This is a key reason for adopting semi-structured interviews in my study of virtual knowledge communication at HR Consult. In the interview guide, I constructed for the present study, I tried to elicit stories of virtual and co-located projects, thereby letting the employees build identities and perceptions of successful knowledge communication practices (see Chapter 4 for details). With this brief introduction to Weick's Sensemaking theory done, the next chapter will lay the theoretical groundwork for my Discursive Sensemaking method.

References

Boje, D. M. (1991). The storytelling organization: A study of story performance in an office-supply firm. *Administrative Science Quarterly, 4*(3), 106–126.

Colville, I., Brown, A. D., & Pye, A. (2012). Simplexity: Sensemaking, organizing and storytelling for our time. *Human Relations, 65*(1), 5–15.

Goffman, E. (1967). *Interaction ritual.* Harmondsworth: Penguin.

Harré, R. (2005). Positioning and the discursive construction of categories. *Psychopathology, 38*(4), 185–188. doi: 10.1159/000086088

Isabella, L. A. (1990). Evolving interpretations as change unfolds: How managers construe key organisational events. *Academy of Management Journal, 33*(1), 7–41. doi: 10.5465/256350

Sandberg, J., & Tsoukas, H. (2015). Making sense of the sensemaking perspective: Its constituents, limitations, and opportunities for further development. *Journal of Organizational Behavior, 36*(S1), S6–S32.

Tsoukas, H., & Chia, R. (2002) On organizational becoming: Rethinking organizational change. *Organization Science, 13*(5), 567–582. doi: 10.1287/orsc.13.5.567.7810

Van Dijk, T. A. (2003). Contextual knowledge management in discourse production. *A new agenda in (critical) discourse analysis* (pp. 71–100). Amsterdam: John Benjamins

Wallemacq, A. & Sims, D. (1998) The struggle with sense. In: D. Grant, T. Keenoy, & C. Oswick (Eds.), *Discourse and organization* (pp. 119–133). London: Sage.

Weick, K. E. (1995). *Sensemaking in organizations*. London: Sage.

Weick, K. E. (2001). *Making sense of the organization*. Oxford: Blackwell.

Weick, K. E. (2008). Sensemaking. In: S. R. Clegg & J. R. Bailey (Eds.) *International encyclopedia of organization studies* (vol. 4, pp. 1403–1406). Thousand Oaks, CA: Sage.

Weick, K. E. (2012). Organized sensemaking: A commentary on processes of interpretive work. *Human Relations, 65*(1), 141–153. doi: 10.1177/0018726711424235

Weick, K. E., Sutcliffe, K. M., & Obstfeld, D. (2005). Organizing and the process of sensemaking. *Organization Science, 16*(4), 409–421.

3 Discursive Sensemaking Analysis – a theory

Chapter Contents

Discourse Analysis (DA) is a contested term. Some scholars even argue that the act of defining the term goes against the basic tenets of the discipline. Nevertheless, this chapter presents some these definitions to tease out some the values underlying then, and argues for why, our in some cases why not, these definitions bit with my approach to DA.

Definition of 'discourse'

Oswick (2010) defined discourse as 'a process of meaning-making through talk and text' (p. 104), which connects well with the Sensemaking focus of the present volume (all capitalised words, such as 'Sensemaking', are defined in the glossary at the back of the book). Keller (2011) defines discourse as, 'regulated, structured passages of sign usage'; 'sign usage' here refers mainly to language, but material objects may also function as signs, e.g. the hammer of a judge has a symbolic function, but using it to pass

DOI: 10.4324/9781003015925-4

sentence in a court of law has very real implications for the convicted felon (Austin, 1962). Keller's general definition, however, does not say anything about the subject position and the level of freedom in discourse production. These issues will be explored in this chapter, but first I'll situate my Discourse Analysis (DA) within the field of other DA approaches within Organisation Studies.

Because the book does not place its main research aims or contribution within Discourse Analysis, this overview may not do justice to the very heterogeneous field Discourse Analysis, in general, and organisational DA, in particular, nor to the heated debate sparked by Alvesson and Kärreman (2011). However, the chapter serves the purpose of providing a theoretical foundation for Chapter 4 which will explicate the Discursive Sensemaking Analysis method.

Organisational Discourse Analysis

Organisational Discourse Analysis is a diverse field loosely connected by a shared perception that discourse constitutes organisations (Grant et al., 2004) and a shared focus on studying language in use in organisations. Alvesson and Kärreman (2011) provocatively state that, 'The only thing that unites much discourse work is the use of the term discourse.' (p. 1141). Other scholars defend the approach, arguing that Organisational Discourse Analysis is a 'plurivocal project – one where a range of approaches and perspectives co-exist.' (Grant et al., 2004). Furthermore, Phillips and Oswick (2012) argue that 'The reason for this methodological variety is simply that the approaches that make up organisational discourse analysis have evolved from an array of different disciplinary traditions' (p. 25).

Over the past three decades there has been a substantial increase in the role of language and communication in Organisation Studies. Grant et al. (2004) state that:

> It is now difficult to open a management or organisational journal without finding that it contains some sort of discursive-based study, and there has been a recent flurry of books, edited collections and journal special issues dedicated to the topic.

Alvesson and Kärreman (2000) are not the only ones to describe this as a 'linguistic turn' in Organisation Studies. For example, Phillips and Oswick (2012) state that the linguistic turn involved a fundamental change in the role of language in organisations:

> Instead of a view of language as a conduit for communication, language becomes something much more complex and dynamic. It becomes an arena where organisational members communicate,

> while simultaneously providing a space for the processes of organising upon which organisations depend.
>
> (Phillips and Oswick, 2012, p. 8).

A similar perspective on the role of language can be found in Alvesson and Kärreman (2000):

> Language use, in any social context, is active, processual, and outcome oriented. Language is used to persuade, enjoy, engage, discipline, criticise, express feelings, clarify, unite, do identity work, and so on. It constructs reality in the sense that every instance of language use is to some extent arbitrary and produces a particular version of what is it supposed to represent.
>
> (Alvesson and Kärreman, 2000, p. 142).

Alvesson and Kärreman (2000) argue that a shared focus in Organisational Discourse Analysis is to study language in use in organisations, rather than studying language itself, as is the case in some DA approaches within Linguistics.

Although studies using Organisational Discourse Analysis represent a diverse body of research, a shared common ground is the perception that organising occurs through language and communication (Jian et al., 2008; Tietze et al., 2003).

A common ground can also be found in the type of questions addressed by Organisational Discourse Analysis; as Phillips and Oswick (2012) found, articles using Organisational Discourse Analysis typically study:

> The nature of organisational discourse, how the texts which make them up are produced, and why some texts are more influential than others … It is this focus beyond simple language-use that differentiates organisational discourse analysis from other forms of language-based inquiry.
>
> (p. 3).

To impose order on this diverse research approach, Grant et al. (2004) provide a useful taxonomy of the journal literature adopting Organisational Discourse Analysis as a method. They divide the articles using into four categories:

1 Conversation and dialogue (typically recording naturally occurring conversations to examine turn-taking rules and other discursive conventions; this body of Research is known as Conversation Analysis).
2 Narratives and stories (attempting to elicit narratives and stories within an organisation, for example, through interviews, such as my study, or through focus groups).

3 Rhetoric (showing how organisational actors adopt rhetorical devices in order to achieve specific goals through communication).
4 Tropes (literary devices: 'the four classic (or master) tropes of metaphor, synecdoche, metonymy and irony' (p. 8)).

As explained in chapter one, the present volume focuses on eliciting employee stories through interviews. In telling these stories about their virtual team practices, employees construct idiosyncratic perceptions of knowledge, and build their professional identities around these perceptions of knowledge and further support these identities by constructing in-groups and out-groups in the relationships they construct in the interview.

Rhodes and Brown (2005) provide a taxonomy to organise the literature on organisational storytelling. They divide the literature in to five categories:

1 Sensemaking,
2 Communication,
3 Politics and power,
4 Learning/change, and
5 Identity and identification.

However, this taxonomy may be too detailed for a multidisciplinary approach such as the one adopted in this book; I primarily focus on *Sensemaking* about virtual knowledge *communication*; this means that both 1 and 2 in the taxonomy are in focus in this book. Furthermore, in their stories, participants invoke or negotiate, resist and enforce powerful organisational discourses, such as the organisational strategies and core values. Participants in my study also construct practices which they see as ideal and argue against other approaches; in other words, they engage in *politics*, thereby putting focus on the third group in Rhodes and Brown's taxonomy, the organisational storytelling literature. Finally, as we shall see in Chapter 8, Identity construction emerged as an important construct when I analysed the interviews conducted for this study, which means that Rhodes and Brown's fifth category is also addressed in this book.

Numerous articles within Organisation Studies adopting a DA approach have focussed on management. For example, Bäklander (2019) interviewed managers to examine employee autonomy, Berkhout (2007) studied leadership in education, and De Cock (1998) studied organisational change by interviewing managers. Fewer articles have studied employees but there are notable exceptions, for example McCabe (2014) studied how employees resist organisational change in a UK bank.

With this brief introduction to the complex field of Organisational Discourse Analysis, I will turn my attention to a discussion of why I do not adopt the most popular DA approach for analysing the intersection of society and language, CDA. Then I'll explain why I selected James Paul Gee's (2011, 2014) sociolinguistic approach. The chapter finishes with a discussion of why I chose interviews as data construction method.

Why not adopt CDA?

CDA is a well-established field with several journals, research groups and centres, and numerous scholars engaged in developing the field. In this section, I will argue for why CDA is not adopted in this book despite its popularity in social analysis.

Teun Van Dijk, a prominent CDA scholar, states that CDA scholars 'are typically interested in the way discourse (re)produces social domination, that is the power abuse of one group others, and how dominated groups may discursively resist such abuse' (van Dijk 2009a, p. 63). This places the object of study ('power abuse, dominance and inequality') as the common ground between an otherwise disparate group of researchers. As argued by Bargiela-Chiappini (2011), CDA aims to 'privilege questions of a political nature, at times explicitly related to an emancipatory or change agenda, and underpinned by a specific ideological apparatus.' (p. 1180).

Rather than focussing on the key CDA and concept 'power', James Paul Gee (2011) argues that text and talk always invoke or reject aspects of macro-discourses (which Gee terms big 'C', Conversations). He defines this discursive process of power-play as one of the seven Building Tasks we constantly construct in language. He terms this Building Task, Politics – the distribution of social goods. Thereby he adopts a more general, pragmatic aspect of language, namely the privileging of some meanings and perspectives over others in everyday (d)iscourse, and the constant evoking and resisting of Conversations in (d)iscourse. Gee also argues for the Building Task, Significance, to describe the way we emphasise some meanings over others and draw attention to certain aspects of the social situation at the expense of others. Thus, Politics (distribution of social goods) is offered as a more micro-level term than the focus of both CDA and Discourse Studies on 'power', and 'hegemony'. These two key concepts may well be important for studying inequality based on gender, religion or ethnicity, but may not have the same importance when studying knowledge communication in organisational settings.

> Another key concept in Discourse Theory and CDA is 'ideology'. This macro-level term may be relevant when analysing racist discourse or political texts, but does not seem to me to apply to the value systems of groups and individuals within organisational settings, unless studying the political viewpoints of participants. I therefore adopt the more micro-level concept 'values'. Jonathan Sachs (2019, February 26) explains the difference between 'values' and 'ideology' from the perspective of a corporate setting. He defines ideology as 'a set of rigid

> beliefs that can limit options and constrict decision making into the small box of dogma.'.
>
> (Sachs, 2019, February 26)

Values, on the other hand, can be seen as a cognitive construct which guides Enactment in the Sensemaking of an Equivocal and changing Ecology in the Sensemaking process (see the introduction to Karl Weick's Sensemaking theory in Chapter 2). Maio et al. (2006) provide an explanation of the differences between ideologies, values, attitudes and beliefs:

- 'By the term "attitudes," we mean tendencies to evaluate an object positively or negatively.' (p. 284)
- Values are regarded as abstract ideals (e.g., freedom, helpfulness) that function as important guiding principles
- 'I deologies are systems of attitudes and values that are organised around an abstract theme' (e.g., "liberalism", "nationalism" or "Nazism"). (p. 284)

However, they are interrelated concepts: 'For example, a liberal ideology may encompass the values of freedom and helpfulness, together with unfavourable attitudes toward censorship and reduced social spending' (ibid, p. 284).

Having explained my reasons for not adopting CDA, I turn to my justification for adopting James Gee's sociolinguistic approach to Discourse Analysis method.

Why I adopt James Paul Gee's sociolinguistic DA approach

First, I'll clarify some terminology, then I'll discuss free will (also known as 'individual agency'). Finally, I'll argue, based on Gee (2011) and Teun van Dijk (2005), for a cognitive dimension in discourse production.

Key terminology in Gee's sociolinguistic DA approach

Because Gee's key concepts can be argued to overlap with that of the other DA approaches we've looked at so far, I'll explain differences and overlaps with the key terminology of the DA approaches outlined in the previous sections.

Gee (2011) tries to clarify the confusing use of the term 'discourse' to designate both micro and macro-level discourse. Gee suggests the term Conversations ('Big "C" conversations') to designate what the CDA scholar Norman Fairclough (2003) terms 'orders of discourse' in accordance with Michel Foucault. Micro-level discourse of specific texts and utterances, on the other hand, are termed (d)iscourse ('little "d" discourse') in Gee (2011, 2014).

When I use '(d)iscourse' rather than simply 'text' it is to emphasise a certain analytical perspective; viewing the text as (d)iscourse entails an analysis of, first, how the text constructs the social reality outside the text or utterance (i.e., the Context and the relations, identities and practices in a given Context). Second, how the texts or utterances negotiate Conversations by referring to them implicitly as a presupposed background, or by explicitly foregrounding aspects of them in (d)iscourse. And third, how the text reflects the speaker/writer's Sensemaking perspective by foregrounding discourse elements, connecting disparate elements and making conscious and subconscious linguistic choices favouring some meanings over others (thereby engaging in what Gee terms Politics). Finally, (d)iscourse constructs social situations. To emphasise the construction of these cognitive and social layers, Gee argues for the use of the term (D)iscourse (Big 'D' Discourse). To quote Gee (2011), talking and writing involve 'acting-interacting-thinking-valuing-talking-(sometimes writing-reading) in the "appropriate way" with the "appropriate" props and the "appropriate" times and in the "appropriate" places' (p. 17). (D)iscourses thus engage both the cognitive level ('thinking-valuing'), the social level ('acting-interacting') and the discursive level ('talking' and 'writing-reading'). Gee coined the two concepts (d)iscourse and (D)iscourse in his book *Social linguistics and literacies: Ideology in Discourses* (1990), but the concept (D)iscourse is confusingly given a new meaning by Alvesson and Kärreman (2000), who use (D)iscourse to describe mega-discourse, which Gee (2011) terms Conversations.

Big 'C' Conversations can be seen as a social level background which remains mainly unspoken, only to be foregrounded in (d)iscourse when a speaker uses presuppositions (for example, the phrase 'my wife is blonde' is not just a neutral description of my wife's hair colour; it presupposes that I have a wife in the first place). As another example, Deictic expressions (referring to previous aspects of the discourse, for example through pronouns, such as 'those' and 'he'), indicate an expectation that the interlocutor shares the Context Model. In other cases, a speaker might explain his or her perception of the Context explicitly to an interlocutor who does not share this Context.

In order to include a cognitive element of mental representations of contexts, Van Dijk (2005) proposes the term 'Context Model'. Context Models constitute one type of several mental models which help interlocutors to decide which aspects of the Context they can presuppose in a given (d)iscourse, and which aspects need to be explained to achieve a shared social Context Model through which the (d)iscourse can be understood. Thus, Van Dijk (2005, 2014) suggests that Context can mainly be examined through the participant's own (d)iscourse about that Context. The identification of Context as a form of Mental Model which is implicitly or explicitly referenced in (d)iscourse also means that the researcher can and should take this cognitive aspect into account when analysing (d)iscourse.

Gee's (2011, 2014) Building Tasks as tools for analysing Discursive Sensemaking

Weick's (1995, 2001) Sensemaking perspective implies that, when describing contexts, interview participants do so from the perspective of their own Sensemaking process, or the perspective of their 'lifeworld' in Schutz's terminology (Schutz & Luckman, 1973). When describing the contexts and practices in which they are embedded, participants can be seen as balancing a (re)presentation of social reality which is consistent enough with others' perspectives to be seen as valid, or 'true', while still remaining true to the values, identities and interpretations which is part of the retention of the participant.

This perspective relates to James Gee's (2011, 2014) Building Tasks which he uses to argue that utterances essentially construct one or more of the following:

- Significance,
- Activities,
- Relationships,
- Identities,
- Politics (distribution of social goods),
- Connections, and
- Sign Systems and Knowledge.

The Building Task *Significance* refers to the use of language to 'build' significance of the reality even in seemingly mundane descriptions by selecting what aspects of reality (physical and social) to draw attention to, i.e. foreground in [d]iscourse. In this process, grammar is not simply a means to construct correct phrases but is used actively and rhetorically to privilege some meanings and interpretations over others. As argued by James Gee, language is:

> not just a code … You're building ways of privileging certain forms of knowledge … You're using it almost like a kit, like a set of colours you can paint with. The grammar is just that. It's a palette of colours and you can paint your own painting and what you're painting is a building.
>
> (Rogers, 2004b, pp. 24–26)

With language as a strategic and rhetorical means to construct social reality, it becomes important for researchers of business studies to analyse the language use of participants. Using Weick's theory, language is used to present the Sensemaking of the speaker. The privileging of interpretations occurs both at the syntactic, Lexical and Prosodic (stress, intonation, pitch, volume and pace) level. At the syntactic, or *synchronous* level, the elements in the words are ordered to attach agency or properties to certain textual elements over others, thereby constructing more significance for some textual elements over others. At the Lexical, or *diachronic* level, the choice of words can be used to represent or construct different perspectives on the same social reality. The act of privileging certain elements over others falls under Gee's Building Tasks *Politics (distribution of social goods)* which is concerned with how language is used to distribute social goods, such as trust, not only literally by granting privileges and setting boundaries, but also more subtly by privileging some value sets over others or some perspectives on reality over others. In this sense, Politics (distribution of social goods) is linked to the Building Task, Significance.

For DA approaches within the critical strand of DA, it is common to set up power, especially with focus on hegemony and subjugation, as a key topic of DA. Gee instead proposes Politics (distribution of social goods) as a more general Building Task of language. In all (d)iscourse some meanings, terms and values are privileged over others, and when aware of this the exposure of power and hegemony in [d]iscourse, the unequal relationships more easily come into focus.

However, Gee's sociolinguistic approach to DA does not assume a priori that unfair hegemony is necessarily at play, as CDA approaches tend to do. Gee's sociolinguistic approach to the concept 'power' thus fits my study well as my aim is not analyse gender or class inequality, racism and other unfair power relations with marginalised voices.

Gee argues that Context both exists 'prior to speaking and is created by speaking', so Context can both be seen as cognitive and social (that is Context is a 'socio-cognitive' phenomenon) and as an aspect of both (D) and (d)iscourse. (Rogers, 2004b). Gee argues that Context is infinite and that this constitutes a 'frame problem' (Rogers 2004b, p. 17); thereby Gee identifies the challenge of limiting the scope of the inquiry to frame Context. In my study, I limit the Context to the organisational Conversations at HR Consult, and thus I exclude national culture and the impact of Conversations beyond the HR Consult as an organisation. The problem with this necessary framing is that it excludes the influence of national culture, and political and religious beliefs.

Gee's approach to DA can be seen as dissociated from CDA; he does not see himself as part of the CDA network described by Norman Fairclough (Rogers, 2004b). He argues that it does not make sense to put emphasis on the analysis of power and hegemony, because all language always has a political aspect (Rogers, 2004b): 'Those things change your standing in social relationships and in groups and therefore they're social goods … solidarity and deference or status are social goods' (Rogers, 2004b, p. 3).

Like Fairclough, Gee does not see his approach as *the* method of DA, but rather as a toolbox from which to eclectically pick out the necessary tools and add others, e.g. from linguistics or the social sciences. Gee also dissociates himself from the grander approaches to discourse analysis in the works of Foucault or Laclau and Mouffe: 'if we want to create more liberating moments, we are going to have to get down in the trenches and understand stuff at micro-level. Grand theoreticians don't like micro stuff,' (Rogers, 2004b, p. 9). Gee on the other hand aims to 'intervene on both levels' (Rogers, 2004b, p. 10), and sees all language as 'doing stuff, we are not communicating information alone, … we are building stuff' (Rogers, 2004b, p. 12).

Some DA approaches question the ability of language to represent the inner state of an individual or the contexts which are described by (d)iscourse, e.g., Wetherell et al. (2001). The strong emphasis on the constructive aspect of language can lead to a neglect to recognise, on the one hand, the ability of language to symbolically represent the physical and social reality and, on the other hand, the values, and identity underlying the perspective from which that reality is (re-)presented. This book tries to integrate these perspectives to argue for a discourse analysis perspective which builds on but problematises two dualities of assumptions about language. First, I problematise the dichotomy between a perception of (d)iscourse as unproblematically representing the inner world of the speaker, and the perception that (d)iscourse is dissociated from such inner meaning. The book also builds on Weick's sensemaking perspective to argue that interpretations of a social situation and of the Conversations at play arise from an individual autonomy in enacting or resisting Conversations in the Social situation. Second, I problematise the duality between the perception of (d)iscourse as always rhetorical, understood as strategically pre-planned to achieve a specific purpose, and the perspectives which ignore the strategic, rhetorical selection of (d)iscourse to achieve specific purposes, and induce action.

As mentioned, Van Dijk (2005) argues for examining Context not as a phenomenon external to social actors, but as a property of cognition in the form Context models. It is on the basis of these Context models that individuals decide how to react to a specific social situation. Therefore, he argues that to understand a Context, we need to examine how the participants interpret that Context. Although Van Dijk does not refer to Weick, Van Dijk's perspective on Context seems to be aligned with the Sensemaking perspective presented in Chapter 2; Weick also argues that people do not understand a changing Ecology as it is, but through the filter of past experiences and current identity. This is a notion at least as old as the 18th century philosopher Immanuel Kant, who argued that an object is never an object in itself ('*das ding an sich*'); it is always an object for someone ('*das ding für uns*') The notion of 'changing ecology' (Weick, 1995, 2001) can be seen as equivalent to a perspective of 'contexts' as never static or fixed, but always negotiated through Sensemaking processes through which Context models are built (Van Dijk, 2005), and through, the (d)iscourses which can be seen as discursive enactments within the Context.

Discussion of choices in constructing my DA approach

This section shifts focus from other DA approaches towards the DA method developed for this book, Discursive Sensemaking Analysis, which I will explain in Chapter 4. In this chapter, however, I want to delimit the scope of my DA to avoid my discourse analysis approach becoming a catch-all for interpretative analysis. First, I will discuss free will, what is known as 'individual agency', in my DA approach, because of the deterministic (or in Alvesson & Kärreman's, 2000, terminology: 'muscular') assumption in some the DA approaches introduced in this chapter. Second, I will argue (in Teun van Dijk's vein) for the ability of DA to analyse the cognitive aspect of discourse – i.e., the norms, values, Context Models and identities of participants. Third, I'll introduce the grammatical analysis tool adopted in the book (and indeed in many linguistically oriented DA approaches), Systemic Functional Linguistics (Halliday & Hasan, 1976/2014). Fourthly, I'll delimit the scope of analysis, a necessary but difficult choice, which Gee (2014) terms the 'framing problem'. Then I turn to a discussion of what type of knowledge can be derived from interview data (also known as 'epistemological considerations'), and finally I'll dissociate my DSA method from some of the radical constructionist DA approaches (known as 'post-structuralism').

Freewill in my DA approach – limited discourse 'muscularity'

I argued earlier that Howarth's definition of 'discourse' represented a muscular view of macro-discourses power over individual agency. A similar formative, or even deterministic perspective of Conversations over individual agency can be seen in Fairclough's concept *orders of discourse*, which he defines as 'a network of social practices in its language aspect... they control linguistic variability for certain areas of social life' (Rogers, 2004a p. 24). Notice the lexical choice 'control', rather than e.g., 'influence'. Howarth's and Fairclough's perspective therefore seem to leave little room for individual agency. This perception may not be shared by all CDA scholars, however.

Gee's (2011) sociolinguistic approach to discourse analysis, on the other hand, grants considerable individual agency through the texts and utterances produced by individuals. From Gee's perspective we invoke, support, refute and negotiate Conversations through our ongoing dialogues and the texts in our daily practices, thereby simultaneously making certain aspects of Conversations real and negotiating them (or 'reify' them to use Etienne Wenger's terminology, see Chapter 7). Through this ongoing process, Conversations may be slowly transformed allowing a shift in power between them. Using Fairclough's terminology, this shift reflects a shift in the power balance of the 'orders of discourse'. For example, what we might call a 'health Conversation' has gained power through ongoing focus within politics, the health sector, mass media, and in daily conversations among people, in short through Conversations, all adding up to reinforce the power of the health Conversation. Part of the influence of the health Conversation comes from extra-discursive phenomena such as the presence of people jogging in the streets and in the forests, riding bicycles or rowing, often wearing outfits designed for their chosen sport, thereby consciously or unconsciously and without speaking or writing, signalling their conformity to the health Conversation. At the same time, you have people resisting or ignoring the health Conversation. But because of the current power of the health Conversation, even ignoring that Conversation will almost certainly be a conscious act on the part of the individual.

The cognitive aspect of discourse

Discourse can be seen not only as language constructing social reality, but as having a cognitive dimension (Gee, 2011; Van Dijk, 2005). Teun Van Dijk (2005) terms his discourse analysis perspective 'socio-cognitive', because he emphasises the cognitive aspect of both Context and social interaction within that Context. Van Dijk's (2005) socio-cognitive perspective on (D)iscourse as a linguistic realisation of mental models can be seen as aligned with Weick's (1995, 2001) theory of Sensemaking as a process through which individuals and groups build selective mental representations of the Equivocal and changing Ecology in which they are embedded. Both Van Dijk and Weick argue that Retention is used as a basis for deciding how to speak and act within a given Context. However, where Weick insists that such interpretation through a filter of Retention is based on spur of the moment decisions only analysed and made rational in retrospect, Van Dijk (2005) sees Context models as a natural part of pre-planning how to speak and act within a given Context.

However, Context models, while cognitive, are simultaneously social in that there are overlaps and negotiations between Context models of social actors: 'Context models embody naïve theories of other minds … language users have learned to build situationally relevant Context models that are mutually tuned to each other' (Van Dijk, 2009b, p. 8). Such Context models should not be seen as static, but as dynamic and constantly evolving in the Sensemaking process. This can be seen as challenging the common post-structuralist assumption (e.g., Kvale & Brinkman, 2009; Wetherell et al. 2001) that discourse analysis can only analyse (d)iscourses and linguistic relations between (d)iscourses. This Post-Structuralist perspective rests on the assumption that the link between language and reality, and between language and cognition, is arbitrary, and linguistic signs only gain meaning in terms of other linguistic signs. As pointed out by Alvesson and Sköldberg (2009) and David (2005), this post-structuralist position is unnecessarily reductionist.

Alvesson and Kärreman (2000) point out that it is difficult to accurately account for both the Conversation level and the (d)iscourse level in the same study (p. 1134). However, I believe that it may be just as difficult to account for one *without* the other. In this respect, I agree with Garzone and Sarangi (2007) as well as Gee (2011, 2014) that discourse analysis must go beyond linguistic description to analyse language in action within applied settings. This argument can also be found in Fairclough (2003):

> one cannot choose between "big 'D'" and "small 'd'" approaches in discourse analysis: discourse analysis is concerned with the relationship between processes/events and practices (as well as structures), texts and discourses (as well as genres and styles), [i.e.] the relationship between "big 'D'" and "small 'd'" discourses.
>
> (pp. 919–920)

This has also been described as conducting research 'at the intersection of language and social structure' (Blommaert & Bulcaen, 2000, p. 450). Please note that Fairclough (2003) uses big 'Đ' Discourse somewhat differently than Gee; Fairclough uses big 'D' discourse to denote what Gee terms big 'C' Conversations. Nevertheless, a common ground between Gee and Fairclough can be found in the linguistic analytical apparatus; this is the topic of the next section.

Systemic functional linguistics – a common linguistic foundation

Both Gee and Fairclough build on the Systemic Functional Linguistics of Halliday and Hasan (1976/2014). They argue that linguistic choices (termed 'Lexico-grammatical' choices in Halliday and Hasan's [1976/2014] approach) consist of both a 'lexical' perspective of selecting one of several available words describing the same phenomenon, and a grammatical perspective in terms of the grammatical choices. These grammatical choices consist of mood (verb expressing attitude towards what you are saying, for example a statement of desire, of command, of likelihood, etc.), agency (who, if anybody, is performing the action expressed by the verb) and predication (for example using adjectives and adverbs). This approach to Lexis and grammar as interrelated aspects of meaning-making represents the 'systemic' view of language. Language is used to represent different perspectives on the Context, activity, or purpose expressed through (d)iscourse. This can be seen as opposed to the earlier Chomskyian view of grammar as consisting mainly of rules of how grammatical phrases are related, e.g. NP-VP-DO (Noun Phrase, Verb Phrase, Direct Object.).

The lexico-grammatical choices can be seen as constructing specific perspectives on the Context invoked by (d)iscourse, the aims of that (d)iscourse, and the practices, persons and objects represented by that discourse. Collectively, these linguistic perspectives can be seen as expressing the 'Sensemaking' perspective of the speaker.

According to Systemic Functional Linguistics, all language performs three so-called 'meta-functions':

- The *ideational* – language is used to represent experience.
- The *interpersonal* – language is used to enact social relations.
- The *textual* (organising the text or oral statement internally).

But whereas SFL tends to analyse the meta-functions through linguistic analysis of the lexical and grammatical level which build the meta-functions, my DSA approach starts from the higher meaning-making level using Gee's Building Tasks. These are used to examine what Sensemaking perspective a statement constructs, which identities are constructed and for what purpose, and which relationships are constructed and for what purpose. Only then does the analysis move to the linguistic level to analyse more specifically how the Lexico-grammatical elements and the prosody (Stress, Intonation, Pitch, volume and Pace) realise this Sensemaking perspective at the linguistic level. This 'top-down' approach is aligned with Gee's (2011, 2014) sociolinguistic approach to DA, and can also be seen as associated with Van Dijk's (2005) focus on socio-cognitive aspects over linguistic aspects.

Delimiting the scope of the analysis – the framing problem

In recognition of Alvesson and Kärreman's (2000) argument that the entire continuum from micro to mega-discourse cannot be spanned, I do not attempt to analyse the grander socio-cultural Conversations of society. In this respect, my analysis of the Conversation level stays within the Conversations in the case company studied, rather than moving to what Fairclough (2005) and Alvesson and Kärreman (2000) consistently identify as 'grand' or 'mega' discourse. Nor does my analysis of (d)iscourse extend to the micro-level of analysing particular Lexical use or syntactic form and function to their full depth; I only analyse the aspects, which support or contradict the Sensemaking level of analysis.

Questioning the assumptions of radical constructionist DA approaches to linguistic data

This section sets the epistemological foundation of DSA in the middle between two radical approaches to DA; the micro-linguistic focus, and a more post-structuralist perspective, which argues that we can never analyse society and cognition, only the play of signs within (d)iscourses (a position which is also criticised by Chouliaraki and Fairclough (2010). An example of a post-structuralist DA approach which is heavily critical of any attempts to analyse discourse as representation of extra-linguistic phenomena can be seen in Wetherell et al. (2001). They argue, in their introduction to their book *Discourse as Data,* that since there is no single truth, there can be no 'true' inner states of language users. Therefore:

> the researcher should not aim [...] to reveal the intentions and meaning or beliefs of speakers or writers, or to see through their words to some underlying meaning, or to uncover attitudes or beliefs of which the speakers themselves are unaware. These are all large and dangerous claims for discourse analysts to make.
>
> (p. 19)

Furthermore, they argue that accounts which assume unproblematically 'that the talk is transparent and the speaker is a fairly truthful, neutral source of information, including information about her or his own view and attitudes [...] would not usually be considered to be discourse analysis' (p. 19).

I do assume that participants are fairly truthful, but that there are nonetheless discrepancies between participant's stories, and others' stories about that person and his/her practices. When these discrepancies occur, they will not be considered in the analysis as signs of lying or as evidence of the inability of language to represent extra-linguistic phenomena. Instead, they will be analysed as signs of differences in Sensemaking perspectives (see Chapter 2), and, therefore, as signs of different Mental Models of both the Context and the identity of self and others. Furthermore, I assume that speakers are highly aware of the attitudes and beliefs which the analyses in the book draw attention to (an opinion I do not share with Some CDA scholars who aim to uncover hidden or tacit attitudes and beliefs which have been imposed on the individual through hegemonic and powerful orders of discourse).

I disagree with Sköldberg (1994) that there is no reality to be found beyond the narrative, even though I accept his premise that organisations are reflexively constructed by storytelling (among other things, by legal documents, office buildings filled with employees and desks which all add up and signal that it is home to an organisation). Contrary to Sköldberg, I share a realist ontology similar to the prominent CDA scholar Norman Fairclough, and to van Dijk's socio-cognitive approach to discourse analysis. This means that we recognise that there is indeed a social reality beyond discourse, and that this impacts on and is in turn influenced by discourse, such as storytelling. Furthermore, I agree with the CDA scholar Teun van Dijk that we need to pay attention to not only the relation between discourse and social reality, but equally to the cognitive aspect of discourse.

In sum, the book will analyse participant stories about their professional lives and the identities of self and others as discursive representations of their Sensemaking perspectives on the virtual work environment in which they live their professional lives (Boje, 1991, 2008). Similarly, with a basis in Weick (1995, 2001) and Van Dijk (2005), the book will consider those same views and attitudes as a basis for an analytical framework for analysing their work environment, and for analysing how they act in relation to it.

But I do not assume this relation between language and extra-linguistic socio-cognitive phenomena 'unproblematically' as warned by Wetherell et al. (2001). I'm fully aware that participants have an interest in presenting themselves as competent professionals when interviewed about their working lives. But what constitutes 'competence' and 'professionalism' differs depending on the participants' perception of first knowledge, second the mental models of Identity Prototypes and, third, the relationships with others which the participants construct through stories about their professional life in virtual teams. The DSA approach in the book therefore aims to examine these socio-cognitive aspects underlying participants' stories in the semi-structured interviews. This epistemological position can be seen as aligned with Teun van Dijk's CDA approach, even though I disagree with the critical theory which underpins his DA approach.

To address another warning of Wetherell et al., I am not arguing that the analysis will 'uncover attitudes or beliefs of which the speakers themselves are unaware' (Wetherell et al., 2001, p. 19). Rather, I assume that the experts on the attitudes or beliefs of a speaker are the speakers themselves. Therefore, the interviews I've conducted attempt to capture participants' own interpretations and reflections about their own virtual knowledge communication practices and the knowledge communication practices of their colleagues, thereby gaining insight into how they Retrospectively make sense of their virtual work environment. The findings can, hopefully, provide indications of how to move us forward in building organisations supporting virtual knowledge communication practices spanning the geographical dispersion of current organisational architecture.

Why interviews?

Interviews have been one of the most popular data collection methods in the social sciences, so much so that Benny and Hughes viewed modern sociology as the 'science of the interview' (1956, p. 137). Interviewing as a data collection method has also grown in applied linguistics (Mann, 2011), and is used 'particularly in qualitative studies that aim to investigate participant's identities, experiences, beliefs, and orientations' (Talmy & Richards, 2011, p. 111). But it has also been one of the most criticised data collection methods. This section reviews the debate and argues for why interviews are the ideal method for studying employee Discursive Sensemaking.

The purpose of adopting the discourse analysis process as one of the steps in the analysis process was to analyse the interviews as sites for Discursive Sensemaking. By 'Discursive Sensemaking' I refer to participants' Sensemaking perspectives as, first, explicitly expressed in the participant's own Retrospective analyses of their knowledge communication practices and the knowledge communication practices of others in their virtual work environment. Second, 'Discursive Sensemaking' refers to participants' discourse as implicitly infused into their stories through prosodic cues (Stress, Intonation, Pitch, volume and Pace), Lexical and syntactic choices, thereby emphasising specific meanings over others. For an explication of Weick's (1995, 2001) Sensemaking theory, see Chapter 2.

Thus, the stories told in the interviews reflect the socio-cognitive Identity Prototypes with which the participants associate themselves, and which can be seen as Mental Models guiding actions in daily practices. However, these prototypes are constantly balanced by the requirements of specific contexts, which explains why we do not always do as we say. Nevertheless, understanding the configurations of identities around specific prototypical approaches to knowledge communication may be important for understanding how to build more effective virtual teams.

The choice of interviews as data collection method in this book imposes a set of limitations on the conclusions that can be drawn from the data. Interview statements will always construct an individual interpretation of the situations they describe, i.e., a particular Sensemaking (Weick, 1995, 2001) perspective.

This can be seen as a constructionist position building on the fundamental insight from Phenomenology that humans always perceive contexts, relationships and practices through the filter of their own subject position (Crotty, 1998). Briefly, Phenomenology can be seen as based on the inseparability of subject and object; as Crotty (1998) states, 'consciousness is always consciousness *about* something. An object is always an object *for* someone' (p. 79, italics in original). In other words, objective reality exists, but has no meaning without subjective consciousness creating that meaning.

This has two consequences for analysing interview data. First, interview statements cannot be taken literally as descriptors of a practices outside the interview situation because individuals do not necessarily do what they say they do. This is not necessarily because they lie in the interview situation, but because, according to Weick (1995, 2001), the Sensemaking process involves attempts at aligning past experiences Retrospectively with current actions and contexts. Second, interview statements cannot be taken literally as descriptors of the participants' inner world and identity as this again will be presented from the Sensemaking perspective of the individual and may be presented with the purpose of positioning the self in a favourable light.

What constitutes a 'positive light', however, is not an objective phenomenon either. On the contrary, it reflects the values and Retention of the speaker in the professional context in which they are embedded. This implies that when participants represent their own practices, they infuse their utterances with the set of values which they see as positive in their professional Context. This process of co-construction of self, the virtual work environment and the Conversations within that environment as realised in the (d)iscourse of interview statements are what I term Discursive Sensemaking. In terms of the present study, this means that I expect participants to offer stories about their local and global projects which are perceived as successes or failures based on the idiosyncratic value system of the participant. I argue that these values are what underlie the participant's professional identity. Because of the social nature of identity argued by Wenger (1998) (see Chapter 8), I assume that this professional identity will be justified with reference to professional relationships with other employees sharing similar identities.

This social aspect of identity is my justification for selecting the three interviews as prototypical examples of the Identity Configurations which emerge as participants associate with or dissociate themselves from the professional identities of others in the organisation.

Despite their individual idiosyncrasies, the participants are embedded in a network of social relations which support, shape and challenge their professional identities. Because of the increasingly dispersed and virtual work environment, the opportunities for building networks of professional identities have increased. These identity constructions may (as we shall see is the case of HR Consult) include identities which are not necessarily aligned with corporate strategy. In this way, technology can be seen as changing mental models as will be argued in Chapter 5, because employees may identify with dispersed employees with different professional identities than the co-located colleagues.

The realisation of the two consequences of a constructionist perspective of linguistic data has led to a radical form of constructionism (post-structuralism). From the perspective of post-structuralism, interviews can only be used to examine the linguistic interaction between interviewer and participant and cannot be used to shed light on the cognition or inner self of the participant (Crotty, 1998). Nor can linguistic data, from the perspective of Post-Structuralism, be considered to have a causal impact on events outside the text (Crotty, 1998). Gergen (1994) is but one scholar who describes this double separation of world from text as a post-structuralist 'crisis of representation' (p. 412). By this phrase, Gergen (1994) refers to the implication of language being understood as an arbitrary meaning system in which terms gain meaning not through their relation to the world but through their Lexical and grammatical relations to other terms.

However, the reflexive epistemology of David (2005) and the reflexive methodology of Alvesson and Sköldberg (2009) question whether the lack of a 1:1 relationship between physical reality, subjective cognition and their discursive realisation means that we should stop researching this relation. Extra-linguistic subject-object relations are represented in language, even if the relation is not straightforward. Alvesson and Sköldberg (2009) propose, in their discussion of what a reflexive position could mean for DA, that we might be able to build more interesting analyses if we include the cognitive and the social perspectives as valid descriptors of a simultaneously subjective and social reality. This should include both individual and social identity. One might argue that since individual actions and (d)iscourses are based on such subjectivity, not attempting to analyse those Sensemaking perspectives can be seen as overlooking an essential aspect of (d)iscourse.

Alvesson and Sköldberg (2009) criticise DA for having a post-structuralist tendency, which reduces the subject of scientific enquiry to language, and thereby reduces science to the study language as linguistic action only. Instead, they argue that DA might fruitfully approach language from three levels of analysis:

1 The discursive level, at which analyses do not go beyond the text, but focus on linguistic interaction and linguistic (grammatical and Lexical) features of that text.
2 The ideational level, at which analyses focus on the inner cognitive meanings, such as identity and values, of the speaker, i.e., a cognitive level.
3 The action and social conditions represented by the text, which may include both relational, behavioural and institutional actions and conditions.

These three levels relate to the foci of my DA approach, although, as I will demonstrate in the analyses presented in Chapters 5–9, I perform Alvesson's and Sköldberg's (2009) levels in reverse order: I start from the action and social conditions level, to look at employee Sensemaking perspectives on knowledge communication practices at HR Consult. I then move to the ideational level to examine the values, identities and practices they construct in the (D)iscourse. And finally, I analyse the discursive level means they use to construct their perspective of the organisational reality at HR Consult, with specific focus on how they mediate, recognise or oppose organisational Conversations.

To sum up, despite the arguments against interview data as a means for accessing the inner life of the participant and the outer reality they represent in interview statements, I choose to use interviews and to analyse them as discursive sensemaking constructions of participants' professional identity through their justification of practices and their choices in enacting or resisting organisational Conversations through their (d)iscourse.

What type of knowledge can be constructed from interview data?

Regarding how (d)iscourse represents (as opposed to constructs) inner meaning or extra-linguistic social situations, the assumption of individual autonomy in the book's DA approach implies that interview statements are seen as representing meaning beyond the particular text. The interview as (d)iscourse is considered to represent, first, meaning in the form of the participants' Sensemaking about the virtual work environment; second, I examine constructions of the knowledge communication practices within that work environment; and third, I examine the values employed to justify those practices.

I use the term 'Discursive Sensemaking' to describe the linguistic expression of this process of participants' interpretations of their practices and identities in the stories they tell in the interviews. To the extent such individually held interpretations are identified among other employees at HR Consult, they can be identified as collective Sensemaking processes and seen as expressions of social Identity Configurations. These social identities can also be seen as Identity Prototypes which exist as socially shared Mental Models. These Mental Models can be seen as reference points which participants associate themselves with or dissociate themselves from (I return to Identity Configurations and Identity Prototypes in Chapter 8).

Having positioned my DSA approach in the field of DA in this chapter, the next chapter will present my Discursive Sensemaking Analysis method for analysing interview data.

References

Alvesson, M., & Kärreman, D. (2000). Varieties of discourse: On the study of organizations through discourse analysis. *Human Relations, 53*(9), 1125–1149. doi: 10.1177%2F0018726700539002

Alvesson, M., & Kärreman, D. (2011). Decolonializing discourse: Critical reflections on organizational discourse analysis. *Human Relations, 64*(9), 1121–1146. doi: 10.1177/0018726711408629

Alvesson, M., & Sköldberg, K. (2009). *Reflexive methodology* (2nd ed.). Los Angeles, CA: SAGE.

Austin, J. L. (1962). *How to do things with words.* Oxford: Oxford University Press.

Bäklander, G. (2019). To see or not to see: Importance of sensemaking in employee self-direction. *Nordic Journal of Working Life Studies, 9*(2), 25–45.

Bargiela-Chiappini, F. (2011). Discourse (s), social construction and language practices: In conversation with Alvesson and Kärreman. *Human Relations, 64*(9), 1177–1191.

Benny M., & Hughes E. C. (1956) Of sociology and the interview: Editorial preface. *American Journal of Sociology, 62*(2): 137–142.

Berger, P. L., Luckmann, T., & Zifonun, D. (1967). *The social construction of reality.* New York: Doubleday & Company.

Berkhout, S. (2007). Leadership in education transformation as reshaping the organisational discourse. *South African Journal of Education, 27*(3), 407–420.

Blommaert, J., & Bulcaen, C. (2000). Critical discourse analysis. *Annual Review of Anthropology, 29*(1), 447–466. doi: 10.1146/annurev.anthro.29.1.447 0019.1/103232

Boje, D. M. (1991). Consulting and change in the storytelling organisation. *Journal of Organizational Change Management, 4*(3), 7–17. doi: 10.1108/EUM0000000001193

Boje, D. M. (2008). *Storytelling organizations.* London: Sage.

Chouliaraki, L., & Fairclough, N. (2010). Critical discourse analysis in organizational studies: Towards an integrationist methodology. *Journal of Management Studies, 47*(6), 1213–1218. doi: 10.1111/j.1467-6486.2009.00883.x

Crotty, M. (1998). *The foundations of social research.* London: SAGE.

David, M. (2005). *Science in society.* New York: Palgrave Macmillan.

De Cock, C. (1998). Organisational change and discourse: Hegemony, resistance and reconstitution. *Management, 1*(1), 1–22.

Fairclough, N. (2003). *Analysing discourse: Textual analysis for social research.* London: Psychology Press.

Fairclough, N. (2005). Peripheral vision: Discourse analysis in organization studies: The case for critical realism. *Organization Studies, 26*(6), 915–939. doi: 10.1177/0170840605054610

Garzone, G., & Sarangi, S. (2007). Discourse, ideology and specialized communication: A critical introduction. In G. Garzone, & S. Sarangi (Eds.). *Discourse, ideology and specialized communication* (Vol. 33). New York: Peter Lang.

Gee, J. P. (1990). *Social linguistics and literacies: Ideology in discourses.* London: Routledge.

Gee, J. P. (2011). *An introduction to discourse analysis.* London: Routledge.

Gee, J. P. (2014). *How to do discourse analysis: A toolkit.* London: Routledge.

Gergen, K. J. (1994). Exploring the postmodern: Perils or potentials? *American Psychologist, 49*(5), 412. doi: 10.1037/0003-066X.49.5.412

Grant, D., Hardy, C., Oswick, C., & Putnam, L. L. (2004). Introduction: Organizational discourse: Exploring the field. In D. Grant, C. Hardy, C. Oswick, & L. L. Putnam (2004). *The Sage handbook of organizational discourse.* London: Sage. doi: 10.4135/9781848608122.n1

Halliday, M. A. K., & Hasan, R. (1976/2014). *Cohesion in English.* London: Routledge.

Howarth, D. (2000). *Discourse.* London: McGraw-Hill Education (UK).

Jian, G., Schmisseur, A. M., & Fairhurst, G. T. (2008). Organizational discourse and communication: The progeny of Proteus. *Discourse & Communication, 2*(3), 299–320.

Keller, R. (2011). The sociology of knowledge approach to discourse (SKAD). *Human Studies, 34*(1), 43–65. doi: 10.1007/s10746-011-9175-z

Kvale, S., & Brinkman, S. (2009). Interview quality. In *Interviews: Learning the craft of qualitative research interviewing* (pp. 161–175). London: Sage Publications Ltd. doi: 10.4135/9781849208963.n7

Lemke, J. L. (2012). Analyzing verbal data: Principles, methods, and problems. In K. G. Tobin, & C. J. McRobbie (Eds.). *Second international handbook of science education* (pp. 1471–1484). Boston, MA: Springer.

Maio, G. R., Olson, J. M., Bernard, M. M., & Luke, M. A. (2006). Ideologies, values, attitudes, and behavior. In J. DeLamater, & A. Ward (Eds.). *Handbook of social psychology* (pp. 283–308). Boston, MA: Springer. doi: 10.1007/0–387–36921-X_12

Mann, S. (2011). A critical review of qualitative interviews in applied linguistics. *Applied Linguistics, 32*(1), 6–24.

McCabe, D. (2014). Making out and making do: how employees resist and make organisational change work through consent in a UK bank. *New Technology, Work and Employment, 29*(1), 57–71. doi: 10.1111/ntwe.12023

Oswick (2010). Discourse. In: M. Tadajewski, P. Maclarn, E. Parsons, & M. Parker (Eds.). *Key concepts in critical management studies* (pp. 104–108). London: Sage Publications Ltd.

Phillips, N., Lawrence, T. B., & Hardy, C. (2004). Discourse and institutions. *Academy of Management Review, 29*(4), 635–652.

Phillips, N., & Oswick, C. (2012). Organizational discourse: Domains, debates, and directions. *Academy of Management Annals, 6*(1), 435–481. doi: 10.1080/19416520.2012.681558

Putnam, L. L., & Nicotera, A. M. (Eds.). (2009). *Building theories of organization: The constitutive role of communication*. London: Routledge.

Rhodes, C., & Brown, A. D. (2005). Narrative, organizations and research. *International Journal of Management Reviews,* 7(3), 167–188. doi: 10.1111/j.1468-2370.2005.00112.x

Rogers, R. (2004a, May). Interview with Norman Fairclough. Retrieved from [http://cw.routledge.com/textbooks/9780415874298/data/Fairclough_interview.pdf

Rogers, R. (2004b, May). Interview with James Gee. Retrieved from http://cw.routledge.com/textbooks/9780415874298/data/Gee_Interview.pdf

Sachs, J. (2019 February 26) *The Difference Between Ideology and Core Values.* Leadership as Practise. https://jonathansachs.net/2019/02/26/the-difference-between-ideology-and-core-values/

Schutz, A., & Luckmann, T. (1973). *The structures of the life-world* (vol. 1). Evanston, Ill: Northwestern University Press.

Sköldberg, K. (1994). Tales of change: Public administration reform and narrative mode. *Organization Science, 5*(2), 219–238. doi: 10.1287/orsc.5.2.219

Talmy, S., & Richards, K. (2011). Theorizing qualitative research interviews in applied linguistics. *Applied Linguistics, 32*(1), 1–5. doi: 10.1093/applin/amq045

Tietze, S., Cohen, L., & Musson, G. (2003). *Understanding organizations through language*. London: SAGE Publications Ltd.

Van Dijk, T. A. (2001). Critical discourse analysis. In The *handbook of discourse analysis* (pp. 349–371). Oxford: Blackwell Publishers Ltd. doi: 10.1002/9780470753460.ch19

Van Dijk, T. A. (2005). Contextual knowledge management in discourse production. In R. Wodak, & P. Chilton (Eds.), *A new agenda in (critical) discourse analysis* (pp. 71–100). Amsterdam: John Benjamins. doi: 10.1007/0–387–36921-X_12

Van Dijk, T.A. (2009a). Critical discourse studies: A sociocognitive approach. In R. Wodak & M. Meyer (Eds.) *Methods of critical discourse analysis*. London: Sage Publications Ltd.

Van Dijk, T. A. (2009b). *Society and discourse: How social contexts influence text and talk*. Cambridge: Cambridge University Press.

Van Dijk, T. A. (2014). *Discourse and knowledge: A sociocognitive approach*. Cambridge: Cambridge University Press.

Weick, K. E. (1995). *Sensemaking in organizations*. London: Sage Publications Ltd.

Weick, K. E. (2001). *Making sense of the organization*. Oxford: Blackwell.

Wenger, E. (1998). *Communities of practice: Learning, meaning, and identity*. New York: Cambridge University Press.

Wetherell, M., Taylor, S., & Yates, S. (2001). *Discourse as data*. London: Sage in association with Open University.

4 Discursive Sensemaking Analysis – a method

Chapter Contents

> The purpose of this chapter is to present my approach to studying virtual knowledge communication practices. There are plenty of method books out there, this is simply one method out of many. That said, none of the other method books offer methods for analysing how employees make sense of their virtual knowledge communication practices specifically.

I focus on the methodological challenges of analysing interviews to the depth that they deserve. The interviews conducted for the case study in this book were supplemented by participation in formal and informal

DOI: 10.4324/9781003015925-5

meetings at HR Consult Denmark, as well as collection of online documents and videos from the corporate intranet and emails (to the extent employees and management permitted access). The two analytical methods to analyse this data consisted first of coding using 'Template Analysis' (King, 2012) and second of Discursive Sensemaking Analysis (DSA. All capitalised words are defined in the glossary at the back of the book). This chapter provides a step-by-step explanation for how this analysis is carried out. But first I'll discuss my sampling strategy and present the case organisation 'HR Consult'.

Sampling strategy – problem-focused sampling

I suggest using a problem-focused approach when selecting a case organisation to study, i.e., find a case organisation based on the problem addressed by the research aims of and the problem addressed by the study. In my study, I was looking for a global organisation which used virtual teams, and where employees worked in multiple teams simultaneously. In terms of knowledge communication of more explicit knowledge, HR Consult represents a critical case because of its high reliance on explicit knowledge (Nonaka and Takeuchi, 1995), i.e., knowledge codified into easily transferable formats such as PowerPoints and PDF files with modular course materials.

The HR Consult consultants interviewed for this research project apply this codified knowledge to build modular solutions for personal, team and leadership development within client companies. My research interest lies with these employees, because I'm interested in the extent to which they engage in Virtual Knowledge Communication to develop their practice and grow professional and trust-based relations on the basis of this form of interaction.

This corporate strategy of applying existing knowledge means that the front-line consultants have little incentive to create and communicate new knowledge. This means that if virtual knowledge communication occurs among consultants in this organisation, it is likely to occur in other organisations, thereby increasing the generalisability of this critical case (Flyvbjerg, 2006).

Another strategic choice in the sampling process was to select offices within HR Consult with different levels of dispersion among case sites. In Denmark employees were mainly co-located with some remote employees; in Benelux, the organisation was distributed across two sites in Belgium and the Netherlands; and in the UK, consultants interviewed were part of a team dispersed across the UK. As the findings presented in Chapter 5 show, these different levels of dispersion did not, as might be expected, impact in any consistent manner on trust and knowledge relations in the different local organisations within HR Consult. The lack of any clear impact of dispersion on knowledge communication suggests that technology does not mediate Virtual Knowledge Communication in a consistent manner. This finding is presented in the case study analysis in Chapter 5. In the following two sections, I will describe the case organisation and introduce the interview participants.

HR Consult – a global HR consultancy organisation

HR Consult is a global organisation with a presence in more than 30 countries. Their core product is their personality profiling system, which consists of a core personal profile of approx. 20 pages with additional modules for team, sales and leadership profiling. The profile has been coded into a database which can build personality profiles based on snippets of text relating to the 72 different personality profiles of the system. The text is put together electronically based on client entries into the online indicator with 100 questions. The workshops to debrief clients on the meaning and usefulness of the profiles have been detailed by the R&D department at HQ. These is so detailed that they include what should be said for each of the PowerPoint slides and the number of minutes each exercise should take, and the HQ marketing department has designed marketing materials and branded props to be used for workshop exercises, including personality type card games, branded juggling balls, and branded building blocks similar to oversized LEGOs.

With this brief case description, I'll address the key challenges of selecting HR Consult as case organisation

Challenges of using HR Consult as a case site

The physical dispersion of HR Consult made it impossible for me to interview all participants face-to-face. This means that only interviews at the Danish site in Western Denmark were conducted face-to-face, while all other interviews were conducted over a Skype connection. This proved unproblematic for most interviews, but in a few interviews, it was difficult to establish a rapport with the participants, particularly in the interviews with two of the consultants from HR Consult Benelux, and in those cases, I found it difficult to establish a good rapport. However, this may not have anything to do with the mediation of technology, but simply the fact that we had not established a relationship before the interview. For the Danish participants, relations were established beforehand, due to my part-time work for HR Consult Denmark from 2005 to 2007.

The importance of a good rapport between researcher and participant could also be seen in participants' willingness to reflect on their own interview statements, and the social situations and practices they described. These reflections can be seen as constituting Discursive Sensemaking, because they are interview statements which reflect on the cognitive and social processes influencing the situations and actions described by interview statements. Participants with whom a good rapport was not established mainly described their practices, but rarely reflected on them. But because practices can be seen as Enactments of particular Sensemaking perspectives (Weick, 1995, 2001, see Chapter 2 in the present volume), these descriptions could be triangulated with other descriptions of similar practices and thereby analysed as being part of a larger Identity Configuration.

Analysing the interviews – the six steps of the Discursive Sensemaking Analysis process

In the following, I'll present the six steps of DSA, a discourse analysis method building on the seven Building Tasks (Gee, 2011, 2014, see Chapter 3 in the present volume) combined with codes for analysing perceptions of knowledge, identity and relationships. This will make it easier for students and researchers as well as for virtual teams' leaders or employees in HR or Project Management positions to use the method.

The steps, which will be elaborated in the rest of the chapter, are:

Step 1. Designing a semi-structured interview guide.
Step 2: Conducting the interviews.
Step 3: Coding the data to identify patterns of knowledge communication practices in a virtual work environment.
Step 4: Discursive Sensemaking level examined through Gee's Building Tasks.
Step 5: Realisation of Discursive Sensemaking at the linguistic level.
Step 5.a: supporting Discursive Sensemaking in research interviews.
Step 5.b: Discourse markers supporting Discursive Sensemaking in research interviews.
Step 5.c: Lexical choices supporting Discursive Sensemaking in research interviews.
Step 5.d: Prosody (Stress, Intonation, Pitch, volume and Pace) supporting Discursive Sensemaking in research interviews.
Step 6: Writing up the analyses.

Step 1: Designing a semi-structured interview guide

In designing a semi-structured interview guide, a key criterion was to elicit stories through which employees address their perception of their knowledge communication practices in the virtual work environment of HR Consult. This criterion is a measure to limit the extent to which the researcher's agenda influences participant response, which Wetherell et al. (2001) criticise on two counts. First, Wetherell et al. (2001) introduce the notion of reflexivity to describe the mutual impact of the world and the researcher on each other. In this study, this influence was made explicit in the introduction provided to participants where I pointed out the challenges of building teams which are able to communicate knowledge effectively in virtual work environments. Second, Wetherell et al. (2001) argue for the influence of the interviewer on interview participants in interviews. They argue that the way the researcher asks questions, and the topics of those questions influence not only which topics the participant is able to address, but also the subject positions the participant can adopt in the interview. Avoiding researcher bias and influence on participant altogether may be an illusion, as argued by Kvale and Brinkmann (2009), but this does not mean that the level of researcher influence cannot and should not be limited through careful interviewer consideration of how the interview guide is constructed.

Therefore, in my study I designed an interview guide which focused on eliciting stories about participants' practices, starting with their role in the organisation, and moving to specific projects in which they were currently engaged thereby eliciting narratives about how organisational knowledge was used and applied in the project. The structure was guided by a section on local projects and relations, and a section on global projects. Both included specific probes centering on elaborations of descriptions of practices and eliciting the participants interpretations of what these practices mean to their work.

The interview stories also provided data for my focus on prototypical identities through the emphasis on values and the justifications for their actions which participants often attached to their stories about their organisational knowledge communication practices. These values and justifications are what I suggest represents Discursive Sensemaking. In designing the interview guide, I did not have specific questions or probes to elicit professional identity constructions. Instead, I expected that when engaging in stories about local and global projects they would construct their identities in accordance with how they believed a good consultant should be. In this sense, I did not expect the stories to be true in an objective meaning of the word, but to be selected and angled to reflect a discursively constructed professional identity and relationships of the participants. In this sense, I expected participants to be true to themselves and their values. The constructions of professional identity through stories presumably represent their mental Prototype of what it means to be a 'good consultant', which can in turn be expected to be the same prototype they try to enact through their knowledge communication practices.

Step 2: Conducting the interviews

I conducted 21 interviews in this study. Each interview started by asking the participant's consent to record the interview and informing them that they would be anonymised in the published versions of the findings.

All participants in my study agreed to this except 'Christian'. 'Christian' had just left a management position at HR Consult Denmark at the time of the interview but was still using HR Consult product solutions for his new employer, and did not like his blatant criticism of particularly the CEO of HR Consult's, (Birgitte), management style to be recorded.

I then briefly informed participants that my study was about knowledge communication in local and global teams and projects and asked them to describe their role in the organisation. This introduction explicitly avoided mentioning my focus on identity and relationships, because I considered it important that constructions of professional identities and relationships arose out of the participants own volition, thereby limiting researcher impact on participants' responses.

My focus on identity (see Chapter 8) and relationships (see Chapter 9) only arose in my analysis of the interviews where I coded for Gee's (2011, 2014) Building Tasks, Identity and Relationships.

The shift in focus from academic research questions and theories into plain interview questions is a challenge when producing an interview guide; interview questions force you to formulate your grand ideas to plain language to elicit the stories which can help you answer those academic questions.

The majority of the participants did engage in elaborate stories about their current projects and teams and required little prompting, and stories about practices were often followed by justifications for why they had done what they had done in a particular situation, particularly when I stayed quiet at the end of a story sequence. Often, they made these values and justifications explicit as conclusions, or morals, to stories about projects or team tasks; they were not 'discovered' by me through analysis and interpretation. In the interaction with participants, I did try to probe for such Discursive Sensemaking from participants when it did not arise naturally.

Towards the end of the interviews, I also became more critical of their perspectives. This often took the form of questioning justifications by rephrasing other perspectives. In the interview situation, I was often able to intuitively link these justifications to my research questions and theoretical concepts from the literature review. When this occurred, I would summarise what the participant had said. Occasionally this led to the participant negating my impression, but often led to their agreement.

In either case, these summaries often sparked further Discursive Sensemaking about the participants' knowledge communication practices and the relations used to support them. So, my probes, questions, and summaries were situated within the interaction of the individual interview rather than following a preprepared formula. Nevertheless, all my interactions with the participants were informed by my review of theoretical concepts and my research questions. From the perspective of more inductive methodologies, such as Grounded Theory (Glaser &

Strauss, 1968), my approach could be seen as a biased perspective. From the perspective of a hypothetico-deductive method at the other end of the scale, my approach could be seen as unsystematic and far too open-ended. But from the point of view of the reflexive epistemology (David, 2005) and reflexive methodology (Alvesson & Sköldberg, 2009), my approach can also be seen as a purposeful inquiry informed by theory, but with an open mind towards the participants' own perspectives, thereby balancing the deductive and inductive approaches.

Nevertheless, the interview situation as a context for interaction had considerable impact on the level of detail participants offered, and the amount of Discursive Sensemaking they engaged in to justify the values and practices in their stories. Rapport between researcher and participant thus had an impact on the level of Discursive Sensemaking in the individual interview. This rapport is symbolised, even, quantified, by the length of the interview: the shortest interview in which a poor rapport was established lasted little more than 30 minutes, while the best rapport resulted in an interview lasting nearly two hours. However, because participants mentioned each other and their different approaches to knowledge communication practices, even interviews which did not contain explicit Discursive Sensemaking could be analysed as reflecting value systems and professional identities made explicit in the Discursive Sensemaking of other participants.

Step 3: Coding the data

The interviews were coded using the theoretical concepts and analytical questions laid out in the tables at the end of Chapters 5–8. These tables include both a priori codes and codes emerging during the coding process. Patterns across the analyses pointed to configurations of three distinct professional identities, of which I selected three interviews as prototypical examples. Gee's (2011, 2014) Building Tasks were part of the coding structure, and the Building Task 'identities' turned out to be the most oft used code. During the coding process, subcategories in the form of 'self', 'other' or 'organisation' were added. When a particular and fairly consistent set of professional identity traits were described by some participants as the basis for their own and others' action, while the same set of professional identity traits was opposed by other participants, I began to analyse these as distinct configurations of professional identity. The identity configurations thus emerged through triangulation between interview passages coded as self-identity and passages coded as identity of others.

The selection of three participants as prototypes of the Identity Configurations does not imply that the boundaries between the identity configurations are not blurred – they are. Nor do I suggest that there are no individual practices – there are. Rather, the intention is to build an awareness of how different professional identity configurations can result in unhealthy in-group/out-group boundaries of virtual knowledge communication if organisations are not aware of the differences between these communities. The analysis also shows that, with the right leadership, the strength of each Identity Prototype can be harnessed to improve organisational virtual knowledge communication.

After coding, I selected three participants as prototypical representatives of each Identity Configuration. The first, which I term the Knowledge Transfer Prototype, was the most common type, and the one most aligned with corporate strategy. This prototype was not analysed as thoroughly as the two other prototypes which can be seen as opposing corporate strategy. These two stand out because of the innovative solutions they create. Those two interviews were subjected to the analytical process of DSA as laid out in step 4 and 5. The purpose was to analyse the interrelations between their perceptions of knowledge, identity and relationships.

Step 4: Discursive Sensemaking level examined through Gee's Building Tasks

At this level of analysis, I focus on how a participant makes retrospective sense of their practices. Practices are one of Gee's Building Tasks, i.e., one of the seven elements we construct when speaking (see Chapter 3). But because the Sensemaking perspective entails that descriptions of practice are never value free or objective, the discursive construction of organisational practices was always infused with the values and the Sensemaking perspective of the participant. Because of this, Gee's Building Task, Politics, can be used as a lens for focusing on how participants use (d)iscourse to render some organisational knowledge communication approaches more valuable than others, and how such privileging of certain approaches are justified by participants. Through the privileging of certain approaches, the Building Task Politics can be seen as closely linked to the Building Task Significance: participants tended to focus on their own approaches to organisational knowledge communication, thereby rendering their own perspective Significant.

These three Building Tasks, Practices, Politics, and Significance were the most important lenses for shedding light on the perception of knowledge of the three prototypes. I used the Building Task Connections as a lens for putting focus on how participants connected their practices to perceptions of knowledge, for example one of the participants, 'Henrik', uses musical improvisation as a metaphor for his use of the organisational knowledge communication approach, thereby emphasising the creativity and transformation entailed by his organisational knowledge communication approach.

The identity focus of Chapter 8 was examined mainly through the directly associated Building Task, Identity. But participants rarely addressed their own or other's identities explicitly. Discursive Sensemaking about identity was embedded in the stories about practices and closely associated to the construction of justifications for these practices as necessary and profitable to the organisation. Thereby, the construction of identity was closely associated with the Building Task Politics.

As the analysis progressed, it became increasingly clear that participants constructed their own professional identity by comparing their own approaches to the knowledge communication practices of their colleagues, and to those encouraged by the organisation. This resulted in the same interview passages being coded as both the participants own identity and the participant's construction of either colleague or organisational identity. These overlaps became important for the emergence in the data of what I have termed Identity Prototypes. As the analysis progressed, I became increasingly aware of interview passages where participants' justified their practices with reference to their perceptions of organisational knowledge. Through these justifications, participants negotiated the conversations of the organisation, in the form of managers' expectations and other colleagues' practices, thereby constructing a professional identity based on these justifications. In negotiating organisational conversations participants can also be seen as engaging in the Building Task, Politics, because they selected stories which supported their prototypical identity, and they justified the actions which they described in their stories with reference to the values underlying their professional identities.

The analysis of these Building Tasks was used to approach the data from a Discursive Sensemaking angle, through their function as a lens for examining how participants' (d)iscourse constructs their perception of their organisational context, and the perception of knowledge, Identity and Relationships which they use to support their perspective on the organisational virtual work environment and knowledge communication practices. This Sensemaking level did not adequately exhaust the data, because the meaning of the interview statements and the value participants attached to particular statements was not only communicated through the written transcriptions. They were also communicated through Prosody (Stress, Intonation, Pitch, volume and Pace) used by participants to build the Significance of certain words, phrases or passages, thereby supporting analyses at the Discursive Sensemaking level of analysis. I provide the details of how I approach this more linguistically focused level of the analysis in the next section.

Step 5: Realisation of Discursive Sensemaking at the linguistic level

I now turn to the linguistic level of analysis, which should not be seen as separate from the Sensemaking level; the two are closely linked. Through selective analysis of participants' grammar, discourse markers, Lexical choices and prosody (Stress, Intonation, Pitch, volume and Pace), I show

how participants use language rhetorically to support their Discursive Sensemaking. I use the word 'selective analysis', because I do not undertake exhaustive analyses of all of these linguistic features. Each of them are fields in their own right within Linguistics, and my analysis process only adopts a limited set of tools based mainly on Gee's (2011, 2014) sociolinguistic approach to discourse analysis. I use a capital 'L' in Linguistics to signify the academic discipline, but a small 'l' when referring to the more general meaning of Linguistics as relating to aspects of language.

In the following, I provide an overview of how each of these linguistic features are examined as part of my DSA. I do not attempt to provide an overview of each of the fields, but instead aim at providing examples and justification for why each element is relevant to DSA. Again, they should not be seen as separate from the Discursive Sensemaking level of the analysis, but more as a different focus in the analysis.

Gee's focus on how language constructs the social world entails a pragmatic view of language in which language is emphasised as performing a construction of reality from the speaker's perspective. Like my orthographic convention for Linguistics, I use a capital 'P' to refer to the field of Pragmatics, a sub-field within Linguistics which is concerned with how language takes on specific meanings within specific contexts, often beyond the literal meaning of grammar and Lexical choices. DSA builds on this position by combining analysis at the Sensemaking level (presented in the previous section) with an analysis of how specific linguistic elements are used to construct the speaker's perspective on organisational knowledge, professional identity and the relationships supporting this professional identity. This distinguishes my DA approach from DA approaches within Linguistics; analyses at what I call the linguistic level are never exhaustive from the point of view of a linguist. But they contain more linguistic evidence than is typically found in DA approaches within the social sciences. The typical social science approach to DA may be seen as focusing on the macro-level of discourse at the expense of the detail offered by closer linguistic analysis. The mainstream DA approaches within Linguistics, on the other hand, may be seen as focusing too much on specific linguistic features at the expense of a more socially focused enquiry examining how language is used to build social reality, enacting and resisting conversations of the context in the process.

Step 5a: Grammar supporting Discursive Sensemaking in research interviews

At what I term the linguistic level of my analyses, I draw attention to participants' grammatical choices when these can be seen as building Significance by positioning certain sentence elements in more salient positions at the end of a phrase or an Intonation Unit. Two examples from my analyses may be the best way to illustrate this.

The first example is the use of the passive voice to avoid placing responsibility when 'Henrik' states that 'I'm told I shouldn't develop so much' ('Henrik', my translation, par. 124, 27:38), thereby implicitly criticising his CEO who, based on the context of his statement, is the one telling him to reduce his development of new organisational knowledge, but by using the passive voice, 'I'm told', he avoids blatant criticism of his CEO.

The other example is when 'Linda' states that she 'simply had to' (select team members from outside the organisation to complete her project, despite her managers' attempts to make her use more local members employed by HR Consult). In this statement, 'Linda' uses the Deontic modal expression 'had to' suggesting that she was obligated to oppose her managers' attempts to enforce organisational practice. Based on the surrounding (d)iscourse of 'Linda's' interview, however, it becomes clear that the values of her own professional identity are the source of her sense of obligation.

Thus, the syntactic choice of a modal verb serves a pragmatic rather than a grammatical function. This evidence from participants' choices of grammar should not be used as determining meaning but should be used in conjunction with other linguistic and Sensemaking evidence to add evidence for favouring some interpretations over others.

Step 5b: Discourse markers supporting Discursive Sensemaking

In identifying passages in which participants discursively made sense of their practices, I also relied on the analysis of discourse markers. Schiffrin (1988) introduced the notion of discourse markers, arguing that certain words ('oh', 'well', 'and', 'but', 'or', 'so', 'because', 'now', 'then', 'y'know', and 'I mean') function to structure. The discourse markers thus signal a relationship between the segment they introduce, S2, and the prior segment, S1 (Fraser, 1999).

In the interviews, participants would often describe a certain practice, which became S1, and follow this up with Discursive Sensemaking justifying this practice. This Sensemaking justification thus performs the function of S2 and was usually signalled by the use of one of the discourse markers 'so', 'well' or 'y'know', preceded and/or followed by pauses. The pauses combined with the discourse marker served to signal that the participant's interpretation of the preceding description was coming. Discourse markers have a core meaning, which is to signal a break before moving to a new topic, not as having a Lexical meaning.

So, in accordance with my perspective on DA, Discourse markers cannot be interpreted in isolation, as simply grammatical functions; Their function can only be interpreted within the context of the larger text, the way they are pronounced (i.e., through Prosody), and the meaning the speaker is trying to convey.

Step 5c: Lexical choices supporting Discursive Sensemaking

Through choice of words, speakers can privilege some meanings over others; this is what I mean by 'Lexical choice'. By considering alternative choices and their implications when analysing the data, this privileging can be seen as a way of making certain aspects of the represented event more Significant than others. In doing so, participants infuse descriptions of their own and the organisational practices with distinct value-laden perspectives, which I see as explicit and discursive aspects of their Retention. Through analyses of these choices, the values underlying the participant's professional identity is shifted from a hidden and tacit aspect of the participant's inner life to a linguistic feature of the speaker's (d)iscourse as they discursively make sense of their practices. As was the case for grammar, analysis of these Lexical choices is not considered in isolation in my analysis, but as co-constitutive of the participant's Discursive Sensemaking.

Step 5d:Prosody (stress, intonation, pitch, volume and pace) supporting Discursive Sensemaking

We recognise and intuitively analyse prosodic clues in daily conversations as a means to understand what our partner in the conversation is saying. These Prosodic Cues are lost in interviews transcription, but can be replaced by transcription codes signalling Stress, Intonation, Pitch, volume and Pace. This section provides definitions of what I mean by these five elements of Prosody, and how they are related to Discursive Sensemaking.

Transcribing and analysing Prosodic Cues can be seen as a means for capturing information which is lost when audio recordings are transcribed (Lemke, 2012). Because the spoken language of a research interview is never analysed directly, but through written transcripts, using interview data for research purposes can challenge data reliability. This is because Prosodic Cues can change the literal meaning of participants' statements. As argued by Lemke (2012):

> The process of transcription creates a new text whose relations to the original data are problematic. What sounds perfectly sensible and coherent may look in transcription confused and disorganised. What passes by in speech so quickly as not to be noticed, or is replaced by the listener's expectations of what should have been said, is frozen and magnified in transcription. Normal spoken language is full of hesitations, repetitions, false starts, re-starts, changes of grammatical construction in mid-utterance, non-standard forms, compressions and so on.
>
> (p. 1472)

Stress can be defined as a grammatical element of how words, phrases and sentences are pronounced in each language, but beyond this grammatical function, Stress is used pragmatically to emphasise particular meanings by stressing certain words or phrases (Gee, 2011). Classic examples of this definition of Stress are the difference between 'I gave John the book' (constative, literal meaning) versus 'I *gave* John the book' (depending on context, pragmatic meaning could be a denial of an accusation that the speaker forgot to give John the book). Wodak and Meyer (2009) argue that Stress is a psychological rather than a physical concept, because it is intuitively heard despite numerous physical combinations of increased volume, increased vowel length and changing Pitch. Change in Pitch to put Stress on a syllable can be expressed as both high and low Pitch or glides up or down on the Stressed syllable. I analyse Stress as an element of my DSA method, because participants often used Stress to build Significance of certain elements of their (d)iscourse.

By 'Intonation', I refer to shifts in the Pitch which occur over pronunciation of an Intonation Unit. I use 'Intonation Unit' in the widely adopted meaning, also used by Gee (2011, 2014), as a spoken unit of discourse which is intuitively analysed by a hearer as distinct from other Intonation Units. The Intonation Unit usually consists of a series of words spoken with a progressive shift in Pitch across the Intonation unit. This can consist in a falling Intonation pattern giving the impression of a matter-of-fact statement if followed by the oral equivalent of a full stop, as in 'I bought an apple.' Rising Intonation patterns are typical of questions, particularly when these are not 'wh'-questions, for example 'you bought an apple?' In Table 4.1, I provide a list of the transcription conventions I used.

I use 'Pitch' to refer to the highness or lowness with which a word or phrase is pronounced. As mentioned above, Pitch is an aspect of the Intonation Unit, but occasionally participants spoke in a generally higher or lower Pitch, making an Intonation Unit or series of Intonation Units stand out from the rest of the participant's statements. Often this coincided with statements or passages relevant to the Discursive Sensemaking level of analysis, thereby Pitch was used to add Significance to the statement or Intonation Unit.

In my data, I found that sudden Pitch shifts were often used to add emphasis to particular words. When this occurred in combination with higher volume in the pronunciation, I simply recorded the word as stressed. The term 'Pitch Range' is used in the analysis to describe the difference between highest and lowest Pitch of an Intonation Unit. While the Pitch Range shifts between different speakers and different dialects, I use Pitch Range only to describe changes relative to the particular speaker's Pitch Range in the particular interview, because this was when changes in Pitch Range made a phrase or statement stand out from the participant's surrounding statements. This often occurred as a sign that a speaker was being ironic.

Again, these analyses are always relative to the individual speaking style of a participant and must take account of individual speaking styles. For example, one of my participants, 'Rasmus' generally spoke with little shift in Pitch Range. On the other hand, 'Dorthe' generally had a very varied Pitch Range. So, when the analysis indicates high Pitch for 'Rasmus', the objectively measured Pitch level may be lower than 'Dorthe's' average Pitch level.

Finally, I use the term Pace simply to describe the speed with which an Intonation unit or series of Intonation Units are pronounced. Pace was relevant for the analysis of Discursive Sensemaking, because it can be used as a sign of hesitation or reflection (in the case of a slow Pace), or excitement (in the case of a fast Pace). As for all elements of prosody, such effects cannot be put into a formula and applied across cases but must be situated within the context of the particular interview.

I use the term Prosodic Cues to describe specific instances of, or combinations of, Stress, Intonation, Pitch, volume and Pace. Often Prosodic Cues are combined for particular effects. For example, you might interpret low volume and small Pitch Range as sign of tiredness or, if combined with hesitations, as signs of uncertainty or non-confrontational lack of agreement with the researcher. As another example, I often analysed the combination of high Pitch and fast Pace as indications of a participant's commitment to and passion for a statement. In the analyses, I also found that Prosodic Cues can signal whether the participant's response, despite agreement with a statement, rests on a dubious foundation, and is uttered by the participant mainly to live up to what the interviewer expects of the participant. While this ambiguity of interview statements can never be unequivocally resolved, the analysis of prosody can offer some indications of speaker attitude towards their (d)iscourse and the organisational conversations invoked by the (d)iscourse.

The analysis of prosody became an important basis for which to analyse the values of each prototypical identity. Thus, shifts in Intonation and Pace can be used by participants to render some phrases or spates of language more salient than others, thereby making the analysis of Prosody relevant for discourse analysis at the pragmatic level, mainly through Gee's Building Task Significance.

The analysis of Prosody, as all discourse analysis, does not result in unequivocal meaning, but when combined with analyses at the Discursive Sensemaking level and with other linguistic evidence from the participant's Lexical and grammatical choices, I would argue that this makes any interpretation both more reliable and more transparent.

Transcription conventions for capturing prosody

The interview passages I selected for deeper analysis on the basis of the first rounds of content coding were re-transcribed to add prosodic details of Stress, Intonation, Pitch, volume and Pace. For this purpose, I needed a set of transcription conventions which fulfilled three needs: being easy to use in practice, being relatively comprehensible to the reader, and having enough detail to show how Prosodic Cues were used by the participant to render some phrases or words more Significant, or to add meaning beyond the literal meaning of the sentence. This added meaning often arose in interaction with other levels of analysis, and were used to render certain elements (phrases, words or syllables) more salient, or to rhetorically organise utterances to achieve specific pragmatic effects. In the transcriptions, Intonation Units are marked by line breaks.

Selecting which transcription conventions to adopt took more consideration than I had expected. Almost every discourse analyst seems to have their own set of transcription conventions, or have at least adapted an existing one to their needs.

Initially, I found this odd because the term 'conventions' connotes some agreement. Yet, as I started working with my data, reflecting on what aspects of the Prosody I needed for my purposes, I realised why there are just as many transcription conventions as there are discourse analysis approaches: Depending on your discourse analysis approach, Prosody may be the research focus in and of itself, or may be entirely irrelevant. As an example of transcription conventions within Linguistics, consider a sentence fragment from a televised interview examined by Cheng and Lam (2011): 'Well, I think I agree with…'. Using Cheng and Lam's (2011) transcription conventions, the sentence fragment from the televised interview looks like this: {\ [< ^ WELL >]} {? [< I >]} {? [< I >]} {\ i [< ^ THINK >]} {= [< ER >]} {= i [aGREE] < WITH > er} (p. 282)

The high level of detail not only seems to obscure the original text but is detailed beyond the needs of my focus on Discursive Sensemaking in the virtual work environment of HR Consult. In the end, I combined and added to the transcription conventions adopted by Wetherell et al. (2001), Cheng and Lam (2011) and Drew and Heritage (1992). This provided me with the set of transcription conventions summarised in Table 4.1. These were selected to suit my needs for detail without overcrowding the transcription with codes as in the example quoted above. I chose not to adopt Wetherell et al.'s practice of measuring pauses in tenths of a second, as I could not, as a listener, identify any significant changes in meaning in pauses with such a small difference.

Instead, I indicate whether a pause is short, typically a fraction of a second indicated by (.) in the transcription; or long, typically longer than a second, indicated by (..) in the transcription. Often meaning beyond grammatical or literal meaning was added through prosodic elements in the interviews. This with the findings and conclusions from Myers and Newman (2007) and Schiffrin (2008). Schiffrin (2008) also notes how pauses, and phrases apparently devoid of Lexical meaning, such as 'y'know', are used to establish cohesion and delimit different sections in oral

Table 4.1 Transcription conventions with brief explanations

Sign	*Description*
/	Rising intonation in the following part of the intonation unit – If this persists throughout the intonation unit it typically indicates a question.
\	Falling intonation in the following words – if the sign precedes the last syllables of an intonation unit, it typically constitutes the verbal equivalent of a full stop.
Word	Italicised word is emphasised.
^	Indicates that the following is spoken in high pitch. As argued by Wennerstrom (Wennerstrom, 2001), 'a high onset in the pitch range, indicates a contrast in attitude with respect to the prior utterance' (p. 23).
_word	Indicates that the intonation unit is spoken in low pitch. This is often used to indicate a foregone conclusion or information which the speaker seems is obvious or a self-evident piece of information. But depending on the context, it may also indicate tiredness or frustration on the part of the speaker.
=	Indicates that the following is spoken in mid pitch. The code is only used if the pitch shifts from high to mid pitch within an intonation unit. If the entire intonation unit is spoken in mid pitch, this is not noted in the transcription.
.	Final contour – the verbal equivalent of a full stop at the end of an intonation unit. Can end a sentence fragment in oral discourse to add emphasis to the preceding constituent as in the following example where emphasis is added to 'guys', who are given the predicate 'good people' in the next intonation unit: '/So ^these \guys. (.) /They're good ^people.' ('Henrik', my translation, 303, 1:00:37).
,	Continuing contour – the verbal equivalent of a comma at the end of an intonation unit. This can occur in mid-sentence to emphasise certain grammatical elements. For example, the continuing contour is used in the following (combined with fronting the adverbial to sentence initial position) to add emphasis to the location where the speaker feels at home: '/and there, (.) \I feel at home there.' ('Henrik', my translation, 303, 1:00:37).
(.)	Pause, less than a second.
(..)	Pause, more than a second.
--	Utterance cut off – interruption by self or another speaker. If the utterance is cut off by another intonation unit (i.e., a new line), the new intonation unit will be started by "--" to indicate that it follows immediately on from the previous intonation unit.
[faster pace]	Pace of enunciation, which can also be described as a faster rhythm has not been assigned a shorthand, but will be indicated in square brackets on a separate line before the passage to indicate that it pertains to all following lines until a new square bracket with e.g.: '[normal pace]'. If the faster pace pertains only to one intonation unit, '[faster pace]' will be inserted at the beginning of that intonation unit and will be assumed to return to normal in the next intonation unit.
£word£	Words between £-symbols are spoken while laughing.

discourse. In Table 4.1 below, I provide an overview of the transcription conventions used throughout the interview analyses in Chapters 5–9 of the book.

Often an Intonation unit combines a rise and fall in Pitch, or fall and rise, within an Intonation unit. To indicate the rise-fall contour, Cheng and Lam (2011) use "/\" before the Intonation Unit. Instead, I use the slash or back slash consistent with the descriptions above, but I insert them within the Intonation unit, rather than before, thereby indicating when fall shifts to rise or vice versa. I considered this information important, because Intonation is usually used to render the highest pitched syllable more salient to the listener, thereby constructing that syllable as Significant. An Intonation unit moving from high onset Pitch to low Pitch and back to high Pitch at the end of the Intonation unit typically renders the last word or words of the Intonation unit Significant. Whether only the last words or all words from the onset of the rising Pitch are constructed as significant can only be determined on the basis of context, if at all (Cheng & Lam, 2011).

Step 6: Writing up the analyses

In writing up the analyses, I have built a macro-structure based on the three focus points of the book: perception knowledge, Identity, and Relationships, and a micro-structure, for the analysis of each interview quote. I explain the structure below.

The micro-structure each interview quote, consists, first, of a lead-in explaining why the quote is relevant in terms of the analytical terminology presented in Chapters 5–8. Second, I provide an analysis from the Discursive Sensemaking perspective, and an analysis focusing on how this Discursive Sensemaking perspective is realised and supported by linguistic evidence. In the first stages of the transcription analysis, the higher level analyses of Discursive Sensemaking were intertwined with closer readings of how the Discursive Sensemaking was realised at the linguistic level. In writing up the analyses, however, I have tried to separate the two perspectives to ensure accessibility and transparency. At the higher order Discursive Sensemaking level, I draw attention to how participants use the (d)iscourse of interview statements to make sense of their practices. This can be seen as a more macro-level analysis.

These linguistic analyses focus particularly on prosody which turned out to be important not only as signposts for the structure of the participants' (d)iscourse, but as evidence for the commitment, resistance, excitement, frustration or indifference with which statements were uttered. Often the selection of quotes to be included in the analyses was based on the analyses of Prosody, which gave clues to whether a statement or issue was important to the participant.

Summary of the analysis process

To sum up the analysis process, I start from a macro-level of Discursive Sensemaking by using Gee's Building Tasks to examine how employees make sense of Practices, Identities, and Relationships, and how they render certain values and practices more Significant than others, build Connections between values and practices, thereby favour some values over others (the Building Task, Politics). Then I move to the linguistic level where tools from grammar, discourse markers, and (in particular) Lexical choices are used to show how Discursive Sensemaking is realised at the linguistic level. Having set out the details of each level of analysis, I will now shift to my considerations of the generalisability and validity of the study.

Shifting from generalisability and validity to quality of craftsmanship as criterion for success

Delmar (2010) argues for shifting focus from generalisability towards 'the quality and validity of qualitative research' (p. 116). Validity should be understood here in a broader sense than in the natural sciences where validity is a statistical test to measure 'whether a method investigates what it purports to investigate' (Kvale & Brinkmann, 2009, p. 327). Though Kvale and Brinkmann (2009) adopt a more Post-structuralist position than Delmar (2010), their argument for validity in qualitative research as shown through 'quality of craftsmanship' (Kvale and Brinkman 2009, p. 247) can be seen as similar to Delmar's (2010) argument for detailed case description. As mentioned, the detailed case description builds a transparency which seems to be an integral part of ensuring quality of research. So, both Delmar (2010) and Kvale and Brinkman (2009) argue for an adoption of 'validation' in its more general meaning: 'to check'. Building on this more general conception of validity, Kvale and Brinkman (2009) argue that validity should permeate all stages of the research process. In arguing for their redefinition of validity within a constructionist framework, they first argue for ensuring 'the logic of the derivations from theory to the research questions of the study' (Kvale and Brinkman, 2009, p. 248). I seek to achieve this by providing detailed descriptions of the steps in the analysis process. Thereby, each section of the methodology chapter adds elements to build transparency in the research design from conceptualisation to write-up. Second, Kvale and Brinkman argue that the methods adopted must match the purpose of the study, which I seek to achieve by adopting a discourse analysis lens to study discursive constructions of Sensemaking in employee interviews.

The transparency in the case description and findings, advocated by Delmar (2010), also impacts on the replicability of the research study.

Yin (2003) argues that in case study research, replicability concerns the possibility of conducting the same case again, not, as in quantitative research, the possibility of replicating the findings in other settings. If a case study is to be replicated in the fashion described by Yin, transparency of the case description, the methods used to analyse the case, and the analysis procedure itself is required. However, even extensive transparency of the research process may not be enough to ensure replicability. In place of replicability, I adopt a focus on transparency through a detailed description of the research process, from the design of the interview guides, to conducting and analysing the interviews and choices in writing up the data. This transparency focus therefore permeates the study.

This method chapter ends part I of the book. Part II presents theory to describe and analyse virtual knowledge communication in global organisations and presents interview analysis to illustrate how the theories can be applied in practise.

References

Alvesson, M., & Sköldberg, K. (2009). *Reflexive methodology* (2nd ed.). Los Angeles, CA: Sage.

Cheng, W., & Lam, P. (2011). Prosody in discourse. In J. P. Gee & M. Handford (Eds.), *Routledge handbook of discourse analysis* (pp. 271–284). New York: Routledge.

David, M. (2005). *Science in society*. New York: Palgrave Macmillan.

Delmar, C. (2010). "Generalizability" as recognition: Reflections on a foundational problem in qualitative research. *Qualitative Studies, 1*(2), 115–128. doi: 10.7146/qs.v1i2.3828

Drew, P., & Heritage, J. (1992). *Talk at work: Interaction in institutional settings*. Cambridge: Cambridge University Press.

Flyvbjerg, B. (2006). Five misunderstandings about case-study research. *Qualitative inquiry, 12*(2), 219–245. doi: 10.1177%2F1077800405284363

Fraser, B. (1999). What are discourse markers? *Journal of Pragmatics*, 31(7), 931–952. doi: 10.1016/S0378-2166(98)00101-5

Gee, J. P. (2011). *An introduction to discourse analysis*. London: Routledge.

Gee, J. P. (2014). *How to do discourse analysis: A toolkit*. London: Routledge.

Glaser, B. G., & Strauss, A. L. (1968). *The discovery of grounded theory. Strategies for qualitative research*. London; printed in U.S.A.: Weidenfeld & Nicolson.

King, N. (2012). Doing template analysis. In G. Simon & C. Cassel (Eds.), *Qualitative organizational research: Core methods and current challenges* (pp. 426–250). London: SAGE Publications Ltd.

Kvale, S., & Brinkmann, S. (2009). *Interviews: Learning the craft of qualitative research interviewing* (2nd ed., vol. 10). Thousand Oaks, CA: Sage.

Lemke, J. L. (2012). Analyzing verbal data: Principles, methods, and problems. In B. J. Fraser & K. G. Tobin (Eds.), *Second international handbook of science education* (pp. 1471–1484). London: Springer.

Myers, M. D., & Newman, M. (2007). The qualitative interview in IS research: Examining the craft. *Information and Organization, 17*(1), 2–26. doi: 10.1016/j.infoandorg.2006.11.001

Nonaka, I., & Takeuchi, H. (1995). *Knowledge-creating company: How Japanese companies create the dynamics of innovation*. Oxford: Oxford University.

Schiffrin, D. (1988). *Discourse markers*. Cambridge University Press.

Schiffrin, D. (2008). Discourse markers: Learning, meaning and context. In D. Schiffrin, D. Tannen, & H. E. Hamilton (Eds.), *The handbook of discourse analysis* (pp. 54–75). Maldrin, MA: Blackwell Publishing.

Weick, K. E. (1995). *Sensemaking in organizations*. London: Sage

Weick, K. E. (2001). *Making sense of the organization*. Oxford: Blackwell.

Wennerstrom, A. K. (2001). *Music of everyday speech: Prosody and discourse analysis*. Cary, NC: Oxford University Press, Incorporated.

Wetherell, M., Taylor, S., & Yates, S. (2001). *Discourse as data*. London: Sage in association with Open University.

Wodak, R., & Meyer, M. (2009). *Methods of critical discourse analysis* (2nd ed.). London: Sage.

Yin, R. (2003). *Case study research* (3rd ed.). Thousand Oaks, CA: Sage.

Part 2

Multidisciplinary perspective on knowledge communication practices in virtual teams

5 Challenges and opportunities of virtual work in global organisations

Chapter Contents

According to the socio-technical theories presented in this chapter, technologies can become both a help and a hindrance to work in virtual teams, depending on the user; the technologies mediate, but do not determine virtual knowledge communication. While many Virtual Teams fail to build mutual understanding and trust, and consequently fail to communicate knowledge effectively, a few virtual teams overcome the challenges and become high performing virtual 'Knowledge Teams'. At HR Consult, Linda is part of such a team characterised by their trust in weak ties, their ability to divide knowledge domains, and their frequent virtual knowledge communication.

Appropriating technology for your own purposes

The trajectory of research into the use of organisational ICT (Information and Communication Technology, all capitalised words are defined

DOI: 10.4324/9781003015925-7

in the glossary at the back of the book) seems to have shifted from a deterministic focus on the affordances of technologies towards a complex view of technologies as embedded in deeper and wider personal, institutional, social and cultural contexts (Kampf, 2005). In fact, more recent studies point to the quality of technology as enabling complex trust-based interaction and knowledge communication in virtual teams (Olaisen & Revang, 2017).

In this section, I outline this trajectory, but argue that the more deterministic view of technology continues to exist alongside the socio-technical perspective. I term the earlier perspective 'deterministic', because it rests on an assumption that the impact of technology can be predicted. As an example of this, I present Media Richness Theory (origin in Daft & Lengel, 1986) in this chapter. I then oppose this theory with the socio-technical perspective which Kampf (2005) represents. From that perspective, the impact of technology on human behaviour seems to be shaped as much by the communities of users as by the affordances built into the technology.

The more deterministic perception of technology originates in Daft and Lengel (1986) who argue that the ability of a technology to communicate complex information depends on its ability to communicate non-verbal cues. From this perspective, face-to-face communication constitutes the richest medium, while email is a 'lean' medium because it is both asynchronous and it's devoid of extra-linguistic cues in the form of intonation, facial expressions or gestures (Daft & Lengel, 1986). In the late 1980s and early 1990s a number of findings began to contradict this deterministic perspective. For example, Walther (1996) cites numerous studies where even 'lean' media, like email and UseNet groups supported deep friendships and even romances. He argues that asynchronous media, based on writing rather that orality, may provide users with more rhetorical choice of how to represent themselves from their best side by emphasising the most positive aspects of their personality. Walther (1996) argues that depending on personal preference some people may find it easier to communicate these positive aspects in writing rather than in face-to-face interactions. Wilson et al. (2006) confirmed Walther's findings, and showed that trust in computer-mediated relationships can and do develop to levels comparable to face-to-face relations, although they start at lower levels. Furthermore, Media Richness Theory has been tested in a study by Dennis and Kinney (1998) showing team performance was not improved by matching task equivocality to media richness. Despite the criticism against the theory Media Richness continues to exist (e.g., Ishii et al., 2017). And if it exists in the research environment, chances are it exists among practitioners too. In short, we can expect, in all organisations and in all contexts, that there will be people with a preference for face-to-face interaction, and some who thrive on online asynchronous communication via ICT. This was also found by Madsen and Johansen (2019), who recorded a comment about an employee who was very quiet in face-to-face interaction, but who was highly efficient with email. In other words, virtual team managers need to be aware of such preferences when deciding on the team's internal communication strategy.

So, the socio-technical perspective I draw on in my theorising about technology appropriation in virtual work environments does not constitute the only or even the dominant view of the impact of technology on human communication. In the following, I will therefore add more empirical grounding for the socio-technical perspective.

Walther's (1996) findings imply a reconceptualisation of ICT use towards viewing the effects of technology mediation as unpredictable and strongly influenced by user Sensemaking about the technology. This perspective is reflected in two strands of research: Lucy Suchman's 'socio-technical design' (Suchman, 1987, 1998, 2007) and Wanda Orlikowski's 'structuration theory' (Orlikowski, 1992, 2007).

The socio-technical perspective on technology is strongly influenced by the work of Lucy Suchman but has its roots in the Tavistock Institute of Human Relations in London (est. 1947), which brought together researchers from a variety of scientific disciplines. Socio-technical systems were seen as combining three types of relations: between human and human (social), machine and machine (technical) and between human and machine (socio-technical). In America the socio-technical perspective evolved at the Xerox Palo Alto Research Center (PARC),[1] where Lucy Suchman worked.

Suchman's (1987) research put emphasis on the situatedness of human planning. By 'situatedness' she refers to the perception that humans always make decisions within the current context in which they are embedded, and only justify and rationalise the actions after the fact, i.e., in retrospect (re. Sensemaking theory presented in Chapter 2). This means that users appropriate technologies for the own purposes to invoke or resist organisational conversations and to affect how others appropriate technology.

Suchman builds on socio-technical design theory to study how users actively appropriate technologies for their own purposes and needs. The aim of the study was to shift the perspective of designers towards thinking more about the users and their needs. This approach to technology sparked the Participatory Design movement in Scandinavian research (Bødker & Pekkola, 2010), again arguing for the need to recognise that users run into challenges unforeseen by designers, and furthermore that users appropriate technologies for their own uses regardless of designer's intentions. In her later works (1998, 2007), Suchman builds on Bruno Latour's Actant Network Theory, which emphasised the agency of non-human actors such as ICT. In these works, Suchman (1998, 2007) emphasises the co-constructive interplay between users and ICT, in which technological affordances may shape user's interactions with technology as much as user's shape how ICT is used or not used.

Independently of Suchman, Wanda J. Orlikowski (1992) found a similar complex interplay between technological affordances and user appropriation of technologies. Briefly, Orlikowski's theory builds on Anthony Giddens (1994) theory of structuration to argue that designers build their own mental models into ICTs; this is the process of structuration, i.e., the projection of existing structures onto new situations or objects. This represents an aspect similar to Weick's Sensemaking (see Chapter 2), even if Orlikowski uses different terminology. Similarly, users build on their existing mental models when utilising the technology: 'While technologies may appear to have objective forms and functions at one point, these can and do vary by different users, by different contexts of use, and by the same users over time.' (Orlikowski, 1992, p. 403).

To sum up, the theoretical perspectives on technology situate my study in relation to them. I outlined a trajectory from more deterministic views of technology to a socio-technical perspective but recognised the continued influence of more deterministic theories such as the Media Richness Theory. The distinction has been sharply drawn both in my arguments above and in Suchman's (1987, 2007), Orlikowski's (2007) and Leonardi's (2009) work. But perhaps they should be seen more as continuum in which I position my study within the socio-technical perspective. I do so because this perspective emphasises the influence of context and individual, situated needs of users in deciding whether, how and for what purposes to use particular technology. Yet the previous deterministic end of the continuum still exists, both among researchers and practitioners, so it cannot be ignored. It seems undeniable that some people still prefer face-to-face interaction.

In relation to my research aims on employee identity in the virtual work environment of HR Consult, the socio-technical perspective adopted seems to imply that organisational technologies are used by employees to build and sustain relations which support and confirm their particular way of being consultants at HR Consult, i.e., their professional identities. But aside from the appropriation of technology as a means for sustaining identities, technology is also a necessary mediator of virtual knowledge communication. In the following section I therefore look at findings from the past 20 years of research on how dispersed work affects communication generally and knowledge communication in particular.

Overcoming challenges to virtual knowledge communication in global organisations

In the previous section, I argued that current theories about ICTs seem to have two co-existing perceptions of technology. In this section, I shift the focus to a practice perspective on the challenges of communicating knowledge in virtual work environments. I do so through a review of work-place case studies of how virtual teams communicate knowledge.

I build on a systematically collected corpus of literature on virtual teams as an entry point for understanding the challenges faced when working in dispersed work environments. The identification of challenges and successes of teams and sectors described in this corpus of articles will be used as a background for the discussion of perceptions of knowledge (Chapters 5 and 6), identity (Chapter 8) and relationships (Chapter 9). It will also offer a theoretical and practice-orientated background for comparison with the case study analyses I present in this chapter and in Chapters 6–9.

I'll start by reviewing literature that looks at communication in virtual teams to examine what current research suggests for improving communication practices in virtual work environments. These communication processes can be seen as a prerequisite for employees to build both a shared sense of identity and an awareness of the different knowledge domains and expertise within the team. While this section focuses mainly on reviewing challenges to communication in virtual work environments, the next section shifts the focus to the challenge of knowing who-knows-what in a virtual work environment.

The literature on virtual teams indicates that the virtual work environment itself is challenging to communication (Gupta & Pathak, 2018). For example, Bosch-Sijtsema et al. (2011) and Golden and Raghuram (2010) provide evidence that tasks are perceived as more ambiguous in dispersed teams than in co-located teams. Part of the reason may be that when team members are not co-located, communication does not arise naturally, as it does in a co-located setting where employees constantly meet and interact in both formal and informal contexts. Hence virtual work requires a more explicit and intentional focus on communication than co-located work.

This intentional focus can be achieved by building a rhythm of frequent communication in the virtual team (Malhotra et al., Majchrzak, & Rosen, 2007; Oshri, Kotlarsky, & Willcocks, 2007; Rezgui, 2007; Rosen et al., 2007; Scott, 2013; Suchan & Hayzak, 2001). By 'communication rhythm', these researchers refer to a formalised and regular interaction between the team members combining synchronous Communication (such as telephone calls, video conferencing or face-to-face meetings) with asynchronous communication (such as email and intranet). Formalised and frequent opportunities for communication help virtual teams to structure team communications. More recent studies, such as Han et al. (2017), find that face-to-face interaction may not be necessary at all.

By 'formalised' I refer to a formally agreed structure which has been decided by the team early in the team life cycle and which is occasionally subjected to review by the team. The purpose of this communication rhythm is not only to focus on knowledge communication about team tasks, but also helps the team focus on problems before they escalate. This can be achieved by specifically addressing any interpersonal issues in the team (Jain et al., Poston, & Simon, 2011; Piri, Niinimaki, & Lassenius, 2012). Furthermore, Piri *et al.* (2012) found that a lack of communication between team members may lead to negative Sensemaking, because team members may start constructing negative perceptions about others' abilities and commitment to the team. This negative Sensemaking may give rise to misunderstandings (Scott, 2013). Olaisen and Revang's (2017) findings suggested that technology is now so far advanced that the importance of face-to-face interaction is no longer needed to support effective team collaboration. The caveat, identified by the authors, could be that their sample was a culturally homogenous sample of Scandinavian virtual teams. Nonetheless, they conclude that:

> Our findings contradict that we need offline social platforms to get online platforms to work to get social relationships and knowledge sharing. We are proposing that online platforms enable knowledge exchange of high quality and social relationships without the support of the physical face-to-face meetings
>
> (p. 1446)

Findings from Suh and Shin (2010) suggest that frequent communication may also boost motivation, which is supported by Scott's (2013) case where the team leader's strategy of very structured and frequent communication seemed to ignite a team spirit and build a foundation for mutual understanding. The case examined by Scott (2013) shows some of the practices which can help teams overcome the challenges of dispersion, such as a lack of shared identity.

First of all, Scott (2013) emphasised the importance of rituals in structuring team communication; the team had a daily communication practice of briefly meeting in a video conference to discuss the previous day's work, and a monthly three-hour conference to discuss and agree on the next months' work. This is the most elaborate and closely described case of communication rhythm in the selection of 73 virtual team articles I examined. By setting up a regular structure of when and for what purposes to meet, this communication rhythm helps set up a ritualised practice which helps build team commitment. Second, the communication rituals in Scott's (2013) case helped establish a common ground for identification and shared understanding between team members, which is often difficult to establish in virtual teams (Casey, 2010; Drouin et al., Bourgault, & Gervais, 2010; Dubé & Robey, 2009; Filstad & Gottschalk, 2010; Oshri et al., 2007; Piri et al., 2012; Rezgui, 2007; Rosen et al., 2007; Suchan & Hayzak, 2001).

Communication frequency should not stand alone, however. Rico et al. (2009) use the concept 'substantive communications' to describe communication which is detailed and elaborate and finds that it facilitates easier conflict handling. Thus, elaboration and detail in communication can be seen as a way to overcome time-consuming misunderstandings when virtual team members are not on the same page.

To sum up, frequent and formalised opportunities for communication, both about task progress and any interpersonal challenges in the team have been consistently found to be a prerequisite for effective work in virtual work environments. The ongoing commitments of team members in other projects and teams (which Chapter 1 identified as a current tendency) makes this requirement all the more important as a means to ensure that team members are aware of different levels of commitment among team members.

Through a frequent communication rhythm dispersed teams can also start to build knowledge of each other's different abilities and competencies, i.e., knowing who-knows-what in the team. This knowledge about who-knows-what is the focus of the next section.

The importance of communicating knowing who-knows-what

Communicating complex knowledge through ICT can be slow (Paul, 2006), and sharing complex knowledge is challenging between parties with little mutual understanding and previous interaction, so-called weak ties (Granovetter, 1973; Hansen, 1999). To suggest possibilities for overcoming both these challenges, this section will review the impact of knowledge about who-knows-what in the team, or in other words meta-knowledge about others' expertise, which ensures that each team member can focus on what they do well, and that they know who to ask when a challenge lies outside their own knowledge domain.

In relation to the virtual work environment, the multi-team commitments and lack of shared physical organisational context challenges the acquisition of this knowledge. However, metaknowledge of who-knows-what can be seen as particularly useful for employees in virtual work environments, because it allows complex knowledge work to be carried out locally by team members with special competencies within a specific, specialised domain, and the coordination of tasks and the resolution of interpersonal issues can be carried out globally in ICT mediated communication.

As a background for the findings in case studies of virtual teams, I'll briefly review the theory developed by Wegner (1986). Wegner (1986) analysed of how humans use knowledge about who-knows-what in a group to coordinate groups tasks. He called this theory Transactive Memory Systems (TMS in the following). Wegner's (1986) TMS theory was originally conceived as a model of how humans in a closely connected network tend to divide knowledge domains, so that knowledge of what the others in the network know can substitute for knowledge which an individual does not possess themself. Through this coordination of knowledge domains, a group can know more than any individual, and the individual can focus on maintaining and specialising in their own knowledge domain. A TMS can both be informal, i.e., held personally in the mind of each group member, or formalised, i.e., codified into a computer database, or a combination of the two.

Although Wegner (1986) developed TMS to describe the coordination of knowledge domains in dyadic private relationships, Andrea Hollingshead (2000) showed that TMS is also a property of work relationships in organisational teams and serves as a basis for allocation of knowledge responsibilities. Although Hollingshead's experiment was conducted with teams of business students, they may be generalisable to professional settings because they fit with my findings from HR Consult. In her experiment, she found that colleagues who shared knowledge domains had a higher tendency to seek knowledge outside their own knowledge domains but had lesser capacity for knowledge retention than colleagues with diverse knowledge domains. The latter group could focus on retaining knowledge within their own domain.

This has implications for employees working together in virtual work environments, because it suggests that cross-functional teams may be able to retain and apply knowledge more effectively than teams working within the same knowledge domain. But this requires knowledge of which domains of knowledge other team members hold, and communication about how the diversity in the team can be leveraged to the advantage of the team. This argument is supported by Hollingshead and Brandon (2003) who found that the teams of business student teams in which the members know each other well have a higher capacity for leveraging the advantage of diversity in knowledge domains. They argue that the reason is probably that knowing who-knows-what provides knowledge about which knowledge domain you need to focus on retaining yourself and which knowledge domain you can expect others in the network to take responsibility for maintaining. Similarly, Wegner (1986) found the effect of TMS highest in close private relations where the parties know each other well.

TMS theory seemed relevant to the findings in 41 of the 73 papers I examined as part of the literature review. In these 41 papers, knowing who-knows-what in the team was either important for the teams' success, or the lack of such knowledge was cited as partial cause for team failure. The lack of co-location may make explicit building of mutual TMS knowledge of who-knows-what even more useful than in co-located teams where employees tend to have more informal opportunities to get to know each other's competencies. This argument does not imply that a focus on TMS could not have been relevant for the teams in the remaining 32 papers, merely that the remaining papers in the corpus did not provide case descriptions detailed enough to establish whether this is so.

Oshri et al. (2008) argue that combining a codified and personalised directory of individual abilities and traits facilitates a mutual understanding and easier knowledge sharing. However, they also found that information tends to stick to within local contexts, and they found that localised work routines and differences in abilities and technical infrastructure may challenge the exchange of knowledge in virtual contexts. This supports my argument in Chapter 1 that the challenge lies more in the lack of mutual knowledge and relationships in a virtual work environment, and less in the mediation of ICT. An understudied proposition is whether a well-functioning TMS may allow team members to divide tasks more efficiently, by allowing completion of sub-tasks within local contexts where a particular expertise is located, followed by communication and a combination of the completed sub-tasks. This could reduce the need to share more complex knowledge, which Hansen (1999) found to be more difficult to share among 'weak ties', that is relations who do not know each other well and who do not interact regularly (Hansen, 1999). I return to the advantages of weak and strong ties in the discussion of relationship theory (Chapter 9).

The use of technology to exacerbate interpersonal issues in virtual work environments

Dispersed teams experience the same problems that co-located teams do – only worse, as Lipnack and Stamps (2000) argue. McNair and Paretti (2010) provide a specific example of how the mediation of technology can be used as a tool to exacerbate a power hierarchy in a virtual team. Their findings demonstrate how technologies are appropriated by users to support the users' own agenda, and the findings demonstrate that this appropriation of technology by users is not necessarily in the best interest of the team. McNair and Paretti (2010) thereby provide evidence for the relevance of the socio-technical perspective in a virtual work environment.

McNair and Paretti (2010) provide a detailed analysis of a dispersed team meeting via video conferencing in a cross-Atlantic virtual team of engineers. Four members were dispersed across Europe, while the fourteen US members were co-located in the US office. The meeting was hosted by the American office. The purpose was to reach consensus on a choice between two models for mathematically determining stress and strain on a consumer product. The US members were co-located with the project manager, who controlled the PowerPoint presentation broadcasted to all members.

Control over the videoconferencing system also meant that the US team members were in control of who was being heard through the video conferencing system. Each time the European members of the team disagreed they were directed to the arguments presented on the slides. Yet, they didn't have the technical advantage of being able to deliver slides themselves to back up their argumentation. Nor could they participate in side conversations which might back up the Europeans' perspectives. In the end, consensus was reached because the Europeans were overpowered and out-informationed by the dominant US team members, thus laying the groundwork for future problems in the interaction between the EU and US members of this virtual team. Even worse, potential problems with the product may not have been solved, since the outcome of the meeting did not necessarily reflect the expertise of all the team participants, or the best possible solution.

Studies such as the one described above demonstrate that users appropriate technologies for their own purposes, and that these may not always be in the best interest of the organisation, the team or the task at hand. Furthermore, this suggests a need to understand how management and organisational culture can be used to cultivate a team climate which supports rather than hinders ICT relationship building and knowledge communication across boundaries.

Some of these strategies seem self-evident, but the virtual team context seems to make them all the more important. For example, the case studied by Suchan and Hayzak (2001) suggests that reward systems favouring individual achievement over team achievement encourages knowledge hoarding. 'Knowledge hoarding' refers to a tendency among employees to hold on to their own knowledge, and not communicate it with others out of fear for losing their bonus. Thus, individual reward systems can be detrimental to collaboration in virtual teams due to their implied encouragement of knowledge hoarding. Reward systems based on team efforts, on the other hand, can foster knowledge communication and employee mentoring in their research context (Lukić & Vračar, 2018; Suchan & Hayzak, 2001).

Studies questioning the intuitive assumptions that ICT mediation inhibits communication

This section focuses more explicitly on organisational case studies which question the generalisability of the findings suggesting that virtuality necessarily presents a barrier to communication and relationship building. Rosen et al. (2007) even argues that well-developed virtual design teams may work more efficiently than traditional teams by sharing cognitive labour.

That some organisational contexts may be more conducive to collaboration despite the challenges of working across boundaries seems evident from the cases studied by Al-Ani et al. (2011), Assudani (2011), Scott (2013) and Han et al. (2017). Key characteristics of these four cases seems to be first an employee attitude, i.e., 'Sensemaking' (Weick 1995, 2001. See also Chapter 2 of the present volume), characterised by commitment not only to the task at hand, but to their individual areas of expertise. Second, the four cases are characterised by teams who have knowledge of and respect for the other team members areas of expertise, i.e., a well-functioning TMS. Third, the employee Sensemaking and TMS seem to go hand in hand with a leadership focusing not only on leading the project tasks, but in facilitating communication about the strengths and abilities of the different team members. Thus, leadership in these articles was focused on supporting the TMS within the team, thereby also fostering trust in the other team members' competencies, and a sense of team identity. This type of leadership support seems to build a positive employee attitude leading to ICT use supporting efficient teamwork.

In short, the findings from the studies seem to contradict findings indicating that a virtual work environment is necessarily problematic. These studies thereby provide counter-intuitive evidence to the expectation that virtual teams should necessarily experience more problems than co-located teams, as argued by Lipnack and Stamps (2000). The counter-intuitive examples of highly effective virtual teams in the studies can be seen as critical cases of how organisations can build more effective virtual teams.

The next section starts by arguing for a different kind of leadership in virtual teams and then focuses more explicitly on the key characteristics of the successful virtual teams described above. I then argue for the possibility of building more effective virtual teams, termed 'Knowledge Teams' based on these characteristics and the more self-managed style of leadership presented first in the section.

From organisationally designed virtual teams to autonomous Knowledge Teams

The review of communication challenges in virtual contexts showed that a lack of mutual knowledge in virtual work environments can lead to negative Sensemaking among employees. This is a strong justification for organisational support for building mutual TMS and a sense of community across boundaries. However, these virtual networks may not arise through corporate decisions; rather, they may require a different kind of leadership than in co-located settings. Wenger et al. (2002) see the leadership required to support communities in global organisations as so different from leadership in co-located settings that that leadership in the traditional sense does not apply. Instead, they suggest the word stewardship. Stewardship implies support for employee commitment through identifying and encouraging the strong networkers in the organisation, both within the local communities and the networkers bridging geographically dispersed parts of the organisation. Stewardship also implies a higher degree of support and respect for the employee autonomy needed to establish shared identities and relationships strong enough to support the knowledge communication practices of a Knowledge Team. Schulze and Krumm (2017) also found a link between a high level of virtual team autonomy and successful virtual team work.

The reward may be high-performing Knowledge Teams which are able to successfully communicate knowledge across a dispersed, global organisation, as seen in some of the more recent studies of successful virtual teams (Al-Ani et al., 2011; Assudani, 2011; Han et al., 2017; Scott, 2013). But the purpose of knowing who-knows-what means that everyone has the same knowledge. Rather, the purpose is to recognise the different knowledge domains both within the team and across the wider networks and communities in the organisation. In ideal cases this could facilitate efficient knowledge communication across organisational boundaries. Knowledge Teams are characterised by their ability to utilise the different domains of expertise both within and beyond the team to solve their tasks. I suggest that Knowledge Teams require a particular type of professional identity. The analysis of the characteristics of this identity is the focus of Chapter 8 of the book. For the present I'll elaborate on the characteristics of a 'knowledge team' by building on existing theory. After the theory of Knowledge Teams, a case analysis of Linda's Knowledge Team will be presented.

Faraj and Sproull (2000) define the term 'Knowledge Team' broadly to mean any team whose work is essentially about creating knowledge, which is the case for the software development teams they study. They argue that:

> members need to develop a common language for describing tasks, assignments, roles, and location of expertise. Knowing the area of expertise of other team members serves an important integrative and coordinative function by stressing metaknowledge about expertise location
>
> (p. 1556).

This metaknowledge of knowledge location is what Wegner (1986) terms TMS. Faraj and Sproull (2000) cite studies showing increased performance in teams which intentionally build a TMS (Transactive Memory State) in the team. However, the definition of 'Knowledge Team' in Faraj and Sproull (2000) is so broad that the definition would include all teams in the service sector under the label 'Knowledge Teams', which seems to make the term redundant. Instead, I propose a narrower definition of Knowledge Team as a team which is focused not only on achieving team goals, but which is also focused on developing their knowledge domain, and their ability to use their networks in the organisation to find the knowledge competencies they need to solve their tasks. The focus on developing knowledge, makes Knowledge Teams similar to Communities of Practice, a concept I will return to in Chapters 7 and 9.

Faraj and Yan (2009) cite findings showing that teams with the ability to build on the extended network beyond the team perform better than teams with more fixed boundaries. Nevertheless, in a team which relies on competencies of colleagues outside the team, a continued challenge to the effective communication of knowledge is the establishment of team boundaries. As argued by Faraj and Yan (2009), the challenge of establishing team boundaries is not unique to Knowledge Teams. Their study of team boundaries demonstrated that most teams disagreed on who was part of the team. This tendency towards fuzzy team boundaries may be exacerbated in a Knowledge Team who rely more on competencies outside the team. But Faraj and Yan (2009) argue that the ability to build on competencies outside the team requires a sense of 'psychological safety' to allow outside knowledge into the team:

> the essential problem for a team is to create boundaries that are porous enough to allow resources and information in but resistant enough to avoid uncertainty about who is on the team and whether these members are accountable for its collective outcomes
>
> (p. 604)

The notion of 'psychological safety' connects with the trust theories presented Chapter 9 where trust is defined as willingness to be exposed to vulnerability. This implies that a sense of psychological safety in a Knowledge Team is a sign of a high level of trust in such teams.

Teams with similar characteristics as the ones described above for Knowledge Teams can also be found in the literature on virtual teams, although they are rare. One example can be found in the work of Armstrong and Peter (2002) who observed teams who 'worked against the incentive plan, the financial control systems, and the priorities of their own local line management for the larger good of the account' (p. 188). Though Armstrong and Peter (2002) do not address knowledge specifically, the case description is detailed enough to show that the individual knowledge domains of each team member are combined and transformed in interaction with both the knowledge embedded in their own organisation and in the client organisation. Thereby the team ensures a high level of client satisfaction.

In this knowledge transformation process, the team does not mind going against the grain of the organisational strategy, according to Armstrong and Peter (2002). To make sense of the (in their organisational context) unorthodox behaviour, the teams observed by Armstrong and Peter (2002) justify their behaviour by referring to 'customer satisfaction and loyalty' (p. 188). 'Loyalty' here refers to the willingness of the client to continue to use the team and their parent organisation for future projects. Armstrong and Peter (2002) point out that such teams are rare, but that an interesting feature of such teams is their ability to 'pull on the very bones of the organisation, straining the existing systems rather than being overcome by them' (p. 189). So, they could be argued to challenge the organisational strategies and practices. In the following sections we will look at three very different approaches to virtual knowledge communication and use of TMS.

Discussion of sensemaking in relation to the virtual work environment

Weick's perspective on Sensemaking as an intuitive response to the interplay between Ecological Change and selective interpretation of that change (see Chapter 2) seems to be aligned with Suchman's (1987) perspective on situated planning. Suchman (1987) argues that planning is most often a Retrospective process which occurs after the action to justify decisions already made. As is Enactment (identity and past experiences in Weick's theory of Sensemaking, see Chapter 2). Weick's model can be seen as action in response to a situation. This action or Enactment is decided on the go and in Retrospect, based on existing mental model or 'Retention' (Weick, 1995). These mental models are then updated in response to the outcome of the newly enacted environment.

Orlikowski (1992) similarly demonstrates the Situatedness of technology use by showing how ICT is appropriated according to the immediate needs and purposes of the user rather than the expectations of designers or decision makers. Therefore, the impact of a technology on a user cannot be predicted by programmers and designers, because the impact and use of a technology will be influenced equally by four factors: the affordances of the technology; the context in which the technology is used; the users' Sensemaking of the technology; and the current, situated needs of the users.

The current, situated needs of the user and the Retention can be seen as mental models which govern how users appropriate ICT in an organisational context. Mental models can be seen as idiosyncratic perceptions of technology and as values underlying professional identities, which together with the selective interpretation of the social situation make up Retention in Weick's model. Because technology use can be seen as being guided as much by the immediate needs and existing mental models of the user, employee practices may not live up to corporate expectations about how ICTs are used, because corporate decisions may not be immediately reconcilable with employee Sensemaking about the corporate ICTs. Linda's use of the corporate ICTs to support her independent network is an example of this. That this argument is grounded in practice as much as in theory can be seen in Leonardi's (2009) study of the reasons why employees neglect to use corporate ICT infrastructure in the form of intranets. Leonardi's (2009) findings show how joint Sensemaking

Table 5.1 Overview of the key concepts in Chapter 5 and how they apply to the three prototypes found in the study

	Knowledge Transfer prototype (Dorthe)	*Knowledge creator prototype (Henrik)*	*Knowledge Broker prototype (Linda)*
Leadership	Need for close, hierarchical leadership	Autonomous/self-managing.	Autonomous/self-managing.
Identity	Values loyalty towards organisational strategies, processes and products. Self-image as able to transfer HR Consult knowledge to client without change in content or form.	Knowledge creator/knowledge leader. HR Consult knowledge as inspiration for knowledge creation. Loyalty to client. Personal knowledge transformation to suit client contexts. Going against the grain of the organisation/shaking status quo.	Knowledge Broker thriving at the boundary of networks. HR Consult knowledge as inspiration for knowledge creation. Loyalty to client. Focus on who-knows-what (relational knowledge). Going against the grain of the organisation/shaking status quo.
Intentional focus on communication *- Rhythm (frequency o of interaction)* *- Substantive communication*	Needs close and frequent interaction with the virtual team leader to coordinate the teams identical Knowledge Transfer practise in each country. Prefers face-to-face team meetings.	Need for substantive communication of complex knowledge to thrive. Face-to-face interaction matters less than the knowledge content in communication.	Need for substantive communication of complex knowledge to thrive. Face-to-face interaction matters less than the knowledge content in communication.
TMS (Who-knows-what)	Limited to local relationships but knows who to call for new customer leads.	His close client relationship means that Henrik knows more about his clients and global colleagues with similar identity than about local colleagues.	Addresses specific client needs by finding the right competencies to solve the problem – co-located or dispersed is less important: it's the client needs that matter.
Technology preference	Prefers face-to-face interaction and telephone. Media richness matters.	Strategic use of email, phone and online meetings. Technology is not seen as a barrier to knowledge communication. Media richness inconsequential.	Strategic use of email, phone and online meetings with virtual team members and clients. Technology is not seen as a barrier. Media richness inconsequential.

among users strongly influences whether users will adopt or reject new technologies. Thereby he extends Orlikowski's and Suchman's theories by showing the impact of Sensemaking on how technologies are appropriated by employees.

For the study of knowledge communication in organisational settings, the findings from the literature on virtual teams have two implications. First, ICT seems to be a given mediator of most knowledge communication in current organisational settings. Second, the impact of this ICT mediation seems to be determined, or 'structurated' in Orlikowski's (2007) terminology, as much by the preferences, needs and interpersonal relations of the users, as by the affordances of the ICTs used. This means that organisations need to both lead and listen to employee Sensemaking about the ICTs implemented in their organisation. But it also means that ICTs need not necessarily be an inhibitor of organisational knowledge communication, if ICT affordances and positive joint Sensemaking about these affordances go hand in hand.

In relation to the findings from the literature on virtual teams, it seems clear that the Knowledge Teams discussed build their successful virtual teams using ICTs similar to those used by more unsuccessful teams. Therefore, it seems that it is not in ICTs the challenge lies, but in the Sensemaking about the ICTs, and in the sense of shared identity and mutual trust built among virtual team members. Therefore, the analysis of the participants' use of ICTs in this book emphasise analysis of their Sensemaking process rather than the specific technologies they use. Thereby, the analyses will show how mental models of employees are changed by the virtual work environment through employee appropriation of ICT to support their perception of knowledge, identity and relationships.

Case study: Dorthe's Transactive Memory System

'Dorthe' is a pseudonym for an employee at HR Consult Denmark. The relationships which Dorthe constructs as most important to her work at HR Consult are built on more personal, Affect-based or personal connections. When asked for examples of how these relations supported her in her work as a consultant, she gave examples of sharing leads for potential clients, and the fundamental feeling of connecting on a personal level with someone. The latter seems to represent Affect-based trust, while the former, i.e., exchange of client leads, seems to suggest that it is not the communication of knowledge which she values in her professional relationships. For Dorthe, the relationship she constructed as most important to her was a co-located consultant and member of staff. When I interviewed Dorthe, this colleague had just left the organisation due to dissatisfaction with the CEO. A few months after the interview, Dorthe left too.

Case study: Shaking status quo at HR Consult Denmark

A similar disregard for the organisational strategy can be found in the interview with Henrik. In his Discursive Sensemaking he constructs himself as being above the skill level of his colleagues. He uses this construction of hierarchy to justify his independence. This becomes very explicit in the following quote. Through his argument in the quote that his level is one that the others need to be pulled 'up to' (l. 9), he discursively makes sense of himself as being above the others. This Discursive Sensemaking constructs his belief in his own competence. He emphasises client needs as an important value: 'I can go in and say what do you need' (l. 3). His Lexical choices underlines this Discursive Sensemaking: he constructs his own competence as a consultant by describing his ability to 'both dig widely and [...] deeply'. He then constructs a Connection to his role as 'product manager', arguing that this role is the reason he needs to pull 'the others up to' (l. 7–9) his own level of competence. Because no one else in the organisation uses the title 'product manager' when describing him, the title seems mainly to be a symbolic manifestation of Henrik's Discursive Sensemaking about his own identity as a knowledge leader in the organisation.

Henrik:

1 '^that's the \level I'm at now, erm,
2 _/In my role as consultant
3 \ I can go in and say \'what do you _need'.
4 /Ask them critical \questions from the outset.
5 ^\knowing that I can both dig widely
6 \and I can dig deeply.
7 [...] \And that is also the level which I,
8 _as Product Manager,
9 /am responsible for pulling the others up to.

(Henrik, my translation, 26, 04:02)

To conclude on the analysis of the quote above, Henrik positions himself as a knowledge leader, and connects his deep and wide knowledge to the value of client satisfaction. Notice that value to his organisation is not brought in as one of his points here, instead he constructs a professional identity built on the values of listening to the client and having a deep understanding of organisational knowledge to be able to understand and 'ask critical questions' (l. 4). Thereby he exhibits a similar Practise as that identified by Armstrong and Peter (2002) where some teams went against the incentive plan of the organisation and justify that Practise by referring to higher client satisfaction as the goal.

A similar finding is evident in the interview with Linda from HR Consult UK. I asked Linda if she saw her time-consuming, client-centred virtual project as a way to generate more business from the client. In her reply, quoted below, she discursively makes sense of her time-consuming project by referring to future orders from the client ('the idea is we take it further', l. 2, and 'I definitely intend for this to be a longer partnership, l. 10). She emphasises 'definitely' in l.1 and repeats the word towards the end of the quote, clearly indicating the importance for her. This quote also serves to position her strategy as successful, thereby becoming an implied justification for her time consumption on the project. From a linguistic perspective, the semantic choice of 'partnership' constructs a close relation with the client. The repetition of 'yes' (l. 1 and l. 9) constructs a sense of strong affirmation that she does expect future revenue due to her Knowledge Teams' knowledge transformation.

Linda:

1 /Yes definitely.
2 \The idea is that we take it further. (.)
3 \And that next time I would like us to be part of it from the start.
4 /it's a two-year programme \where we are on the last year, er, (.)
5 \So there were other suppliers doing stuff before that,
6 \and it would be really good to be part of it from the start.
7 /and arrange \the whole programme
8 \even if we still only deliver the latter part of the programme [...] _So ^yes, \yes.
9 /I definitely \intend for this to be a longer par--partnership.

(Linda, my translation, 223, 31:31)

Linda's knowledge transformation approach does seem to be paying off, because she explains that the client wants to expand the project to a global level. However, Linda does not quite have the power to roll the project out globally; she does not say so directly but implies this information by stating that rolling the project out to a global level is easier for her contact at Soft Tech, because the contact has a leadership function in the client organisation, giving her power to leverage the project beyond the UK. Linda on the other hand needs to 'sell' the project to offices in the other countries and 'find people in the different countries who I can work together with' (Linda, my translation, 201, 22:29). This shows a lack of organisational support for her independent strategy as a Knowledge Team leader. Linda's approach seems break new ground in the organisation, but because it goes against the corporate strategy, the organisation doesn't benefit from her team's knowledge creation.

In the interview situation, her statement about the global roll-out of the project could be seen as having the purpose of constructing herself as competent. Testifying to the truth value of Linda's proposition, however, HR Consult Denmark employees confirmed that they were starting up a project with Soft Tech based on Linda's work. I received this information when I debriefed HR Consult about my findings approximately six months after interviewing Linda. The project she designed for 'Soft Tech' was being rolled out in other European countries, Canada and the US simultaneously. This shows that when she tries to position herself in the interview situation as a competent consultant with a successful project, she seems to have a firm basis on which to do so. But when it came to a global roll out of the project, Linda felt that the project was taken away from her. She told me that this was one of the key reasons she left HR Consult.

Linda's insistence on adopting a different knowledge communication practice than others at HR Consult UK, thereby resisting the Conversation in the organisation, suggests a strong professional self-identity attached to this knowledge transformation approach. Summing up, this implied self-identity in her narrative about her project for Soft Tech. I prompted her to confirm this interpretation, to which she replied: 'Yes that's definitely correctly understood.' (Linda, my translation, 324–336, 46:31). But after a brief pause, she then shifted the topic from knowledge transformation to what emerged as one of her key values: the autonomy and freedom to pursue her own strategy. By introducing this topic when prompted quite explicitly to comment on her knowledge transformation practice, she builds a Connection (Gee, 2011, 2014) by associating 'freedom' with the ability to construct and transform organisational knowledge to her clients' needs. From a linguistic perspective the use of high key onset when shifting the topic (l. 1) signals that the coming (d)iscourse is important to her. I do not attach any particular significance to the high key pronunciation of 'freedom' (l. 3), because it may just as well be a signal that she feels she found the right word after the brief pause (l. 3).

Linda:

1 (.) ^Well the reason I like this role
2 _ compared to some of the old roles is
3 /precisely \because I have that (.) ^freedom.

(Linda, my translation, 325, 46:40).

The quote above is mainly relevant because Linda choses to shift the topic from knowledge construction, which was my agenda as interviewer, to her own agenda, by introducing a topic that was important to her own Sensemaking. The importance she attaches to the freedom to pursue her own strategy could be seen as similar to Henrik's arguments for the value of autonomy to pursue a different knowledge communication practice than his colleagues. This shift in focus also shifts the focus from the professional identity of Linda to a focus on the implication of her professional identity for her knowledge communication.

Case study: Linda's Knowledge Team

Linda at HR Consult UK, on the other hand, has built her own high-performing Knowledge Team without involving her managers. This behaviour is similar to the team described by Armstrong and Peter (2002) which went against the grain of their organisation to achieve a higher level of client satisfaction. As we will see in this section, she uses her network within and beyond the organisation to go against a corporate strategy of using modular, predesigned solutions for solving client needs for individual, group, sales and leadership development. Linda cherishes her autonomy and doesn't mind putting in extra hours to satisfy her client, a global software company, which I will call 'Soft Tech'. With her ability to build virtual knowledge communication networks across the global organisation she works in, she can be described as a Knowledge Broker (Wenger, 1998), a concept I'll return to in Chapter 7.

Networking skills are an essential aspect of being a Knowledge Broker. In the quote below, Linda's Discursive Sensemaking builds a Connection between the value of autonomy to network and manage her project and her professional identity as a Knowledge Broker. She starts with an explicit marker of identity construction ('someone like me' l. 1), and then expresses a sense of personal ownership over her project here ('my own project', l. 2). In terms of prosody, she emphasises 'completely', l. 2) as post modifier of her ability to run the project. Notice also that after emphasising autonomy in the first three lines she constructs a Connection to her network, i.e., her TMS thereby constructing her TMS, as Significant. I explore her network relations deeper in Chapter 9.

Linda:

1 --Someone like me, --
2 --I run my own project *completely*. --
3 --/I almost work as an \independent consultant,
4 /and have made my network as an experi--
5 --half way in and half way out of [HR Consult].

(Linda, my translation, 236, 32:59)

To sum up on key aspects of a knowledge broker in the Discursive Sensemaking above, Linda constructs the value of her TMS network and her autonomy both in her role as consultant and in building a network of relations within the organisation as important values. She has built a strong network which goes beyond her own team, thereby demonstrating Faraj and Yan's (2009) finding that Knowledge Teams have fuzzy boundaries, and that, as found by Armstrong and Peter (2002) some knowledge workers work autonomously against the incentive plan of their organisation for the larger good of their account. A final characteristic of a Knowledge Broker could be described as a stewardship approach to leadership in her team: She trusts the abilities of the people she finds in her network and is able to transfer that trust to the team through frequent and substantive communication.

Linda uses her network to transform HR Consult knowledge and tailor it to her client's organisation, thereby exhibiting a key trait of her Knowledge Broker approach. Because their organisation is dispersed, they needed a solution tailored to a virtual platform. This had not been done before at HR Consult and required that Linda not only constructed a solution which fitted the client's problem, but also transformed the HR Consult products used in the solution into a virtual platform of Blended Learning. Blended Learning is an academic field in its own right with its own literature, which Linda asserts she spent considerable time reading up on for the project. Time consumption of this and the task of transforming organisational knowledge to suit the client and the platform became a theme several times in the interview, not least in the quote below. Thereby Linda demonstrates Armstrong and Peter's (2002) finding that some knowledge workers work against the strategy of their organisation for the larger good of their account. Notice that Linda does not distinguish between online and offline relationships. In fact, as we'll see in Chapter 9, she prefers her online relationships, because she can identify more with their knowledge communication practice.

In terms of Discursive Sensemaking, her perspective on organisational knowledge in the quote below can be seen as emerging in her statement that her team used 'ideas' (l.4) from the HR Consult's product portfolio. Had she followed the organisational strategy, we might have expected that she used more than just 'ideas' from the existing products. Furthermore, she undermines the importance of these organisational 'ideas' by placing her team's construction of 'completely new stuff' after the existing organisational knowledge. She connects this practice of constructing new organisational knowledge to the time consumption of that practice. She also suggests that the time consumption of the knowledge transformation her team has undertaken has been questioned in the organisation (l. 9–11). This information seems to construct her own approach as rather unique in the organisation; otherwise, no one would question it. But in the quote below, she also constructs her team member, Susan, as spending as much time on the project as Linda does (l. 14–15), and by stating that Susan does not put every hour on the bill, Linda suggests that Susan, too, works overtime because she thinks it's 'fun' (l. 13). By attributing to Susan the expectation of future work on the same project, Linda implies that such future work for the client is a possibility. In terms of motivation for adopting the time-consuming knowledge transformation practice, Linda constructs two sources of motivation as part of her Discursive Sensemaking in the quote below: first, she constructs the intrinsic reward of her practice: 'I think it's fun' (l. 13), and second, through her interpretation of her team member, Susan's, motivation, she implies that the project may spark future projects from Soft Tech (l. 17). It is because of the expectation of future business from Soft Tech that Linda concludes her Discursive Sensemaking in the quote by arguing that the time consumption is an investment.

From a linguistic perspective, her Lexical choice of using the first-person plural pronoun 'we' in the quote below contrasts with Henrik, who represents the Knowledge Creator. Henrik uses the first-person singular 'I' when describing his knowledge transformation practice. Linda's repetition of the amount of time spent on the project (l. 2, l. 9. l. 13) renders time consumption as a Significant concept in the quote. But she connects the labour involved in 'editing' (l. 3) and creating 'new stuff' (l. 7) to her justification: 'I think it's fun' in l. 13. It seems that, like Henrik, she finds intrinsic value in the creation of new knowledge. In terms of prosody, her high key enunciation of 'quite' (l. 2) suggests that she uses the word to amplify the amount of time spent, rather than to tone down the time consumption as would be expected from the lexical meaning of 'quite'. Through the high key enunciation of 'ideas' (l. 4), she implies the difference between the Knowledge Transfer approach of adopting HR Consult learning programmes as they are, and her own transformation of the knowledge of the programmes into a new solution. Her high key enunciation of 'completely' (l. 7) adds Significance to the team's creativity and innovation in their transformation of HR Consult's 'ideas'.

Linda:

1 /Well, we have--
2 --\we have spent (.) ^quite \a lot of time on erm
3 _\editing the materi--\editing it. (..)
4 \We've definitely used _erm ^ideas,
5 \from the existing exercises. Erm (.)
6 [faster pace]/to see what we could use [normal pace]\in this space[1]. Erm (.)
7 ^\but we've also created ^completely \new stuff. [...] we erm (.)
8 [slow pace]\time was spent on it. (.)
9 _ \And then people are saying
10 \'well what does that cost'.(..)
11 (slower pace) And that's a bit harder for us. (.)
12 (faster pace) ^\I just spend that time /because I think it's fun, (.)
13 \and my impression is that 'Susan'
14 \she spends more time on it that she-- (.)
15 \She doesn't put every hour spent on the project on the bill,
16 \because \it makes sense for her to have it in the future as well. (..)
17 So erm so there's definitely an investment for us in it.

(Linda, my translation, 205, 27:10)

Note on quote:[1] 'Space' in l. 6 is used as an abbreviated anaphoric reference to a virtual space, i.e., the online platform through which training and workshops were conducted for Soft Tech. 'Anaphoric reference' was introduced by Halliday and Hasan (1976/2014) to describe reference to a word or phrase introduced earlier in a text.

To conclude on the analysis of the quote above, through her description of the knowledge communication Practices Linda and her Knowledge Team engaged in for the Soft Tech project, Linda constructs a desire to spend time improvising and transforming HR Consult's knowledge to situate the knowledge within the client's context, thereby going against the grain of her organisation, which bases it's strategy of reusing modular solutions designed by the R&D department.

Case study: A sense of autonomy as an aspect of the Knowledge Broker Prototype

Linda carries on her time-consuming laborious approach to client-centred knowledge transformation in spite of organisational strategy and Conversation encouraging a different approach. As I will show in the following analysis, Linda seems to avoid any interference by management, if possible, thereby demonstrating her need for a different type of leadership, such as the 'stewardship' described earlier in the chapter. In the UK, part of the reason Linda is able to do so seems to be the physical distance between consultants and managers.

Autonomy as a value is also evident in her Sensemaking about the team she has put together for the project with Soft Tech. In terms of Discursive Sensemaking, Linda constructs a sense of personal ownership and autonomy when speaking about her project in the quote below. She constructs herself, rather than HR Consult or any of her managers as being in charge of the project. This sense of ownership is also reflected in her construction of herself as being in charge of colleagues on the project. This is evident even when she speaks about colleagues she has invited to participate and whom she constructs as trusted equals in another part of the interview. From the linguistic perspective, the hierarchy she constructs is evident not only in her use of the first-person personal possessive pronoun 'my', identifying her as owner of the project, but also through the choice of the verb 'use', which constructs her as team leader in charge of who should be on the team. The Lexical choice of the verb 'use' in this quote signals a sense of ownership, metaphorically constructing her colleague as an instrument or tool:

Linda:

1 Ed, I even use on (.)
2 \on my project. Erm
3 (,) _so he is one of my coaches.

(Linda, my translation 363, 54:50).

In the interview, I commented on the autonomy to define a variety of roles and strategies within Linda's job title as Client Relations Manager, a title she shares with a virtual team of seven other consultants spread across the UK, including Ed from the quote above. My prompt was: 'it's definitely broad, so broad a job title that it can cover almost anything, you know?' (Linda, my translation, 278, 39:06). In my prompt, 'it' refers to the job title Client Relations Manager.

This prompted a passage of Discursive Sensemaking where Linda makes sense of the autonomy of her role, but also about her managers' inability to understand what she is doing in the organisation.

In terms of Discursive Sensemaking in the quote below, she chooses to centre her (d)iscourse on the notion of freedom and autonomy in her role, but builds a few hedges to qualify her argument: she emphasises that it is a requirement that 'you're doing well' (l. 2), i.e., that the consultants meet the target revenues set by the organisation, and that you stay within 'our values and our product portfolio'. But these hedges seem like a wide frame in which her colloquialism ('bloody' l. 3) signals her strong feeling that in her organisational role you're 'allowed to do almost what you want' (l. 4), and that there's an 'incredible amount of freedom in how' (l. 8–9). She then shifts the topic to her managers (l. 10), claiming they 'do not understand' what she is doing (l. 12). This Discursive Sensemaking about the role of her managers constructs a professional identity as someone unique in the organisation through her adoption of an approach (the 'how' in l. 9) which does not conform to the norms in the organisation, and which is either too complex or too different for her managers to understand: 'they don't really understand what I'm doing' (l. 12). Because of this she undermines the traditional hierarchy of manager-employee by providing her Discursive Sensemaking interpretation that 'they can't really challenge me' (l. 13) and 'they are learning as much as leading' (l. 16). In short, the leadership she experiences does not live up to the ideals of the stewardship approach described earlier in the chapter.

This Sensemaking analysis is supported by a linguistic analysis of the quote below. In terms of grammar, although she does refer to the organisational Conversation in the form of requirements for her role (in l. 2: 'doing well', and l. 6: 'our values and our product portfolio'), she refers to these organisational requirements in sub-clauses, thereby constructing them as less Significant hedges to her argument in the main clauses: 'you're actually allowed to do almost what you want' (l. 4), and 'there is an incredible amount of freedom' (l. 8). In terms of prosody the lack of Significance she attaches to the organisational requirements also seems to be signalled in the low-key enunciation of l. 5–6 'you have to stay within our [...] values and our product portfolio.' This can be juxtaposed with the colloquial 'bloody' (l. 3) which, although the sentence is broken off, seems to function as a clausal amplifier to the phrase 'allowed to do almost what you want' (l. 4). The drawing out of the vowel sound in 'incredible'

(l. 8) adds emphasis to the word, thereby constructing 'freedom' as highly Significant. The drawing out of the vowel sounds in 'values' and 'portfolio' (l. 6), on the other hand, is combined with a low-key enunciation. Because of the low-key enunciation, the long vowel sounds seem to suggest that Linda feels obliged to mention these organisational requirements but that she does so out of obligation rather than passion. By giving a full intonation unit to 'in how' (l. 9), she adds emphasis to phrase, thereby constructing the difference between her own and the mainstream knowledge communication practice as Significant.

Linda:

1 _There's not really, erm (.)
2 \as long as you're doing well,
3 /you can bloody--
4 \well, you're actually allowed to do /almost what you want. (..)
5 _Well, of course you have to stay within (.)
6 _within erm our \what we call our _value:s \and our product pro--portfolio:
7 \and so on.
8 So (.) But there is an incre:dible amount of freedom, erm, in--
9 /in how (.)
10 /and there is definitely stuff which actually [names of her closest managers],
11 _well, that's one of their problems
12 ^/they don't really understand \what I'm doing [...]
\13 They can't really challenge me in--
\14 --in what I'm doing (.)
\15 because for them
\16 /they're learning just \as much as leading.

(Linda, my translation, 278, 39:06)

To sum up on the analysis of the quote above, Linda's Discursive Sensemaking builds a professional identity of opposition to the mainstream organisational knowledge communication approach of reapplying standardised solutions. By constructing her managers as unfamiliar with what she's doing as long as she meets her targets, she amplifies this sense of herself as both an outsider, but also as someone more knowledgeable than her managers. Again, this Discursive Sensemaking is strikingly similar to Henrik's, as we shall see in the section below: he also constructed himself as being above his CEO in terms of knowledge and understanding, and also emphasised his autonomy and freedom to pursue a different knowledge communication strategy than the mainstream Knowledge Transfer approach.

The analysis above seems to suggest that in order for the organisation to benefit from the knowledge creations of the Knowledge Broker Prototype (as exemplified by Linda) and the Knowledge Creator Prototype (As exemplified by Henrik), organisations need to provide a considerable level of autonomy to pursue their innovative knowledge creation strategy. The need for employee autonomy to pursue knowledge creation is also emphasised by Nonaka and Takeuchi (1995) who argue for allowing space for creativity and flexibility which is required for creation of new knowledge. I return to Nonaka and Takeuchi's theory of the Knowledge Creating Company in Chapter 6.

As an epilogue, Linda chose to leave HR Consult four months after the interview. She told me that the reason was that her managers insisted she complied with the corporate strategy. Linda joined a competing HR Consultancy founded by another disgruntled HR Consult employee.

Implication of Knowledge Teams for global organisations

By challenging the organisational status quo, Knowledge Teams, as well as more individual knowledge creators such as the Knowledge Creator exemplified by Henrik, seem to be able to shake and shift the conversations or cultures within the organisation, thereby contradicting findings suggesting that teams are 'fragile social structures that lose when placed in opposition to the dominant cultural forces' (Hackman, J., 2000, cited in Armstrong & Peter, 2002, p. 189). This capacity for temporarily driving organisational change and overcoming inertia in the organisation is the reason organisations should pay attention to such teams when they emerge and start challenging the organisational status quo. If the organisation is able to realign systems, measures, objectives and talent management to support the Knowledge Team and its strategic objectives, these teams may be potential drivers of innovation and organisational evolution.

To sum up, I adopt the concept 'Knowledge Teams', to distinguish them from organisationally formed virtual teams which often exhibit challenges in communicating knowledge within the team, building team relationships and establishing a team identity. Knowledge Teams on the other hand can be seen as an emerging type of autonomous, virtual team with the ability use their professional networks to support their practice of transforming organisational knowledge, and question existing conversations in the organisation.

Notes

1 Xerox PARC (Palo Alto Research Center, est. 1969) has had considerable impact on technology use through the development of technologies such as the GUI (the Graphic User Interface, the basis of interfaces on Windows, Apple and all smartphone interfaces) the laser printer, the ethernet (aka. Local Area Network or LAN connecting computers and other electronic devices, such as printers, in local computer networks.

References

Al-Ani, B., Horspool, A., & Bligh, M. C. (2011). Collaborating with 'virtual strangers': Towards developing a framework for leadership in distributed teams. *Leadership, 7*(3), 219–249. doi: 10.1177/1742715011407382

Armstrong, D. J., & Peter, E. B. (2002). Virtual proximity, real teams. In P. Hinds (Ed.), *Distributed work* (pp. 167–190). Boston, MA: MIT Press.

Assudani, R. H. (2011). Role of familiarity in affecting knowledge gaps in geographically dispersed work. *IEEE Transactions on Professional Communication, 54*(3), 314–332. doi: 10.1109/tpc.2011.2161805

Bødker, S., & Pekkola, S. (2010). Introduction the debate section: A short review to the past and present of participatory design. *Scandinavian Journal of Information Systems, 22*(1), 4.

Bosch-Sijtsema, P. M., Fruchter, R., Vartiainen, M., & Ruohomäki, V. (2011). A framework to analyze knowledge work in distributed teams. *Group & Organization Management, 36*(3), 275–307. doi: 10.1177%2F1059601111403625

Casey, V. (2010). Developing trust in virtual software development teams. *Journal of Theoretical and Applied Electronic Commerce Research, 5*(2), 41–58.

Daft, R. L., & Lengel, R. H. (1986). Organizational information requirements, media richness and structural design. *Management Science, 32*(5), 554–571. doi: 10.1287/mnsc.32.5.554

Dennis, A. R., & Kinney, S. T. (1998). Testing media richness theory in the new media: The effects of cues, feedback, and task equivocality. *Information Systems Research, 9*(3), 256–274. doi: 10.1287/isre.9.3.256

Drouin, N., Bourgault, M., & Gervais, C. (2010). Effects of organizational support on components of virtual project teams. *International Journal of Managing Projects in Business, 3*(4), 625–641. doi: 10.1108/17538371011076082

Dubé, L., & Robey, D. (2009). Surviving the paradoxes of virtual teamwork. *Information Systems Journal, 19*(1), 3–30. doi: 10.1111/j.1365-2575.2008.00313.x

Faraj, S., & Sproull, L. (2000). Coordinating expertise in software development teams. *Management Science, 46*(12), 1554–1568. doi: 10.1287/mnsc.46.12.1554.12072

Faraj, S., & Yan, A. (2009). Boundary work in knowledge teams. *Journal of Applied Psychology, 94*(3), 604.

Filstad, C., & Gottschalk, P. (2010). Knowing in mobile organisations-trust and knowledge sharing in virtual teams. *International Journal of Mobile Learning and Organisation, 4*(3), 1–12. doi: 10.1504/ijmlo.2010.033555

Gee, J. P. (2011). *An introduction to discourse analysis.* London: Routledge.

Gee, J. P. (2014). *How to do discourse analysis: A toolkit.* London: Routledge.

Giddens, A. (1994). Elements of the theory of structuration. In A. Giddens (Ed.), *The polity reader in social theory.* Cambridge: Polity Press.

Golden, T. D., & Raghuram, S. (2010). Teleworker knowledge sharing and the role of altered relational and technological interactions. *Journal of Organizational Behavior, 31*(8), 1061–1085. doi: 10.1002/job.652

Granovetter, M. (1973). The strength of weak ties. *American Journal of Sociology, 78*(6), 1360-1380.

Gupta, S., & Pathak, G. S. (2018). Virtual team experiences in an emerging economy: A qualitative study. *Journal of Organizational Change Management, 31*(4), 778–795.

Halliday, M. A. K., & Hasan, R. (1976/2014). *Cohesion in English*. Abingdon: Routledge.

Han, S. J., Chae, C., Macko, P., Park, W., & Beyerlein, M. (2017). How virtual team leaders cope with creativity challenges. *European Journal of Training and Development, 41*(3), 260–277.

Hansen, M. T. (1999). The Search Transfer problem: The role of weak ties in sharing knowledge across organization subunits. *Administrative Science Quarterly, 44*, 82–111.

Hollingshead, A. B. (2000). Perceptions of expertise and transactive memory in work relationships. *Group Processes & Intergroup Relations, 3*(3), 257–267. doi: 10.1177/1368430200033002

Hollingshead, A. B., & Brandon, D. P. (2003). Potential benefits of communication in transactive memory systems. *Human Communication Research, 29*(4), 607–615. doi: 10.1111/j.1468–2958.2003.tb00859.x

Ishii, K., Rife, T. S., & Kagawa, N. (2017). Technology-driven gratifications sought through text-messaging among college students in the US and Japan. *Computers in Human Behavior, 69*, 396–404. doi: 10.1016/j.chb.2016.12.022

Jain, R. P., Simon, J. C., & Poston, R. S. (2011). Mitigating vendor silence in offshore outsourcing: An empirical investigation. *Journal of Management Information Systems, 27*(4), 261–298. doi: 10.2753/MIS0742-1222270409

Kampf, C. E. (2005). *Kumeyaay online: Dimensions of rhetoric and culture in the Kumeyaay Web presence*. Saint Paul: University of Minnesota.

Leonardi, P. M. (2009). Why do people reject new technologies and stymie organizational changes of which they are in favor? Exploring misalignments between social interactions and materiality. *Human Communication Research, 35*(3), 407.

Lipnack, J., & Stamps, J. (2000). Virtual teams: People working across boundaries with technology. New York: Wiley.

Lukić, J. M., & Vračar, M. M. (2018). Building and nurturing trust among members in virtual project teams. *Strategic Management, 23*(3), 10–16.

Madsen, V.T., & Johansen, W. (2019), A spiral of voice? When employees speak up on internal social media, *Journal of Communication Management, 23*(4), 331–347. doi: 10.1108/JCOM-03-2019-0050

Malhotra, A., Majchrzak, A., & Rosen, B. (2007). Leading virtual teams. *Academy of Management Perspectives, 21*(1), 60–70. doi: 10.5465/amp.2007.24286164

McNair, L. D., & Paretti, M. C. (2010). Activity theory, speech acts, and the "doctrine of infelicity": Connecting language and technology in globally networked learning environments. *Journal of Business and Technical Communication, 24*(3), 323–357. doi: 10.1177/1050651910363275

Nonaka, I. & Takeuchi, H. (1995). *The knowledge-creating company: How Japanese companies create the dynamics of innovation* (vol. 105). New York: OUP USA.

Olaisen, J., & Revang, O. (2017). Working smarter and greener: Collaborative knowledge sharing in virtual global project teams. *International Journal of Information Management, 37*(1), 1441–1448. doi: 10.1016/j.ijinfomgt.2016.10.002

Orlikowski, W. J. (1992). The duality of technology: Rethinking the concept of technology in organizations. *Organization Science, 3*(3), 398–427. doi: 10.1287/orsc.3.3.398

Orlikowski, W. J. (2007). Sociomaterial practices: Exploring technology at work. *Organization Studies, 28*(9), 1435–1448. doi: 10.1177%2F0170840607081138

Oshri, I., Kotlarsky, J., & Willcocks, L. P. (2007). Global software development: Exploring socialization and face-to-face meetings in distributed strategic projects. *Journal of Strategic Information Systems, 16*(1), 25–49. doi: 10.1016/j.jsis.2007.01.001

Oshri, I., van Fenema, P., & Kotlarsky, J. (2008). Knowledge transfer in globally distributed teams: The role of transactive memory. *Information Systems Journal, 18*(6), 593–616. doi: 10.1111/j.1365-2575.2007.00243.x

Paul, D. L. (2006). Collaborative activities in virtual settings: A knowledge management perspective of telemedicine. *Journal of Management Information Systems, 22*(4), 143176. doi: 10.2753/mis0742-1222220406

Piri, A., Niinimaki, T., & Lassenius, C. (2012). Fear and distrust in global software engineering projects. *Journal of Software-Evolution and Process, 24*(2), 185–205. doi: 10.1002/smr.476

Rezgui, Y. (2007). Exploring virtual team-working effectiveness in the construction sector. *Interacting with Computers, 19*(1), 96–112.

Rico, R., Alcover, C. M., Sanchez-Manzanares, M., & Gil, F. (2009). The joint relationships of communication behaviors and task interdependence on trust building and change in virtual project teams. *Social Science Information Sur Les Sciences Sociales, 48*(2), 229–255. doi: 10.1177/0539018409102410

Rosen, B., Furst, S., & Blackburn, R. (2007). Overcoming barriers to knowledge sharing in virtual teams. *Organizational Dynamics, 36*(3), 259–273. doi: 10.1016/j.orgdyn.2007.04.007

Schulze, J., & Krumm, S. (2017). The "virtual team player". A review and initial model of knowledge, skills, abilities, and other characteristics for virtual collaboration. *Organizational Psychology Review,* 7(1), 66–95.

Scott, M. E. (2013). "Communicate through the roof": A case study analysis of the communicative rules and resources of an effective global virtual team. *Communication Quarterly, 61*(3), 301–318.

Suchan, J., & Hayzak, G. (2001). The communication characteristics of virtual teams: A case study. *IEEE Transactions on Professional Communication, 44*(3), 174–186. doi: 10.1109/47.946463

Suchman, L. (1987). *Plans and situated actions: The problem of human-machine communication.* Cambridge: Cambridge University Press.

Suchman, L. (1998). Human/machine reconsidered. *Cognitive Studies/Japanese Bulletin of Cognitive Science, 5*(1), 5–13.

Suchman, L. (2007). *Human-machine reconfigurations: Plans and situated actions.* Cambridge: Cambridge University Press.

Suh, A., & Shin, K.-S. (2010). Exploring the effects of online social ties on knowledge sharing: A comparative analysis of collocated vs dispersed teams. *Journal of Information Science, 36*(4), 443–463. doi: 10.1177/0165551510369632

Walther, J. B. (1996). Computer-mediated communication impersonal, interpersonal, and hyperpersonal interaction. *Communication Research, 23*(1), 3–43.

Wegner, D. M. (1986). Transactive memory systems. In B. Mullen & G. R. Goethal (Eds.), *Theories of group behavior* (pp. 185–208). New York: Springer-Verlag.

Weick, K. E. (1995). *Sensemaking in organizations.* London: Sage

Weick, K. E. (2001). *Making sense of the organization.* Oxford: Blackwell.

Wenger, E. (1998). *Communities of practice: Learning, meaning, and identity.* New York: Cambridge University Press.

Wenger, E., McDermott, R., & Snyder, W. M. (2002). *Cultivating communities of practice: A guide to managing knowledge.* Boston, MA: Harvard Business School Press.

Wilson, J. M., Straus, S. G., & McEvily, B. (2006). All in due time: The development of trust in computer-mediated and face-to-face teams. *Organizational Behavior and Human Decision Processes, 99*(1), 16–33. doi: 10.1016/j.obhdp.2005.08.001

6 A vocabulary for describing virtual knowledge communication

Chapter Contents

The purpose of this chapter is three-fold: first, to position the study within the knowledge management literature which seems divided into a more cognitivist tradition tending towards viewing knowledge as mainly static and mainly a property of the mind, and a more constructionist tradition tending towards viewing knowledge as dynamic, evolutionary and a property of communication and interaction in communities of knowers ('epistemic communities'). The second purpose is to build a vocabulary in the form of theoretical concepts for describing the knowledge communication practices constructed by participants in their interview statements. Finally, extensive case study analysis demonstrates how different knowledge communication perceptions impact on knowledge communication in a global organisation.

DOI: 10.4324/9781003015925-8

This chapter extends concepts from knowledge management into a framework based on Karl E. Weick's theory of Sensemaking (all capitalised words, such as 'Sensemaking', are defined in the glossary at the back of the book; for more on Sensemaking theory, see Chapter 2). In this Weickian framework, professional identities and the values underlying those Identities shape and influence the types of knowledge perceived as useful. This understanding of knowledge in a professional context builds on a view of knowledge as evolutionary rather than static. 'Evolutionary' here refers to the perception that knowledge changes and evolves as it is reproduced among knowers, between groups or encoded in knowledge objects such as documents and emails (Heylighen 1993). Even computer hardware can be seen as knowledge objects encoded with the specialised knowledge of computer designers and engineers, albeit a highly codified knowledge which is difficult to decode even by specialists. Yet even knowledge encoded into the computer as a physical object can be de-coded to a high enough degree to allow competitors in the market to produce very similar computers, tablets, smartphones, etc.

Perceptions of 'useful' knowledge

The trajectory in the knowledge management literature could be argued to be a shift in the perception of what 'useful knowledge' is. In this sense, the knowledge management debate in the second half of the 20th century seems to have been foreshadowed by Aeschylus' 2,500-year-old quote 'who knows useful things, not many things, is wise' (Aeschylus, 2000). This trajectory of knowledge management theory can be seen as shifting from a focus on a need for more information and the Internet as the 'information superhighway', to Tsoukas and Vladimirou's (2001) argument that information only becomes knowledge if it is the property of a human knower. Tsoukas and Vladimirou's (2001) define knowledge sharing as: 'the availability of the right knowledge at the right time' (p. 33). But what the 'right' or 'useful' knowledge is, depends on the perception of the knower, the context and tasks at hand.

This book extends this knowledge management perspective by building on the Sensemaking[1] perspective (see Chapter 2) to argue that the perception of knowledge usefulness depends on the knower or the community of knowers. Elaborating on the evolutionary metaphor of knowledge communication, Heylighen (1993) argues that only knowledge adapted to fit to a particular environment of knowers will be reproduced in that environment. So, the evolutionary metaphor for knowledge can be seen as resting on the argument that knowledge 'survival' depends on its reproduction (i.e., communication) between knowers who find the knowledge both valid and applicable within that specific environment, and the ability of that knowledge to be adapted and applied within other environments.

This evolutionary perspective on knowledge fits with Teun Van Dijk's (2005) definition of knowledge as:

> Shared beliefs satisfying the specific (epistemic) criteria of an (epistemic) community. … Each community, or historical moment of a community, has its own criteria that allow members to establish that some beliefs are treated and shared as knowledge, whereas others are not.
> (p. 73)

I adopt Van Dijk's definition of knowledge because it shares Weick's insight that human beings do not perceive the world as it is, but through the filter of their simultaneously individual and social identities and experiences. This is reflected both in the notion of 'beliefs' which only gain status as knowledge through the (epistemic) community. Knowledge as a property of a community can be seen representing, first, a dynamic view of knowledge, because knowledge changes depending on which community adopts it and for which purposes. This links Van Dijk's (2005) definition to the notion of 'usefulness' of knowledge as an (inter)subjective quality of knowledge, as in 'useful for whom' and 'useful for which purposes'. Second, perceiving knowledge as a property of communities can be seen as a social view of knowledge, because the forms and applications of knowledge depend on the relations within the (epistemic) community, and the same knowledge may be perceived differently and applied differently by a different (epistemic) community.

The SECI model presented in the next section provides a vocabulary for describing different perceptions of which knowledge is found to be 'useful' by different epistemic communities.

The SECI model as a vocabulary for describing virtual knowledge communication

Von Krogh (1998) argues that the current perspective on knowledge as a co-creation and as an ongoing process rather than a static product is linked to an understanding of knowledge as having both a Tacit and an Explicit dimension. He attributes this distinction to Nonaka and Takeuchi (1995), though rightfully the concepts were coined by Polanyi (1966). The same mistake was made by Fong (2003).

Nonaka and Takeuchi's (1995) book on knowledge creation is one of the most often cited texts in the prolific knowledge management literature. I adopt their knowledge creation model, both because I use the vocabulary of their model to describe the knowledge communication practices of the three prototypes later in this chapter, and because a description of their model is necessary before examining the criticism against the model and discussing this criticism in the latter half of the chapter.

Nonaka and Takeuchi's theories of the knowledge creating company are centred on their knowledge conversion model termed the 'SECI model' after the four knowledge conversion processes. These four processes are Socialisation, Externalisation, Combination and Internalisation, see Table 6.1, and the explanation below the table.

Table 6.1 lists the four types of knowledge conversion processes in Nonaka and Takeuchi's (1995) SECI model. The table provides brief definitions and examples to illustrate the concepts. Each of the four knowledge conversion processes in Table 6.1 focus on the transformation of knowledge along two dimensions. These are the Tacit-Explicit and the personal–social dimension. 'Social' should here be understood in the broadest form of the term as being shared by two or more individuals, so it can be seen as moving from individual to interpersonal, organisational and beyond.

The Tacit and the Explicit dimension of knowledge should be seen as mutually interdependent. To illustrate this, Brown and Duguid (1998) argue that Explicit Knowledge is like the knowledge of a dictionary: the dictionary provides definitions of the meaning of words, but they do not tell you how to speak a language. It seems that the dictionary is of no use if you do not already possess a Tacit (silent) knowledge of speaking the language because the Explicit Knowledge provides you with knowledge of how the Explicit Knowledge of the dictionary should be de-coded and applied in practice. As another illustration of the mutual dependency of the Tacit and Explicit dimensions of knowledge, Brown and Duguid (1998) argue that 'trying to reduce one to the other is a little like trying to reduce a two-dimensional drawing to one dimension' (p. 134).

Table 6.1 Overview of the SECI model

Knowledge Conversion Processes	*Definition*	*Examples*
Socialisation	Sharing of tacit, personal knowledge between two individuals	Apprenticeship: learning a craft through close interaction and communication
Externalisation	Converting personal, explicit knowledge to explicit interpersonal knowledge	Writing a 'How-to' guide or manual. Using metaphors and illustrations to explain insights and intuitions
Combination	Combining Explicit Knowledge objects into new Explicit Knowledge	Finance department Combines financial reports of each department into the annual report of the company
Internalisation	Making explicit knowledge tacit through learning	Learning how to use intuitively, using a computer through use of a how-to guide

Similarly, in defining Tacit and Explicit Knowledge Nonaka and Takeuchi (1995) argue for a continuum between the two and argue that they are mutually dependent. Yet in their knowledge conversion model, Tacit and Explicit are separated into independent knowledge conversion processes (see Table 6.1). They offer extensive case studies to support their arguments.

One of the book's key examples of Socialisation as a means for communicating tacit knowledge is the construction of the Matsushita bread making machine (Nonaka & Takeuchi, 1995). The challenge for Matsushita was to build a bread machine, which would make bread that tasted as good as that made by hand by a professional baker. However, the breakthrough in the design of the machine didn't come until an employee got the idea to spend considerable time with the master baker of a hotel famous for its bread. Only through careful observation and practice of the master baker's technique did the engineer understand the Tacitly held knowledge of the baker's special kneading technique. Through the close, master-and-apprentice-like interaction between the master baker and the Matsushita employee, they were able to help each other to articulate the Explicit Knowledge of master baker's kneading technique, thereby Externalising it. By combining their different types of Tacit Knowledge both the master baker and the Matsushita employee gained new insights, i.e. the learning process which Nonaka & Takeuchi term 'Internalisation'.

In this case story, we see how that the knowledge conversion theory of Nonaka and Takeuchi (1995) follows the spiralling motion mentioned above, starting with individually held, Tacit Knowledge, but which spirals outward to groups, the entire organisation and potentially further out into the interorganisational and social level.

Despite the emphasis on the dialectic relationship between personal and more interpersonal or institutionally held knowledge, Nonaka and Takeuchi (1995) do not build a satisfactory theory of the interpersonal mechanisms influencing the flow of knowledge by employees and between employees. Part of this gap can be seen as being addressed by Wenger's (1998) theory of Communities of Practice (see Chapter 7). Furthermore, Chapters 7, 8 and 9 fill this gap by providing theories and case study analysis of personal and social identity theory, and the interpersonal mechanisms of relationships.

Criticism of the SECI model

In this section, I review the criticism of Nonaka and his associates by building on Gerard (2001), Tsoukas (2004), and Virtanen (2010). This criticism has mainly been targeted at Nonaka and Takeuchi's (1995) use of the concepts 'Tacit' and 'Explicit'. This section of the book examines the positions within the debate, and builds on the growing body of work arguing for a complex understanding of Tacit and Explicit Knowledge as a continuum where one will always contain an element of the other (e.g. Gerard, 2001; Tsoukas, 2004; Virtanen, 2010). This 21st century literature contrasts with knowledge management literature primarily from the 1990s which has a more dichotomous ontological distinction between Tacit and Explicit Knowledge. The primary source of this tendency in the 1990s seems to stem from Nonaka and Takeuchi's (1995) use of the concepts in the knowledge conversion processes (see Table 6.1). Nonaka and Takeuchi's (1995) theories of the knowledge creating company have had considerable impact on, within and beyond the field of knowledge management (more than 30.000 citations on Google Scholar). Because the conceptual distinction between Tacit and Explicit Knowledge has been essential in describing my analyses of how employees at HR Consult make sense of their knowledge communication practices, I will discuss the concepts at some length.

The critique against the SECI model centres on the very notion of making Tacit Knowledge into Explicit knowledge, based on close readings of Polanyi's original arguments for the concepts. Polanyi argued for a personal coefficient in all knowing and argues that this entails a fusion of personal and objective knowledge (Polanyi, 1966, p. vii). In Polanyi's theory all conscious acts have a Tacit dimension (Virtanen, 2010). Consequently, the concept has a much wider application than the narrower focus in some knowledge management literature where Tacit Knowledge is described as context-specific knowhow (Brown & Duguid, 1998) and intuition and hunches (Nonaka & Takeuchi, 1995)

Furthermore, Virtanen (2010) criticises the description in Nonaka and Takeuchi (1995) of the Externalisation as a process of using figurative language to articulate what Nonaka and Takeuchi (1995) label as intuition and insights. Virtanen argues that Nonaka and Takeuchi (1995) thereby imply that intuitions and hunches can be equated with Tacit Knowledge. However, it seems that verbalising intuitions is not particularly problematic. Polanyi, on the other hand, argued that tacit knowledge is both difficult and time consuming to Externalise.

Virtanen cites the examples of Explicit Knowledge objects provided by Nonaka and associates, such as manuals, data and scientific formulae. When I refer to 'Nonaka and his associates', I use it as a shorthand for citing the following: (Nonaka & Takeuchi, 1995; Nonaka & Toyama, 2005; Nonaka et al., 2000; Nonaka & von Krogh, 2009). These examples (manuals, data, scientific formulae), Virtanen argues, suggest a separation between Explicit and Explicit Knowledge: 'the aim, after all, is to convert knowledge existing in a Tacit form to more exploitable Explicit forms.' (Virtanen, 2010, para. 2). Based on Polanyi's writing, Virtanen (2010) argues for Tacit and Explicit as inseparable, co-existing in all knowledge forms, and argues that the Tacit element of any knowledge can never be articulated, because it forms a subsidiary element to any conscious act, and according to Polanyi's theory, the Tacit, subsidiary element will change if put into focus. In other words, the Explicit Knowledge objects used as examples by Nonaka and Takeuchi (1995), such as manuals and scientific formulae, contain Tacit presuppositions which are required to access the knowledge potential of the object. For example, highly specialised texts within a particular academic field may presuppose that the reader has the Explicit Knowledge of the field required to understand the text, and even then, may require considerable learning effort to Internalise the knowledge embedded in the object and apply it within the context of the learner/knower.

But it seems that Tsoukas' (2004) statement that all knowledge requires a human knower goes too far in the criticism against the SECI model by not allowing for the embedding of knowledge into knowledge objects, such as books and databases. Instead, I would argue that for knowledge to be perceived as useful to a knower, it requires that the knower can see a potential for application of the relevant knowledge within their own situation.

Virtanen (2010) goes as far as arguing that the knowledge management literature accepting the possibility of making Tacit Knowledge into Explicit knowledge rests on two conflicting epistemologies, the objectivist notion of Explicit Knowledge as easily transferable, and Polanyi's epistemology resting on a notion of knowledge as always situated and with an inseparable Tacit element. However, if we accept, as it seems that Nonaka and his associates do, that Tacit and Explicit are a continuum where knowledge is always both Explicit and Tacit, though to differing degrees, then it would seem that Virtanen (2010) is overstating his claim when arguing that the notion of making Tacit Explicit rests on irreconcilable epistemological foundations.

Furthermore, Virtanen's argument that the Tacit dimension changes if put into focus, just as atoms can appear as particles or beams depending on how they are observed, may not necessarily be problematic: if we consider knowledge as dynamic and evolutionary (Heylighen, 1993), and as a living entity (Kastberg, 2007), then shifts in knowledge as it moves between knowers could be seen as fruitful rather than problematic. If knowledge didn't change as it moved between knowers and between more Tacit or more Explicit forms, then it loses its innovative potential. Additionally, Virtanen (2010) limits his discussion to the Tacit/Explicit dimension, without regard for the individual/social dimension discussed in the next two chapters of the present volume. Briefly, foreshadowing later arguments, individuals retain the autonomy to oppose and correct what they may see as misunderstandings and misapplications of their more Tacit knowing in the knowledge conversion process.

But Virtanen does have a point when arguing that Tacit and the Explicit are not separate knowledge types but are aspects of all forms of knowing. Gerard (2001) too points out that Polanyi's notion of the Tacit cannot be defined by his oft cited utterance (e.g., Smith, 2001) that 'we can know more than we can tell' (Gerard, 2001, para. 1). Tacit knowledge goes beyond being knowledge we cannot articulate to being an aspect of all knowledge, even in its most Explicit forms. So Explicit Knowledge has Tacit presuppositions – i.e., it can presuppose unstated, Tacit Knowledge needed to decode, understand and Internalise the Explicit knowledge embedded in a text.

Virtanen's argument about the impossibility of making Explicit Knowledge Explicit does seem to hold true for some of Polanyi's examples of Explicit Knowledge, e.g., Polanyi's (1966) example of the Tacit process of face recognition. Despite the almost infinite range of different faces, we can easily recognise and distinguish between the people that matter in our lives, but none of us will ever be able to articulate how we do it. The concept of language provides a good example of the complex nature of the relation between Tacit and Explicit Knowledge. On the one hand, a language can be seen as knowledge shared and held in common among large groups of people allowing often unproblematic exchanges of meaning without ever putting or being able to put this Explicit Knowledge into focus and making it Explicit. The number of disciplines devoted to understanding language testifies not only to the complexity of language as an object of knowledge, but also to the human need to make such knowledge Explicit. On the other hand, despite the shared nature of language as a linguistic sign, a shared signifier ('significant' in Ferdinand de Saussure's semiotics) may have different signified ('signifié' in de Saussure's semiotics) to different individuals sometimes causing misunderstandings. An example of such misunderstanding can be seen in the case studied by Lehtonen and Kampf (2014) where Finnish and Indian team members attached different, Tacitly held meanings to the same concepts, causing misunderstandings in the team communication. In terms of knowledge communication, this argument implies that knowers within the same epistemic community may have different understandings and applications of the community's knowledge domain.

Nonaka and Takeuchi (1995) do not mention Polanyi's example of inarticulable, Tacit Knowledge, but instead provide the previously mentioned example of the Matsushita bread maker. Polanyi's and Nonaka and Takeuchi's examples of Tacit Knowledge entail two opposing perceptions of the nature of Tacit Knowledge; Polanyi's example of sensory impression entails a perception of Tacit Knowledge as unable to be made Explicit. Nonaka and Takeuchi's example on the other hand provides an example which entails a perception of Tacit Knowledge as difficult but possible to articulate.

However, the disagreement between Nonaka and Takeuchi's examples of Explicit Knowledge may not be as notable as Gerard (2001) and Virtanen (2010) claim, because Polanyi (1966) also argues for communication of Tacit Knowledge through close personal interaction, using master–apprentice interaction in a laboratory as empirical grounding for Tacit learning between scientists.

In other words, even in Polanyi's writing, the boundary between Tacit and Explicit Knowledge seems to be blurred. Virtanen (2010) argues that part of the debate about Tacit and Explicit Knowledge stems from the lack of clear definitions in Polanyi's writing leaving the texts open to interpretation. Similarly, Nonaka and Takeuchi (1995) argue that 'Tacit Knowledge and Explicit Knowledge are not separate but mutually complementary entities. They interact with and interchange into each other in the creative activities of human beings' (p. 61). This suggests that Nonaka and Takeuchi's concept of Tacit Knowledge is more nuanced than it is given credit for by Virtanen (2010) and Gerard (2001), as Nonaka and Takeuchi (1995) argue for Tacit and Explicit Knowledge as a continuum. But the continuum argument and the idea of conversion between Tacit and Explicit levels still suggests that the Tacit and Explicit are distinct knowledge types for Nonaka and Takeuchi (1995). This is supported by the fact that they never argue for the Tacit aspect of knowledge as a background to all Explicit Knowledge as Virtanen (2010) and Gerard (2001) do in their readings of Polanyi's Tacit concept.

Revisions of Nonaka's knowledge creation theory in the light of the criticism

In more recent articles, Nonaka and his co-authors (Nonaka et al., 2000; Nonaka & von Krogh, 2009) seem to widen the criteria for when Tacit Knowledge is truly Tacit. Using the notion of a continuum, it could be argued that Nonaka and associates in their later writings have slid towards the more Explicit end of the continuum, because they argue that the location for Socialisation need not be a physical place, but can be either physical, mental, virtual or any combination of the three. They use the term 'Ba' to signify this space. From their arguments for Ba as a site for Explicit Knowledge sharing through Socialisation, Nonaka and his co-authors thus implicitly argue against the close physical contact which Nonaka and Takeuchi (1995) argue is necessary for sharing Tacit Knowledge. Nonaka et al. (2000) also summarily introduce the importance of intangible knowledge assets into the equation, devoting one paragraph to each of their four categories of intangible assets. These are divided into four categories: first, the experiential knowledge assets, including knowhow as well as 'emotional knowledge' of who to trust. Second, 'conceptual assets', including mental models of the organisation and its brand. Thirdly, 'systemic knowledge assets' consisting of organisational knowledge objects such as technologies and documents with information about the organisation and its stakeholders. And finally, 'routine knowledge' assets including shared stories in the organisation as well as Explicit Knowledge that is 'routinised and embedded in the actions and practices of the organisation'

(p. 30). But with the focus on leading the knowledge creating process in their paper, the knowledge assets are not really developed – for example, the concept trust is not defined, nor do they attempt to theorise on how it impacts on the knowledge creating cycle. I address trust theory in Chapter 9 as part of a review of a relationship theories. Another gap seems to be that the influence of identity (individual, social or organisational) is not mentioned. I address this in Chapter 8.

How the book uses the SECI model to describe perceptions of knowledge

In the light of the criticism against the SECI model, this section presents three reservations with which the SECI model is adopted in the book as a vocabulary for describing the perceptions of knowledge and the communication preferences and practices which are grounded in these perceptions.

First, the Tacit and Explicit always coexist in all forms of knowledge, and therefore also in all the knowledge conversion processes of the SECI model. This implies for example that Socialisation will almost always involve oral and/or written communication. It is impossible to imagine that two people engage in any form of knowledge communication without interacting using language as well as physical interaction.

Second, the more recent articles by Nonaka and his associates include the notion that complex knowledge may be communicated over ICT if, and only if, a shared mental space, such as shared identity and mutual trust, also exist between the parties communicating and converting knowledge. This strong need for a relation between the parties highlights my arguments from Chapter 5 that knowledge communication across ICTs is possible, but that it requires that parties have a sense of mutual identification and trust. I explore trust theory in more detail in Chapter 9).

Thirdly, the discussion of Tacit and Explicit Knowledge can be linked to my focus on identity configurations centred on different perceptions of knowledge. I would argue that some identity configurations may consider more Explicit forms of knowledge as being more useful, while others may consider more Tacit Knowledge forms to be useful. Furthermore, these differences in perception of knowledge may be reflected in different knowledge communication practices. Through this argument, I extend Nonaka and Takeuchi's (1995) to include an aspect of Sensemaking (Weick, 1995, 2001. See Chapter 2 out the present volume), because knowers can be expected to make sense of knowledge as useful or not based on their personal perception of the context as well as their retention of identity and past experiences.

With this critique and revision of the SECI model in mind, the next three sections will apply the SECI model to analysis of the perception of knowledge of the three Prototypes: the Knowledge Transfer Prototype, the Knowledge Creator and the Knowledge Broker Prototype.

Discussion of knowledge theory in the light of Weick's (1995, 2001) theories of sensemaking

Sensemaking theory shifts the perspective from understanding contexts as objective and factual to perceiving contexts as subjective and interpreted through the filter of Retention (Identity and experiences). The same applies to knowledge, which, if understood from the evolutionary perspective presented in the introduction to Chapter 6 will change and adapt to contexts depending on the needs and sensemaking of the knowers within that epistemic community. Deciding which knowledge could be useful within a given context can therefore be seen as a Sensemaking process. The subjective and selective aspect of Sensemaking also implies that knowledge cannot be transferred without loss or transformation because people select the parts and aspects that fit their Retention. But Retention in Weick (1995, 2001) can also be seen as social; the people we identify with and have shared experiences with can be seen as a strong influence on which knowledge is perceived as useful.

The knowledge theories presented in Chapter 5 and in this chapter suggest that knowledge in general and communication of knowledge in particular can both be seen as a cognitive and a social process. As a cognitive process, knowledge can be seen as a property of knowers, but also includes what could be described as 'social cognition'. For example, through the notion that a group can have mutual knowledge of a knowledge domain.

In relation to Tacit and Explicit Knowledge, the Tacit aspect of knowledge can be seen as part of Retention in Weick (1995, 2001). Thereby the Tacit aspect can be seen as an essential part of understanding the extracted cues from the explicit elements of new knowledge in the Changing Ecology. Communication of knowledge can therefore be seen as founded on the mutually constitutive elements of Tacit and Explicit. The Externalised forms of knowledge, e.g., documents or oral communication of knowledge, can thus be seen as having both Explicit and Tacit aspects, where the Tacit in Explicit knowledge forms can be seen as a presupposed and therefore unarticulated aspect. Externalised forms of knowledge might therefore only be adopted by the receiver, if the retention of the receiver holds the necessary Explicit Knowledge to understand what was not made explicit in the knowledge communication. The very status of an aspect of knowledge as Tacit also implies that knowers can never communicate the exact same knowledge, which implies that knowledge communication can always be misunderstood regardless how Explicit it is. In a semi-dispersed work environment, it may be more difficult to know whether receivers of knowledge communication share the necessary Explicit Knowledge to understand the knowledge communication as intended. This suggests a need for virtual work environments to include meta-communication about how core concepts are understood at each site. Thereby, the semi-dispersed employees can begin to build a shared understanding of the knowledge communicated.

But the subjective element of Selection and Retention, which determine which knowledge is perceived as useful, also has implications for Nonaka and Takeuchi's (1995) SECI model.

The subjective aspect of Retention can be seen as a filter influencing, first, how and whether new knowledge is retained; and second, how and whether that knowledge will communicated to others as part of the Enactment process. This means that different employees or groups of employees may have preferences, as part of their Retention, for different knowledge processes. For example, a preference for Externalisation and Internalisation of existing knowledge may mean that the employee or group does not see the more creative knowledge processes of Combination and Socialisation as useful. Within a virtual work context, meta-communication about such knowledge preferences could be seen as an important initial step for a virtual team. Thereby the semi-dispersed team might understand how to build on the strengths of different perceptions of knowledge, rather than allow them to emerge as possible interpersonal conflicts when team members do not recognise differences.

Such differences in preferences for different knowledge communication processes can also be seen as an aspect of the professional identity of an employee and may be a more stable identity trait which is applied across an employee's multiple projects and teams. This makes the study of how employees perceive knowledge and how they build professional identities centred around this perception relevant to the book's larger research aim of improving communication, relationships and the efficiency of knowledge communication in virtual work environments.

To sum up, the knowledge theories presented in the chapter focus on knowledge and it's changing forms or qualities as it moves from individual to interpersonal to organisational and social levels

Case study: The Knowledge Transfer Prototype's perception of useful knowledge

This section provides an analysis of the perception of knowledge of the most common professional identity prototype at HR Consult Denmark and UK, the Knowledge Transfer Prototype. I do not analyse this prototype in depth using step 4 and 5 of my discursive Sensemaking Discourse Analysis (DSA) approach explained in Chapter 4 (the discourse analysis steps), because my focus is on the critical cases represented by the Knowledge Creator and the Knowledge Broker Prototype.

Instead, I use examples primarily from my interview with Dorthe at HR Consult Denmark, and secondarily from the HR Consult UK virtual team of consultants, the so-called Client Relations Management Team, where I interviewed two of the members. These two UK participants represented the Knowledge BrokerPrototype and the Knowledge Creator Prototype, and in their Discursive Sensemaking they explicitly dissociated themselves from the members of the team that represent the knowledge transfer prototypical identity. Despite their bias, they did describe the knowledge communication practice of the knowledge transfer prototypical identity, and it is these descriptions in addition to description of managers in the UK, which I build on in this section when providing examples of the Knowledge Transfer Prototype in the UK. But first I'll focus on the Conversations at HR Consult Denmark and UK.

There seems to be an organisational Conversation in these two organisations which leads to an expectation that the consultants should mainly communicate the highly Explicit knowledge products produced by HR Consult UK, to ensure a high revenue, rather than engage in transforming them to Situate them in client Conversations. I use the term 'situate' throughout the analyses in the sense of Lave and Wenger (1991). i.e., learning (or knowing) which is adapted to specific contexts and practices, rather than being general and abstract. This Conversation emerges in (d)iscourses on the corporate intranet, at meetings in the organisation and in formal documents and presentations on organisational strategy emphasising growth of the organisation through market penetration. The means for achieving this goal seems to be to sell HR Consult knowledge in the form of highly codified learning modules with workshop programmes, PowerPoint presentations and workshop exercises. The core of the strategy builds on the ability to Combine, to use Nonaka and Takeuchi's (1995) term, these modules into learning programmes to address client demands and challenges, without engaging in time-consuming knowledge creation and transformation at the front-line consultant level.

The key characteristic of the Knowledge Transfer Prototype at the consultancy level seems to be the construction of a professional identity centred on the value of these HR Consult learning modules. This does not seem to be based solely on organisational requirements for generating revenue, but also a professional identity built on a high respect and passion for communicating knowledge products designed by HR Consult R&D.

In the following, I use these examples to show how the perception of knowledge, identity and relationships of the Knowledge Transfer Prototype impact on the knowledge communication practices at HR Consult. The analysis provides details for comparison between the Knowledge Transfer Prototype and the two other prototypes presented in the latter two sections of the chapter.

The perception of knowledge valuing Explicit Knowledge products seems to lead to knowledge communication practices focusing on transferring existing HR Consult knowledge to clients. When analysed using Nonaka and Takeuchi's (1995) SECI model, this knowledge communication practice can be seen as missing a knowledge creation step at the frontline consultant level. From the perspective of the Knowledge Transfer Prototype, knowledge creation occurs at the central R&D department, and the task of consultants becomes a transfer of this Explicit knowledge to the client through learning development programmes built from the modules constructed by the R&D department.

The Knowledge Transfer Prototype can be seen as first Internalising HR Consult knowledge. Through this Internalisation of the products, consultants learn to Combine the training modules designed by R&D into training programmes adapted to the needs of a client organisation. This Combination step builds on combining mainly Explicit Knowledge products designed by R&D. Consultants with a Knowledge Transfer Prototype then Externalise this knowledge within different client contexts to ensure a new process of Internalisation within the client organisation. Ideally, the client is then able to apply the knowledge to solve the challenges which brought them to HR Consult in the first place. Because the Externalisation of HR consult knowledge in the client organisation builds on existing knowledge, new HR Consult knowledge does not seem to be created in this process. The main criterion for success in their role as consultants thus seems to be the extent to which existing HR Consult knowledge is Internalised and applied within the client organisation.

This focus on applying existing knowledge within client organisations means that little new knowledge is created by the Knowledge Transfer Prototype. This means that the Knowledge Transfer Prototype has little incentive to engage in knowledge communication with colleagues, except to exchange client leads.

Case study: The Knowledge Creator's perception of useful knowledge

Henrik's, a Knowledge Creator Prototype, perception of organisational knowledge seems to be aligned with Nonaka's arguments for a knowledge creation spiral which does not just occur in one department, R&D, but is funnelled in and out between the personal, interpersonal and organisational levels throughout the organisation in a process of ongoing transformation and creation. This first section of the analysis focusses on the individual level of Henrik's perception of knowledge, which can be seen as centred on a belief that even at the consultant level in Denmark, far away from the R&D department in the UK, the full SECI circle should be completed. From the perspective of the organisation, adaption to client context should consist of selecting and combining predesigned training modules from the product portfolio. I use *adapt* here to describe minor changes in the learning programmes designed by the R&D department, and selection and combination of the predesigned modules to address client needs for training and development. Each module consists of PowerPoints, exercises and learning guides (booklets) for a particular aspect of personal, team, sales or leadership training.

In the quote below, Henrik argues for his perception of organisational knowledge as a process constantly in need of transformation, however. His case demonstrates that a full SECI circle can be seen by some consultants as imperative. I use 'transformation' here to signal a more complete (re-)creation of organisational learning programmes to tailor the development programme specifically to the client's context. So even though the R&D department of the organisation has produced workshop materials, PowerPoints and exercises for consultants to use to communicate HR Consult knowledge to clients, Henrik feels a need to transform that knowledge to particular client contexts, thereby building a more Situated learning developed through full SECI funnels. I've divided the following rather long quote into three parts, allowing for an analysis of each part.

Henrik's Discursive Sensemaking about his perception of knowledge can be seen in his construction of an analogy comparing organisational knowledge to musical improvisation. This metaphor, which he lays out in the three excerpts quoted below (both from Henrik, my translation 73, 10:23), shows that to him organisational knowledge is not static: like a jazz tune you can play an infinite number of improvisations over it as long as you 'understand the scales' (l. 4–5) and 'what to play over this chord' (l. 6). At the linguistic level, he uses prosody to support his Discursive Sensemaking. The prosodic cues in the first part of the quote (l. 1–9 below) indicate his passion and commitment by use of a faster pace and a generally higher key throughout the quote. The initial high key onset helps set this quote apart from the surrounding (d)iscourse, thereby, in combination with the impression of passion and commitment, rendering it Significant. The sharp intake (.h) and exhale (h) of breath at the onset of the last two intonation units give the impression that he is straining to get his point across:

Henrik:

1 "^\I play the piano.
2 --so it's really,
3 \It's from ^that process ^there[1]
4 \which _if you understand
5 (.h)\the scales
6 \if you under/stand \what to play over this chord[2]

7 \if you under/stand,
8 _mm ^tones should be put together so they sound
9 \(h) good-- if you're /going \in this direction (.)

(Henrik, my translation, 73, 10:23)

Quote notes:

[1] Henrik plays piano with his fingers on the table.

[2] Henrik taps the table to indicate the piano keys he has just pretended to play.

Henrik then (see quote below) uses this description of musical improvisation as a metaphor to discursively make sense of his perception of organisational knowledge as a process which needs to be transformed to be applied within different contexts. He argues that an exercise from a learning module designed by the HR Consult R&D department (corresponding to the chords and scales in a tune) can be transformed to fit training in sales (corresponding to musical improvisation): 'I'll turn it ninety degrees this way' (l. 18) or transformed to management development if 'I take this out' (l. 20). But this ability to transform, or 'improvise' over organisational knowledge, he argues, builds on deep understanding, or to use Nonaka and Takeuchi's (1995) terminology, a deep level of Internalisation.

The linguistic analysis of three same quotes underlines the importance for Henrik of this knowledge creation approach. The repetition of 'understanding' renders this Lexical choice Significant (1.2). Grammatically, this Significance is amplified by his breaking off the sentence after 'understanding', thereby putting the word in a salient end-of-clause position. This choice puts 'understanding' as the object of 'it's about'. Had he not broken off the sentence, it would have been the focus of the direct object. He elaborates on how the same exercise, equivalent of musical notation, can be transformed and used for training within 'sales' (l. 15) and 'management' (l. 19):

Henrik:

10 /it's ^precisely \the same here[1]
11 _so that--that--that transformation there[2] [...]
12 \It's about /understanding--(.h)
13 \understanding an exercise.
14 \and then looking at it.(.h)
15 /well, if that's used \within sales /well then
16 /well then
17 \it needs to look like ^this--
18 -_so I'll turn it ninety degrees this way
19 /If it's used within management
20 \then I take /^this out
21 \turn it 50, na, 60 degrees /this way (.)'

(Henrik, my translation, 73, 10:23)

Quote notes:

[1] Points to the words 'product manager' which he has written on a piece of paper in front of him.

[2] Points to the words 'product manager' again.

In the final part of the quote (see below) he uses the discourse marker 'So' to indicate that a conclusion or, in this case, a Sensemaking interpretation is coming (l. 22). The 'so' in l. 22, unlike the 'so' in l. 18, is preceded by a pause (end of l. 21) and 'so' in l. 22. is repeated twice, thereby establishing a break from the (d)iscourse that came before and constructing the following (d)iscourse as a conclusion or Discursive Sensemaking interpretation. His Discursive Sensemaking here (l. 22–25) centres on his own acquisition of the ability to transform organisational knowledge to 'different areas of expertise' (l. 23).

Finally, the high key repetition of 'that' (l. 24) adds emphasis and Significance to the following Intonation Unit's statement about his skill acquisition.

Henrik:

22 _So, so \that ability to to
23 \look at a thing and make it relevant within different /areas of expertise
24 /which we (.)\ have. ^that, that
25 /is one I've definitely \acquired.

(Henrik, my translation, 73, 10:23)

To conclude on the analysis of the three parts of the quote above, Henrik uses his perception of organisational knowledge as complex, processual and in need of transformation to be situated within different knowledge domain. By linking his own acquisition of this skill to another skill, playing the piano, which he implies he masters, he constructs an image of himself as a highly competent consultant. This whole passage (Henrik, 73, 10:23) gives a good impression of Henrik's approach to organisational knowledge.

To him, organisational knowledge is not a static product which should be delivered as intact as possible to the client. It is in an ongoing process of transformation. This is not to say that the knowledge is changed beyond recognition and entirely new products emerge. In that sense knowledge transformation might be a better description of his process, rather than knowledge creation used by Nonaka and Takeuchi (1995). Henrik's identity as consultant is closely linked to a need to transform HR Consult's product portfolio to suit particular clients' needs, the other consultants interviewed are more focused on selling the existing HR Consult products as they are produced by HR Consult R&D in the UK. Exceptions among the participants are John and Linda who like Henrik, transform HR Consult knowledge to build situated learning solutions for their clients. I explore the concept Identity more fully in Chapter 8 and provide more case analyses to link the theory to organisational Practices.

One physical example of Henrik's knowledge transformation is a card game he designed for a workshop at a major Danish client, a pharmaceutical company (the card game was observed at HR Consult Denmark's offices before the workshop). The 170 glossy full colour cards can be seen as a combination of the existing leadership development programme of the pharmaceutical company and HR Consult's leadership development programme, which thereby allowed the client to build on the strengths of both perspectives and to see how they fit together. Like Linda, Henrik admits that the card game probably didn't have a very good return on investment in the short term, but in making sense of the effort he put into it, he argues that his approach would keep the client coming back for more. While I debriefed HR Consult Denmark about my findings, Henrik was actually in Switzerland at a meeting with the pharmaceutical company's other local European offices to brief them about the project, because the pharmaceutical company was rolling the learning programme designed by Henrik out at a global level. The card game was but one element of this learning programme; other elements included the custom designed PowerPoints and training materials for the workshops and interventions of the learning programme.

Henrik has not only Internalised HR Consult's leadership programme, he has also Internalised the clients' existing leadership programme, vision and values through Socialisation with his client. So, the Socialisation step in Henrik's approach to knowledge transformation transcends the organisational boundaries of HR Consult to include the client organisation and his relations there, thereby reaching the interorganisational level of the SECI funnel. In this process, he transforms and re-creates organisational knowledge and Externalises his new solution, first through his sales pitch to sell his solution to the client, and second through workshops and ongoing learning supported by himself. In this process the card game performs just one example of his knowledge transformation strategy, which in this case can be understood as a combination of both Explicit and Tacit aspects of the leadership development of the two organisations. However, Nonaka and Takeuchi's SECI model constructs Combination as a process of combining only Explicit Knowledge. This can be seen as a weakness in Nonaka and Takeuchi's (1995) theory arising from the separation of Tacit and Explicit Knowledge in the SECI model. Rigid application of their model to the data presented here would mean ignoring the high level of Tacit Knowledge construction in Henrik's combination of the two leadership programmes into a new, Explicit knowledge in the form of the card game. Thereby, his solution can be understood as starting a new process of Internalisation at the client organisation.

In terms of communicating his deep knowledge with his colleagues at HR Consult Denmark, Henrik seems to have a challenge due to the difference between his own perception of useful organisational knowledge, and that of his colleagues at HR Consult Denmark. This lack of knowledge communication is highlighted by Henrik's statement that there is a pressure on him from the CEO to share his knowledge more. However, the difference in perceptions of knowledge, between Henrik on one hand and the CEO, Birgitte's, perception on the other hand is highlighted in his recollection of her words: '[Henrik] we really need to empty your head and give it to someone else' (Henrik, my translation, 132 (28:08). Henrik interprets her meaning for me, saying, 'y'know, we need to make sure more people have competencies.' (Henrik, my translation, 132, 28:08). To me, with the knowledge theory in mind presented earlier in this chapter, it seems that Birgitte with the knowledge-out-of-head metaphor is making sense of knowledge as a static product which can be transferred 1:1 to another head. This suggests alignment with the cognitivist tradition within knowledge management. To prompt him into stating the differences in perception of knowledge more explicitly, I therefore commented, 'Yea, that's sort of an odd metaphor, that you can just take things out of your head and give them to someone elses.' (Henrik, my translation, 134; 28:21)

In his response to this prompt to comment on the metaphor of 'taking knowledge out of someone's head', Henrik confirms that his own Sensemaking about the nature of organisational knowledge was opposed to Birgitte's perception of knowledge. In his response, quoted below (Henrik, my translation, 135; 28:25), notice his immediate, high key confirmation of my questioning of Birgitte's knowledge metaphor, suggesting that he feels understood (l.1); the prompt fits his own Sensemaking perspective that it was an odd metaphor about knowledge. He even laughs at Birgitte's perspective, before dismissing it as 'not possible' (l. 2), as seen from his own Sensemaking perspective. He then elaborates on his own perspective of knowledge internalisation and transformation as time consuming (requiring him to work at 'night', l. 4) and hard work (thus requiring 'blood, sweat', l. 4).

At the linguistic level, the effort he argues is required to Internalise, transform and communicate complex knowledge is evident. In terms of prosody, his scorn for Birgitte's perspective on the knowledge which he has worked hard to acquire can be seen in the short pause before shifting to high key (on 'push', l. 5), and descent into low key (on 'button', l. 5). The intensity with which he makes this argument is signalled in both the scorn just mentioned and in the emphasis he adds to the enunciation of 'motivated' and 'work hard' (l. 6). Lexically, you would expect 'blood' and 'sweat' to be collocated with 'tears', but by choosing 'night work' instead he renders his own effort significant.

Henrik:

1 £^Yes, isn't it? He, he£.
2 /And we know a\that it's not possible. (.)[1]
3 \We're talking about skills,
4 /which have been acquired through \blood, sweat and night work. (.)
5 /And you can't just (.) ^push \a _button and then the man's updated.
6 /The man has to be both motivated \and work hard for it. (.)
7 _So, so,
8 \there are no easy fixes _but it's I--I
9 ^from ^my perspective,
10 _and it may well be a perception,
11 ^I don't \hold on to my knowledge. (.)
12 /Y'know, \a lot of what I've done is on the G-drive.[2]
13 ^People can just access \it y'know. (.)
14 But I don't make a manual for people to understand it, y'know.

(Henrik, my translation, 135; 28:25)

Quote notes:

[1] Points at the interviewer and himself.
[2] The 'G-drive' is the name of the networked server at HR Consult.

To conclude on the analysis of the quote above, Henrik offers the Explicit forms of the fruits of his labour and puts them on the network drive but does not offer a 'manual' – it seems that the Tacit presuppositions are not explained, making it difficult for others to reapply the Explicit version of his work in other contexts. Henrik on his part feels justified in his Sensemaking belief that others should simply buckle down and do the hard work he himself has undergone to Internalise and transform organisational knowledge. As a consequence of Henrik's Sensemaking belief, and the lack of knowledge creation identity among other consultants, Henrik's knowledge does not seem to be communicated wider into the organisation. The network drive seems to become what von Krogh (1998) termed a 'data warehouse' and Davenport and Prusak (1998) termed a 'knowledge repository'. During one of my visits to HR Consult Denmark, two of Henrik's colleagues discussed who could find the time to 'tidy up' this network drive because they argued it had become cluttered with information without any easy entry points.

Case study: The Knowledge Broker's perception of useful knowledge

A significant difference in knowledge communication practices between the Knowledge Broker Prototype and the Knowledge Transfer Prototype became an important theme in the analysis of the interview with Linda, who represents the Knowledge Broker Prototype. This is the difference between, on the one hand, employees with a static perception of useful knowledge as product, emphasising standardised solutions. And on the other hand, employees with a dynamic perception of knowing as a process emphasising knowledge transformation to suit client needs. Linda constructs her knowledge communication approach as being client-centred. This can be seen in the quote below where her Discursive Sensemaking constructs her client-centred knowledge solutions as being diametrically opposed to the use of standardised knowledge solutions in her organisation. By first rejecting the use of an 'out-of-the-box-solution' (l. 3), and juxtaposing this with sitting down and talking 'for several days' with the client, she engages in the building task *Politics (distribution of social goods)* by building a value hierarchy between her own, client-centred approach and, from her perspective, the less valuable standardised solution. This Discursive Sensemaking is also constructed at the linguistic level. Her time-consuming choice not to adopt an 'out-of-the-box-solution' seems to devalue the knowledge work involved in designing the highly Explicit knowledge products constructed by the R&D department at HR Consult. Her scorn for such a standardised solution is signalled in the high key pronunciation of the phrase 'out-of-the-box-solution' (l. 3). This sets up a dichotomy between her approach of transforming organisational knowledge to tailor a solution, on the one hand, and the standardised and highly Explicit knowledge product designed by the R&D department at HR Consult on the other hand:

Linda:

\The client likes that when they come with a problem then erm,
/I don't offer some (.)
\^out-of-the-box-solution. (.)
\So--so we sit down and /talk for several *days*
\about how are we going to address this

(Linda, my translation, 326, 47:40)

She then makes a point of stating that she is rather unique in her organisation for adopting this approach:

Linda:

And it's also--(.)
\It's really me doing this.
\My colleagues don't do that as much'.

(Linda, my translation 326, 47:52).

In terms of Discursive Sensemaking, this statement shifts the opposition constructed in the previous quote from a difference in practice to a difference between individuals, among which she constructs herself as rather unique. Her construction of herself as unique in the organisation, which is similar to Henrik's self-image, may seem to be an attempt to construct a positive image of herself in the interview situation, because she moderates it later through statements about like-minded colleagues in her network.

Nevertheless, an image of a small group of employees who see themselves as different from the norms, i.e., the Conversation and official strategy at HR Consult emerges. Her perception of knowledge thus seems similar to Henrik's perception of HR Consult knowledge as requiring time-consuming knowledge transformation to be Situated within the client's context.

As a description of organisational knowledge communication practice, the construction of this difference can be triangulated, and the opposition between the two knowledge communication practices can consistently be identified in other interviews, despite considerable nuances within approaches and Sensemaking.

However, the quote above is not only a description of organisational knowledge communication practice, but also Linda's Discursive Sensemaking about her perception of useful organisational knowledge as a process which requires ongoing transformation to be situated within the client context, rather than being a predesigned product which can be applied in a variety of contexts.

To sum up on the analysis of the quote above, Linda constructs her perception of HR Consult knowledge as a process which can and should be transformed to suit client needs; she goes through a full SECI knowledge creation process in order to fulfil client needs. She constructs this perception of organisational knowledge as different from the typical knowledge communication approach at HR Consult which she describes as emphasising 'out-of-the-box-solutions'.

The implication for her knowledge communication practice seems to be that she engages in time-consuming knowledge transformation through Socialisation with people sharing her perception of knowledge. On the other hand, she devalues the knowledge communication practice of colleagues with a Knowledge Transfer identity. Through her use of value-laden descriptions when describing the Knowledge Transfer Prototype, we can begin to see a professional identity based on values attached to her knowledge communication practice. This will be explored further in Chapter 8.

Case study: A sense of autonomy as an aspect of the Knowledge Creator identity

Henrik carries on his time-consuming approach to client-centred knowledge transformation in spite of organisational Conversations and practices encouraging a different approach, thereby maintaining the values underlying his professional identity as a prototypical Knowledge Creator. The following analyses suggest that a high level of autonomy in deciding how to complete tasks is required for this knowledge creation approach and can therefore be seen as a characteristic of the Knowledge Creator Prototype. Henrik seems to be granted this autonomy by the organisation because he has demonstrated the success of his approach by bringing in more orders from his clients. As an employee at HR Consult Denmark, Henrik seems to be a special case in terms of the autonomy granted to him. Most other participants I interviewed in Denmark construct an image of a management practice where no one has time to build knowledge communication practices to develop their domains, because the CEO Birgitte loaded new responsibilities onto their shoulders when she believed they had time for them.

In the following quote, Henrik makes sense of this granting of autonomy by management. The first part of the quote is his answer to a question about what he meant by saying that Birgitte thought products were 'fun'. Central to his Discursive Sensemaking in the quote is the ending where he focuses on his own need for making what he describes as 'a really cool product' (l. 9). He emphasises that Birgitte has granted him the space needed to fulfil this need. But by discursively constructing her as not really understanding the workshops and learning programmes he has designed (l. 3–6), he builds an image of his autonomous labour to transform existing products to different client needs, and to translate and transform new HR Consult products into a Danish context. Through his prosody he underlines his perception of Birgitte as disconnected from his practice and not understanding his knowledge communication approach.

The pause before 'nice' (l. 1) and the rise-fall intonation pattern isolating the word 'almost' suggests scorn or mockery of what he, through the value-laden Lexical choice 'nice', constructs as an unreflecting management practice. In lines 2–4, he seems hesitant in making his criticism more overt; his hesitation is signalled in the pauses at the end of each of the intonation units in l. 2–4, and the faster pace in l. 5 seems to reflect a decision to just get it over with. His redeeming remark that she has always granted him autonomy is made in quick succession from the previous intonation unit, suggesting he wants to change the topic quickly. Finally, the combination of high key pronunciation of 'academic' (l.7) and the shift from low key pronunciation of 'really' (in the middle of l. 9) to high key pronunciation of 'product' (end of l. 9) puts emphasis on this perception of his own knowledge transformation as the key focus of the quote.

Henrik:

1 \she thinks i:t's (.) ^nice
2 \that we have several things to offer _others.
3 Erm \our clients, erm (.), without (.)
4 \understanding what (.)
5 (faster pace) what they really are.--
6 --^\But she has always allowed space for (.) erm
7 \ me to /satisfy the ^academic \need,

8 Which I also have
9 \for (.) making a _really/ cool ^product.

(Henrik, my translation, 20, 0:03:00)

To conclude on the analysis of the quote above, Henrik both constructs his need to bring new HR Consult products to market, and his CEO's inability to understand those products although she does provide him with the autonomy to continue this practice. Even though Henrik attributes Birgitte's acceptance of his time-consuming knowledge creation to a desire to have 'several things to offer', it seems more likely that she tolerates his practice because it has led to more revenue from clients. Henrik is known in the organisation for his ability to bring in new clients and generate more revenue from existing clients by offering them additional learning programmes. The learning programmes, which can extend over weeks or months of workshops, exercises and ongoing learning within the client organisation, are what is summarily described as 'products' in the quote above.

Although Henrik has made the choice of working overtime to fulfil his own expectations for what useful organisational knowledge should be, he complained a couple of times about the amount of work he had. I therefore challenged him by saying that this seemed to be his own choice. This led to Discursive Sensemaking to justify this choice in the quote below. As Discursive Sensemaking the quote justifies his time-consuming practice by referring to a sense of ownership: 'it's my organisation' (l. 5) and describes this as a 'good experience' (l. 4). But he is fully aware that this experience may be 'erroneous' (l. 3). So, despite his criticism of organisational knowledge communication at HR Consult Denmark, Henrik has a strong need to identify with the organisation. This sense of identification with the organisation was, despite his criticism, also seen in the analysis of his opposition to organisational (D)iscourse mentioned earlier in the chapter. He then shifts to the consequences of his knowledge communication approach (l. 7–8). The shift in topic is signalled by the discourse markers 'y'know' (l.7) and 'so' (l. 8). He points to neglect of his family (l. 10) and his own sleep (l. 11) but justifies his choice by arguing the sacrifice has to be made to 'succeed' (l. 13). Whether he refers to personal success or organisational success remains unclear. Had I asked him, he would probably have said the organisation, but based on the way he spoke about his colleagues as not competent enough, it seems that he is highly concerned about maintaining his organisation's reputation and his self-image.

Henrik:

1 \Well I think /it's a cool \organisation a:nd
2 (faster pace) _and \the more /I do \here the more I
3 (normal pace) _/I get \the erroneous ^experience\that
4 (faster pace) /but nevertheless good experience that \that it's my

5 \that it's my organisation
6 (normal pace)_\that I'm part of this organisation (.)
7 \Y'know(.)
8 \so it's all about--it's well --
9 --\it's an ownership which I choose to take both at (..)
10 (.hhh)/at my familiy's \expense too
11 /a:nd at the expense of my own ^sleep
12 _and whatever else there might be
13 (..)_ But that's what it takes for it to /succeed in the end. (.)

(Henrik, my translation, 111, 20:50)

To conclude on the analysis of the quote above, autonomy to pursue a time-consuming practice of knowledge transformation has implications for both family life and health (through sleep deprivation and working long hours). Despite these consequences, Henrik's professional identity as a knowledge creator seems to compel him to undertake the work, despite the lack of backing from the organisation.

To sum up on Henrik's professional identity, Henrik's Discursive Sensemaking about his knowledge creation practice builds a professional identity centred on this knowledge creation Practice of customised client solutions. Through his professional identity construction, he attaches a set of values to this Practice. These values are Enacted as a (d)iscourse requiring a deep internalisation of HR Consult knowledge before starting a new knowledge creation cycle through Socialisation with the client and Externalisation of knowledge into a learning programme for client employees and Internalisation of the new knowledge in the client organisation. But because Henrik does not communicate his knowledge with other consultants at HR Consult Denmark, the knowledge never leads to an internalisation process within HR Consult, resulting in loss of an innovation opportunity. Another value attached to his professional identity is the need to work autonomously without interference from management. As part of his Discursive Sensemaking he even constructs his CEO as not understanding the learning programmes the organisation sells to clients.

He emphasises his professional identity as rare in the organisation, citing the name of another consultant in Austria and vaguely referring to 'somebody in Canada'. Although Henrik seems to be isolated at HR Consult Denmark with his knowledge creator identity, he has been able to find a social basis in the small, globally dispersed Strategic Community to support this identity centred on knowledge creation; this will be explored further in the next chapter.

Case studies conclusion

Perception of knowledge as a key aspect of virtual knowledge communication emerged from interaction with the case context rather than from existing theory. The relevance of perception of knowledge for knowledge communication practices arose through the iterative process of conducting interviews, reflecting on and analysing the data.

The findings indicate three main tendencies in perceptions of knowledge at HR Consult: a *Knowledge Transfer approach*, a *Knowledge Creation approach* and a *Knowledge Broker approach*. At HR Consult the three approaches, or perceptions of knowledge, tended to be polarised, and therefore seemed to have considerable implications for virtual knowledge communication practices at HR Consult. The Discursive Sensemaking of employees sharing the Knowledge Transfer perception of knowledge tended to have a high respect for HR Consult knowledge. They perceived organisational knowledge as encoded into the tried and tested organisational knowledge products, such as PowerPoints, exercises and workshop materials. From this perspective of knowledge, the main role of the consultant in communicating organisational knowledge seemed to be to make sure that client understood and applied the knowledge as intended by HR Consult. For some consultants, such as Dorthe at HR Consult Denmark, this still meant considerable interaction with the client organisation to follow-up and make sure that the development programme was applied. But to others, such as the *Knowledge Transfer Prototype s* identified at HR Consult UK, this perception of knowledge meant a high focus on selling standardised HR Consult licences (known as accreditations) to clients combined with selling standardised, computer-generated personality profiles to all client staff, thereby ensuring maximum profit at little expense to HR Consult UK. Client practitioners with such licences would then be left with the responsibility for applying HR Consult training and development within their own company.

The perception of knowledge adopted by Henrik, exemplifying the Knowledge Creator, and by Linda, exemplifying the Knowledge Broker Prototype, differs from the Knowledge Transfer Prototype by seeing organisational knowledge as a process in ongoing transformation. This perception of knowledge means that organisational knowledge is used as ideas which form the basis for their time-consuming work to understand client challenges and to integrate client knowledge with HR Consult knowledge. However, the Knowledge Broker differ from the Knowledge Creator in their use of their networking skills to this the right expertise to solve the task.

This difference in perceptions of knowledge has two implications for knowledge communication at HR Consult. First, employees with different perceptions of the same knowledge products seem to have no incentive to communicate knowledge with each other. In fact, both Henrik and Linda express frustration that their colleagues and managers do not understand what they are doing and are not willing to commit to similar time-consuming knowledge creation. Using the vocabulary from Nonaka and Takeuchi's (1995) SECI model, the Knowledge Transfer Prototype can thus be seen as mainly Internalising and Externalising existing, codified knowledge, while the Knowledge Creator and the Knowledge Broker Prototype engage in completing a full SECI spiral of knowledge creation. The Knowledge Creator does not involve colleagues in this work, while the Knowledge BrokerPrototype uses their dispersed global network within and beyond the organisation to build Knowledge Teams with the ability to leverage the diversity of knowledge expertise within and beyond the team.

Notes

1 All capitalised words are defined in the glossary at the back of the book.

References

Aeschylus. (2000). E-text: Aeschylus, fragments 3. Retrieved 13-01-2015, from: http://www.theoi.com/Text/AeschylusFragments3.html

Brown, J. S., & Duguid, P. (1998). Organizing knowledge. *California Management Review, 40*(3), 91. doi: 10.2307%2F41165945

Davenport, T. H., & Prusak, L. (1998). *Working knowledge: How organizations manage what they know*. Boston, MA: Harvard Business School.

Fong, P. S. W. (2003). Knowledge creation in multidisciplinary project teams: An empirical study of the processes and their dynamic interrelationships. *International Journal of Project Management, 21*(7), 479–486. doi: 10.1016/s0263-7863(03)00047-4

Gerard, J. (2001). The tacit knowing framework: A look at sustained competitive advantage under a unified tacit and Explicit Knowledge. Paper presented at *the Fourth International Conference on Organizational Learning and Knowledge Management*, Ontario, Canada.

Heylighen, F. (1993). Selection criteria for the evolution of knowledge. Paper presented at *the Proc. 13th Int. Congress on Cybernetics*.

Kastberg, P. (2007). Knowledge communication – Formative ideas and research impetus. *Programmatic Perspectives, 2*(1), 59–71.

Lave, J., & Wenger, E. (1991). *Situated learning: Legitimate peripheral participation*. Cambridge: Cambridge University Press.

Lehtonen, M., & Kampf, C. (2014). Virtual teams and knowledge communication: Drawing on semiotics for making knowledge about virtual teams and collaboration visible. *International Journal of Sociotechnology and Knowledge Development (IJSKD), 6*(3), 1–25. doi: 10.4018/ijskd.2014070101

Nonaka, I., & Takeuchi, H. (1995). *Knowledge-creating company: How Japanese companies create the dynamics of innovation*. Oxford: Oxford University.

Nonaka, I., & Toyama, R. (2005). The theory of the knowledge-creating firm: Subjectivity, objectivity and synthesis. *Industrial and Corporate Change, 14*(3), 419–436.

Nonaka, I., Toyama, R., & Konno, N. (2000). SECI, Ba and leadership: A unified model of dynamic knowledge creation. *Long Range Planning, 33*(1), 5–34. doi: 10.1016/s00246301(99)00115-6

Nonaka, I., & von Krogh, G. (2009). Tacit knowledge and knowledge conversion: Controversy and advancement in organizational knowledge creation theory. *Organization Science, 20*(3), 635–652. doi: 10.1287/orsc.1080.0412

Polanyi, M. (1966). *The tacit dimension*. London: Routledge.

Smith, E. A. (2001). The role of tacit and Explicit Knowledge in the workplace. *Journal of Knowledge Management, 5*(4), 311–321.

Tsoukas, H. (2004). Do we really understand Explicit Knowledge? In H. Tsoukas (Ed.), *Complex knowledge: Studies in organizational epistemology* (pp. 141–161). London: OUP Oxford.

Tsoukas, H., & Vladimirou, E. (2001). What is organizational knowledge? *Journal of Management Studies, 38*(7), 973–993. doi: 10.1111/1467-6486.00268

Van Dijk, T. A. (2005). Contextual knowledge management in discourse production. In R. Wodak & P. A. Chilton (Eds.), *A new agenda in (critical) discourse analysis* (pp. 71–100). Amsterdam: John Benjamins.

Virtanen, I. (2010). Epistemological problems concerning explication of Explicit Knowledge. *Journal of knowledge management practice, 11*(4). Retrieved from Journal of Knowledge Management Practice website: http://www.tlainc.com/articl246.htm

Von Krogh, G. (1998). Care in knowledge creation. *California Management Review, 40*(3), 133. doi: 10.2307%2F41165947

Weick, K. E. (1995). *Sensemaking in organizations*. London: Sage

Weick, K. E. (2001). *Making sense of the organization*. Oxford: Blackwell.

Wenger, E. (1998). *Communities of practice: Learning, meaning, and identity*. New York: Cambridge University Press.

7 Knowing as learning in Communities of Practice (CoP)

Chapter Contents

> The focus on communication in Etienne Wenger's (1998) Community of Practise (CoP) theory warrants its inclusion in this book. Through this focus, the theory fills a gap in Nonaka and Takeuchi's (1995) theory of knowledge creation (see Chapter 6). Wenger argues that it is through participation in the construction, evolution and maintenance of a specific knowledge domain that we find a sense of meaning and professional identity.

This communication focus of CoP theory is also recognised by Iverson and McPhee (2002), who argue that: 'CoP theory offers a complex conceptual structure that illuminates connections and processes of knowledge based on a model that centres communication in KM [Knowledge Management]' (p. 264; All capitalised words are defined in the glossary at the back of the book). Additionally, CoP theory focuses on knowledge as always embedded in practices and relationships (Wenger et al., 2002), This conceptualisation of the 'situated nature of knowing' (Østerlund & Carlile, 2003, p. 91) has led to an understanding of knowledge communication as complex and goes beyond mere transfer of bodies of knowledge.

Rather than seeing knowledge communication as an end in itself, CoP theory (Lave and Wenger 1991; Wenger 1998; Wenger et al., 2002) regards 'knowing in practices' as constructing and constituting the organisation itself (Iverson & McPhee 2002, p. 264). The core concepts of Lave and Wenger (1991) and Wenger (1998) describe social processes such as 'participation', 'joint enterprise' and 'mutual engagement'. Wenger (1998)

DOI: 10.4324/9781003015925-9

emphasises this process perspective by arguing that knowing should not be considered in abstract terms but should be examined as inextricably tied to practice and to the people engaged in the act of knowing, i.e., the 'communities' of knowers. This reflects his and Lave's argument that learning is situated within communities and within specific knowledge domains (Lave & Wenger, 1991). The 'Tacit' from this perspective seems to become the underlying assumptions and presuppositions shared by the community.

'Learning' and 'knowing'

Although CoP theory focusses on 'learning' rather than 'knowledge', a point of convergence between learning theory and knowledge theory can be seen in the link between learning as the process of 'coming to know'. The concept 'knowing' is used by Wenger (1998) to describe the dynamic, processual nature of knowledge. The gerund, 'knowing' can thus be contrasted with the connotations of the noun, 'knowledge', which suggests knowledge-as-object (Wenger, 1998, pp. 134–141).

Wenger (1998) emphasises this process perspective by arguing that knowing should not be considered in abstract terms but should be examined as inextricably tied to practice and to the people engaged in the act of knowing. A consequence of the process perspective on knowledge for Wenger seems to be that knowing and learning are situated within specific practices, within the knowledge domains attached to them, and within the communities sharing those practices (Lave & Wenger, 1991). This perspective fits well with Van Dijk's (2005) notion of epistemic communities introduced at the start of Chapter 5. The 'Tacit' (silent) dimension of knowledge seems to become the underlying assumptions shared by the community, which, because they are shared by the community, need not be stated when community members interact.

Just like Von Krogh (1998) positions Nonaka's and Takeuchi's (1995) theory of the knowledge creating company in opposition to cognitivist theories of knowledge management, Fuller (2007) positions Community of Practice theory (Lave & Wenger, 1991; Wenger, 1998) as opposed to cognitivist learning theory. The cognitivist perspective on learning has also been termed the 'standard paradigm' of learning (Beckett & Hager, 2002). Cognitivist learning theory, as (perhaps rather crudely) simplified by Fuller, sees learning as the acquisition of a knowledge product by a learner. Learning from this perspective involves knowledge transmission from an expert to a novice. Typically, this transmission occurs within the formal learning setting of a classroom and implies a 1:1 transfer rather than a process of mutuality implied by 'knowledge communication'. As a consequence, the cognitivist perspective sees learning as an individual process, whereas Community of Practice theory constructs learning as a social process, or 'joint enterprise' (Wenger, 1998).

Meaningful participation

Wenger's (1998) Communities of Practice theory constructs meaning and identity as closely intertwined with the practices and relationships of the community. Wenger (1998) argues that humans constantly and voluntarily engage in learning and developing different knowledge domains. While this perspective may hold a general truth when looking at society as whole and the continuing knowledge development and technical progress of humanity, the argument seems to rest on less solid ground in specific organisational contexts, where some employees may find meaning in developing organisational knowledge while others may be more committed to doing their job as it has always been done using the practices and knowledge required by the task at hand. Lave and Wenger (1991) deals with this through the notion of a core and a periphery of a CoP. The 'core' can be seen as knowledge developers whereas those engaging in 'legitimate peripheral participation' (pp. 35–37) may either be accepted as practitioners continuing doing 'business as usual' or newcomers on an inbound trajectory into the community.

CoP theory seems to rest on the assumption that humans find meaning in engaging with other knowers around a shared 'domain' of knowledge, regardless of whether they are at the core or periphery of a CoP centred on that specific knowledge domain. The domain can be anything from a shared hobby, the shared, situated knowledge of how a couple maintains their family and marriage, to the professional domains of how be to an engineer at Danfoss (my examples), or how to be a claims processor (Wenger's example, 1998). Different knowledge domains thus become the foci of different Communities of Practice in a person's life, entailing multiple memberships in a variety of communities.

Through participation in the community, members build a shared knowledge of the domain, and develop a shared language, or 'shared repertoire', i.e., a terminology and jargon used to facilitate knowledge development and learning about the domain (Lave & Wenger, 1991). Participation in the community may occur at different levels of expertise, with expert members visualised as the core of the community and newcomers visualised as being on the edge of the community. Newcomers are introduced into the community through 'legitimate peripheral participation' (Lave & Wenger, 1991, pp. 35–37). But participation in a community, according to Wenger (1998) is inextricably bound to 'reification'.

Reification and the tacit/explicit dimensions of knowledge

'Reification', meaning 'making (something abstract) more concrete or real' (The New Oxford English Dictionary, 1998), is the process of turning expressions of participation into objects, such as documents, artefacts and instruments. Through the continued reproduction of the community's knowledge domain, the sense of participation and meaning is revitalised.

Like the Tacit/explicit dimensions of knowledge, participation and reification are not mutually exclusive; they form a mutually constitutive duality. Additionally, the affinity between the tacit/explicit and participation/reification can also be seen in reification as the process of turning more Tacit understandings of the community into more explicit forms, just like the socialisation and externalisation steps of the SECI model (see Chapter 6).

Though Wenger (1998) does not make the link himself, the mutually dependent process of participation and reification seems similar Polanyi's notion of explicit (reified) knowledge as always having a Tacit element.

But where Polanyi (1966) focuses on the 'Tacit' as a 'personal coefficient' of knowing, it seems Wenger would argue for an equally 'Tacit', but 'social coefficient' of knowing (my term).

This social coefficient implies an understanding of 'Tacit' knowledge as that which does not need to be voiced because it is shared rather than meaning that which cannot be voiced because it is outside human understanding (see the discussion of the Tacit/Explicit Knowledge dimension in Chapter 6). Both the personal and the social coefficients of knowledge can thus be seen as Tacit aspects of knowledge but differing in their emphasis of the individual and the social.

Organisational Communities of Practise

In Wenger (1998), CoPs are conceptualised as voluntary. But organisations also have an interest in the value of employees voluntarily developing organisational knowledge. In the book *Cultivating Communities of Practice*, Wenger et al. (2002) examine the challenge of building successful CoPs in organisations. Through a series of case studies, they arrive at guidelines for building successful CoPs in organisations.

Central in these guidelines is the recommendation for providing a high degree of autonomy to the employees. This autonomy is also signalled in the choice of 'Cultivating' rather than 'managing' in the title of the book. A high degree of autonomy can thus be seen as a prerequisite for the relationships in CoPs. These relationships are the foundation of an ongoing loop of knowledge communication and knowledge creation (thereby producing ongoing spirals of SECI processes). Wenger et al. (2002) suggest replacing the term 'management' with the term 'stewardship' in recognition of the need for autonomy in CoPs. In this respect, CoPs can be seen as sharing similar traits as the Knowledge Teams introduced in Chapter 5.

Wenger et al. (2002) also differ from Wenger (1998) by putting more emphasis on oppositions and disagreements within CoPs. In Wenger (1998), the key concepts 'mutual engagement', 'joint enterprise' and 'shared repertoire' seem to emphasise the common ground built in a CoP.

In Lave and Wenger's (1991) original theory, which is carried into Wenger (1998), the main difference between CoP members seems to be the level of expertise and participation, rather than their differences in perspectives on the knowledge domain. This can be seen in the notion of 'legitimate peripheral participation':

> In order to become a member, legitimacy must be granted to the joiner and the joiner must engage in the practices to learn the domain and the CoPs specific forms and practices of participation and reification to start an 'inbound trajectory'
>
> (p. 101)

So legitimate peripheral participation can be seen as describing a process of becoming an accepted and a contributing part of the core CoP but does not account for the possibility that new-comers may not just be on an inbound trajectory to learn the knowledge domain and the practices of the CoP; they may bring new areas of expertise into the CoP, thereby challenging the notion of a core of expertise and periphery of inexperience. Without reference to Wenger (1998), it seems to be this traditional idea of a knowledge asymmetry between expert and layman which Kastberg (2011) questions. He argues that often the so-called 'layman' will be an expert in another knowledge domain, and that learning should therefore be considered as occurring on both sides of the knowledge asymmetry.

Wenger (1998) uses the concept Knowledge Broker to describe persons building bridges between such knowledge asymmetries. Knowledge Brokers can be seen as having a key function in global organisations, because they can build cross-functional, cross-boundary collaboration.

To sum up on organisational Communities of Practice: they have the double purpose of providing meaning to and building a sense of shared identity between participants, on the one hand, and developing organisational knowledge for the benefit of the wider organisation, on the other hand. In light of the Transactive Memory Systems theory presented in Chapter 5, organisational communities can also be seen as a way to strengthen employee networks of knowledge about who knows what in the organisation, and where specific knowledge expertise is located. Organisational communities are relevant to the study of identity configurations, because in an organisational context Communities of Practice may constitute a forum for the maintenance and nurture of such identities and may provide the level of autonomy needed to develop and transform organisational knowledge domains.

To sum up the whole section on CoP theory, CoP can be seen as connecting knowledge creation and learning on one hand with identity and relationships on the other. This is achieved by arguing for the sense of meaning and identity arising from the shared development of a knowledge domain. Thereby CoP theory links knowledge communication, the focus on identity (Chapter 8) and the focus on relationships (Chapter 9).

With regard to identity, CoP theory emphasises the social over the individual aspect of identity; this will be discussed in relation to other theories of relationships in Chapter 9.

Discussion of the relation between Sensemaking and Communities of Practise

Weick's (1995, 2001) theory of Sensemaking can be seen as relevant to Wenger's (1998) Communities of Practice theory because of their mutual focus on identity and construction of 'sense' (Weick) or 'meaning' (Wenger). Both theories have a Tacit belief system based on identity formation and previous experiences (which Weick terms Retention). And in both theories the belief systems and actions (i.e. 'Enactments' or 'Reifications') are mutually constitutive; actions are seen as based on identity and past experience, which in turn is updated based on the actions of others and, in Weick's theory at least, based on the interpretation of changes in the context (which Weick terms 'Changing Ecology').

However, while Wenger's focus in his discussion of identity lies in the social aspect of identity, Weick's concept of identity builds more on an understanding of identity as an aspect of cognition. This cognitive aspect impacts on how we perceive contexts and communities. With regard to actions, Wenger's concept 'reification' focuses more on the reproduction and sustenance of the community, while Weick's focus in the concept 'enactment' emphasises the reaction of individuals and groups to changes in the environment. A difference can also be seen in Weick's focus on Enactment as the individual's or group's response to the Changing Ecology in order to establish a new status quo, whereas reification focuses more the shared practices of the community as a material realisation of the sense of participation, shared identity and community. This does not mean that reification should be seen as focussed on maintaining status quo, but rather that the focus in reification seems to be the maintenance or advancement of knowledge practices of the community, whereas Enactment focuses on reacting to changing, ambiguous or uncertain situations, termed 'Equivocal' situations (Weick, 1995), in order to realign them with the Retention of the group or individual.

Because Weick (1995, 2001) argues that a sense of coherent identity across different social contexts, or changing ecologies is a core aspect of Retention, the perception of different knowledge processes as useful can be seen as a more stable element of professional identity. Specific epistemic communities can be seen as adopting a perception of Explicit knowledge as useful, while others view more Tacit knowledge and the socialisation process as useful. Thus, different perceptions of knowledge can be seen as a basis for professional identity formations and may also be a basis for forming relationships and CoPs with employees sharing similar perceptions of knowledge. This will be taken up in the next chapter, which reviews identity theory, and finishes with a discussion of how identity theory can be seen as linked to Sensemaking theory. For now, I'll shift to a case study analysis of the sense of meaning which an organisational CoP can provide.

Case study: Henrik's organisational Community of Practice

In this section, I focus on the selected group of internationally dispersed relations with whom Henrik finds support and understanding for his identity as a Knowledge Creator and where he receives the admiration of like-minded Knowledge Creators.

After Henrik had presented his perspective on organisational knowledge as requiring laborious and ongoing transformation to be situated within client contexts, I summed up his perspective, and addressed the time needed to communicate and share such situated knowledge. I then asked him whether this kind of time is invested in sharing knowledge between consultants in the global organisation he works in, HR Consult. After a brief hesitation, he shifted his answer from the local, Danish context we had been discussing to an international, so-called *Learning Solutions Communication Network* (LSCN), which is a global community instigated by the global Head of Development at HR Consult. Henrik provided me with all the emails of the team and recordings of the online team meetings. He explains than the purpose of the team is for employees with a knowledge creation focus to meet and share their knowledge creations and new solutions. So, the community can be understood as a sign that HR Consult is becoming aware of the knowledge creation taking place at the consultancy level, and the so-called LSCN team is an attempt to start to leverage that knowledge creation.

In terms of identity, the social aspect of community identity seems to be more an outcome of the deliberate selection of employees who, through their work, had already demonstrated that they had a practice of creating new organisational knowledge. The selection of Henrik for participation in the community can also be seen as evidence that the knowledge transformation practice he describes does add value to his clients and that this is recognised even at the international level of the organisation. During the time of the case study, the community included 12–15 members. Because of the importance Henrik attaches to these globally dispersed relations in the community, the majority of this section will be devoted to the analysis of his global relationships within this CoP.

In the quote below, Henrik contrasts the lack of knowledge communication at HR Consult Denmark with the virtual knowledge communication of the community. I have summarised his perception of knowledge focusing on deep understanding of both HR Consult knowledge and client context in Chapter 5. To follow up on this in the interview with Henrik, I argued that communicating knowledge gained through such a practice would require time for interaction and communication and asked him whether the consultants at HR Consult used that time. He responded without hesitation that this was what they did in the LSCN community (l. 1 in the quote below). As Discursive Sensemaking, this shows his understanding of the community as a place where he feels he can engage in deep knowledge communication with people who share his perception of knowledge and the identity built around it. He contrasts this with the lack of knowledge communication at HR Consult Denmark (l. 4–6), which he identifies as not being at a level 'where it should be'. At the linguistic level, the choice of deontic modality ('should', l. 6) is used to refer to his personal standards of what useful knowledge is. His prosody indicates a matter-of-factness in stating that he sees the LSCN community as a place where he feels he is able to communicate his complex understanding of organisational knowledge. This is indicated by his lack of hesitation before answering, and the simple falling intonation contour spoken in low key (but not low volume). The certainty with which the statement is made is underlined by the repetition of 'we do that' (in l. 1 and l. 2), and the shift to high key in the repetition makes the answer stand out as Significant, thereby underlining his Discursive Sensemaking of the community as site for sharing of complete and situated knowledge.

Henrik:

1 '_\We do that here[1] (.)
2 ^\We do that at a global level here (.)
3 _erm we don't (h)
4 /we (.) don't do that at \[HR Consult] Danmark at the moment
5 /At, at a level which i:s (.)
6 _(faster pace) where it should be, y'know.

(Henrik, my translation, 139, 29:35)

Quote note:

[1] Indicates the words 'LSCN team' on a note in front of him.

To conclude on the analysis of the quote above, it builds on Henrik's Sensemaking about the Danish organisation as a place where the level of knowledge communication is not at the level he expects with his Knowledge Creator identity. In contrast to this, he perceives the LSCN community as a site for communicating his complex understanding of knowledge. So, despite the mediation of technology, the quality of the relationships in the globally dispersed community seems to be strong enough to support communication of complex knowledge.

But as is evident in the quote below, Henrik is also aware of the organisation goal of the community. At the Discursive Sensemaking level the organisational goal of harvesting 'initiatives' (l. 1–2) is contrasted with the consultants' outcome of building a 'network' (l. 7). It's impossible to determine the underlying meaning of his interpretation of the organisational goal as being 'pretty clever' (l. 5), but whether he means it slightly ironically or not, the phrase serves the purpose of demonstrating that he is very aware of the strategic goal of the community. But in the quote below Henrik also draws attention to a 'network' (l. 7) built among the consultants in the community as part of his Discursive Sensemaking about the community's purpose and meaning. At the linguistic level, the Discourse Marker 'So' (l. 1) indicates the status of the quote as Discursive Sensemaking about the value of the community. The frequent use of high key onset (l. 1, 5 and 7) makes the quote stand out as Significant in relation to the surrounding discourse. He suggests that the knowledge transformation practice which he and the rest of the community share is not common in the organisation: he uses low key onset (l. 4), suggesting a certain frustration at the perception that their knowledge communication practice is 'strange'. Through the lexical choice 'strange' he seems to point to his own Sensemaking about how his colleagues see him.

Henrik:

1 _So, so ^\they harvest these, erm (.) \initiatives (.)
2 /from people like me \for example. _Who are doing something strange.
3 ^And that's pretty \clever--
4 --/while they're collecting \this knowledge,
5 /They're also building this ^network \among,
6 \among us people. (.)

(Henrik, my translation, 156, 0:32:15)

To conclude on the analysis of the quote above, although he points to the organisational goal of harvesting initiatives, Henrik also constructs the relations built between the consultants as an important outcome. Through participation in the community and reification of their practices in PowerPoints and discussions at team meetings, the community seems to be building a strong Transactive Memory System between themselves: the value of the community arises not only from their communication of knowledge about their projects, but their increasing awareness about who has expertise in creating solutions for specific problems. In the minutes of meeting from the community's fourth online meeting, the value of this knowledge was highlighted as key outcome even in this early stage of the community.

The quote below highlights the sense of meaning (Wenger, 1998) which Henrik finds in participating in the community. I showed earlier how Henrik constructs a contrast between, on the one hand, his disappointment with his local colleagues and their lack of willingness to construct new knowledge, and on the other hand, the colleagues in the LSCN community. I asked him whether the contrast was what made it 'fun' to be in the network, the prosody of his confirmation ('^Yes _it ^is', l. 1) suggests that my question fits his own Sensemaking well: moving from high key to low key and back to high key again suggests almost incredulity that anyone might think otherwise. His Discursive Sensemaking in the quote below demonstrates that despite the lack of time to put into this community, Henrik's commitment to the community goes beyond identification; he cites it as one of the reasons he stays in the job (l. 4–6). Thereby, he constructs the community as providing a sense of meaning, but simultaneously constructing his local work environment as unsatisfying. This sense of meaning and identity which he experiences from participation in the community was identified by Wenger (1998) as being the core motivation for participating in CoPs. Yet the community is strategic in the sense that it was instigated by the Head of Development at HR Consult to leverage the knowledge created at the consultant level and learn from it at an organisational level. Thereby new products or product modules may be built based on the knowledge creation of the consultants in the community.

Henrik's construction of this importance of the community is supported by the prosodic cues; he does not hesitate before replying (l. 1), and the falling to rising intonation in l. 1 suggests a matter-of-factness. Yet the lack of hesitation before the next intonation unit renders l. 2 equally salient, thereby constructing his frustration about the lack of time to commit to the community as just as important as the sense of belonging he finds in the group. That he is frustrated about this lack of time is signalled in the exhalation at the end of l. 2. The Discourse Marker 'so' in l. 4 is used to signal a shift to a remark commenting on the previous passage, a form of conclusion on the meaning of the community. In this passage, from l. 4 onwards, he hesitates more, draws out vowel sounds at the end of intonation units (l. 4 and 5), and exhales (l. 7), suggesting that he is reflecting on the importance of the community as he speaks, and the care with which he selects his words suggests that the passage is important to him. It also suggests that this Sensemaking argument has not been verbalised before, because unlike some of his other Sensemaking reflections, his grammar does not flow unproblematically; he hesitates (pauses and exhalations at the end of l. 6–8 and 11–13) and uses grammatical structures with repeated phrases to pick up where a clause or sentence was broken off (l. 5, l. 8, l. 10). This broken sentence structure also causes intonation units to be shorter than in the rest of the interview.

Henrik:

1 '^Yes _it ^is—
2 --\although there hasn't been (hh)--been
3 \much opportunity for me to spend that much time on it (.)
4 \So it's definitely this / he:re[1]

/which is the reason\ I:m (.)
\reason I'm down /here. (.)[2]
/because there (h)
/there I \have the(..)
\there I find /understanding for my own \role
\and there I'm among equal
\equals (.)
_erm (.)
/and that's cool --/ that's cool (..)

(Henrik, my translation)

Quote notes:

[1] Indicates the words 'LSCN team' on a note in front of him.

[2] Indicates 'HR Consult Denmark on a note in front of him.

The PowerPoint presentations and sharing of the learning solutions for discussion in the meetings can be understood as evidence of their Reifications and the commitment to the Joint Enterprise of transforming HR Consult knowledge to Situate it within specific client contexts to address a particular client's unique challenges.

To sum up on the importance of relationships for his identity, Henrik seems to consider the community to be a haven where he can be with colleagues who share his perception of knowledge, and the professional identity attached to that perception. But he does not seem to use the community to solve the specific client challenges he faces. In this respect he differs from the Knowledge Broker Prototype analysed in Chapter 5. Instead, he builds his learning solutions in cooperation with his clients. However, through participation, he finds meaning in communicating these knowledge solutions and the experience gained in the community. In this work, the solutions of other community members can be understood as a source of inspiration and feedback. The importance of this social basis for his identity is underlined by his statement that the community is the reason he is still working at HR Consult Denmark, regardless of how literally the statement is meant to be taken. The mediation of technology in all interactions of the dispersed community does not seem to be a problem to Henrik, suggesting that the sense of meaning he finds in participating outweighs the challenge of communicating knowledge using ICT.

This case study rounds off Chapter 7. Chapter 8 reviews identity theory and analyses how the three Identity Prototypes build professional identities based on the perceptions of useful knowledge, which we have looked at in Chapters 6 and 7.

References

Beckett, D., & Hager, P. J. (2002). *Life, work and learning: Practice in postmodernity*. London: Routledge.

Fuller, A. (2007). Critiquing theories of learning and communities of practice. In J. Hughes, N. Jewson, & L. Unwin (Eds.), *Communities of practice: Critical perspectives* (pp. 17–29). London: Routledge.

Iverson, J. O., & McPhee, R. D. (2002). Knowledge management in communities of practice: Being true to the communicative character of knowledge. *Management Communication Quarterly, 16*(2), 259–266.

Kastberg, P. (2011). Knowledge asymmetries: Beyond "to have and have not". *Fachsprache, XXXIV*(3–4), 137–151.

Lave, J., & Wenger, E. (1991). *Situated learning: Legitimate peripheral participation.* Cambridge: Cambridge University Press.

Nonaka, I., & Takeuchi, H. (1995). *Knowledge-creating company: How Japanese companies create the dynamics of innovation.* Oxford: Oxford University.

Østerlund, C., & Carlile, P. (2003). How practice matters: A relational view of knowledge sharing. In: M. Huysman, E. Wenger, & V. Wulf (Eds.), *Communities and technologies* (pp. 1–22). Dordrecht: Springer. doi: 10.1007/978-94-017-0115-0_1

Polanyi, M. (1966). *The tacit dimension.* London: Routledge.

The New Oxford English Dictionary. (1998). Reify/reification. In J. Pearsall (Ed.), *The New Oxford English Dictionary.* Oxford: Clarendon Press.

Van Dijk, T. A. (2005). Contextual knowledge management in discourse production. *A new agenda in (critical) discourse analysis* (pp. 71–100). Amsterdam: John Benjamins Publishing Company.

Von Krogh, G. (1998). Care in knowledge creation. *California Management Review, 40*(3), 133.

Weick, K. E. (1995). *Sensemaking in organizations.* London: Sage

Weick, K. E. (2001). *Making sense of the organization.* Oxford: Blackwell.

Wenger, E. (1998). *Communities of practice: Learning, meaning, and Identity.* New York: Cambridge University Press.

Wenger, E., McDermott, R., & Snyder, W. M. (2002). *Cultivating communities of practice: A guide to managing knowledge.* Boston, MA: Harvard Business School Press.

8 Professional identity as (d)iscursive construction

Chapter Contents

This chapter reviews and synthesises two traditionally opposing perspectives on identity: firstly, the traditional cognitive perspective where identity represents the 'inner core' of an individual. Secondly, a more constructionist perspective seeing identity as a social performance which, in the more radical constructionist approaches, has no 'inner core'.

Cognitivist theory of identity

The cognitivist approach to researching identity rests on the assumption that the researcher can access the inner world of the research subject through language, according to Benwell and Stokoe (2006). Identity from this perspective can evolve and change over time, but it remains relatively stable. More important from the research perspective, because of the assumed correlation between inner identity and its linguistic representations, examining identity is relatively straight forward from the

DOI: 10.4324/9781003015925-10

cognitivist perspective. Benwell and Stokoe (2006) argue that focus in the cognitivist tradition shifted in the latter half of the 20th century from a focus on individual identity to a focus on social identity, using identity labels 'such as "adolescent", "black" or "working-class", [as] indisputable identity formations' (p. 24). Benwell and Stokoe (2006) argue that this position can be seen as 'essentialist', i.e., the categories describe an inner essence of the research subject's identity. Billett (2007) outlines a similar trajectory within cognitivist identity research, though he places the shift towards collective identity focus in the 1990s. This shift came, Billett argues, after a realisation within the field of learning that 'the theories within cognitive psychology were inadequate in understanding human learning as something shaped not only by individuals' capacities to secure, effectively organise and deploy their knowledge structures but also by the social world beyond individuals' (p. 58). Despite the disagreement on chronology, Billett (2007) and Benwell and Stokoe (2006) agree that the cognitivist approaches to identity research rest on an assumption of possible access to a pre-discursive inner self of the research subject.

Billett (2007) argues for a link between identity and learning by emphasising the importance of the interplay between personal and social identities for shaping the level of retention and re-application of learning. 'Learning' as used in Communities of Practice (CoP) theory can, as mentioned in Chapter 7, be defined as the process of 'coming-to-know' (all capitalised words, such as 'Communities of Practice', are defined in the glossary at the back of the book). For Wenger (1998) learning is closely intertwined with the process of being initiated into a CoP with its own social identity attached to it and centred around the CoP's knowledge domain and the practices attached to it.

At the other end of the continuum of identity research, Benwell and Stokoe (2006) place discourse analysis approaches examining identity, which could also be framed as the constructionist position, within identity research. From this perspective the researcher can never access cognition. Identity is seen as constructed and performed through actions and through language, and consequentially this perspective sees identity as constituted in (D)iscourse, rather than (D)iscourse being reflections of an inner, cognitive self (Benwell & Stokoe, 2006). A subject can thus have multiple identities each suited to different contexts, and each constructed through different sets of actions and different (d)iscourses.

James Paul Gee's approach to Discourse Analysis reflects this social aspect of identity. For example, one may act out an identity as a parent in the context of the family but act out a professional identity as an engineer in a work context. (D)iscourse in each identity domain would employ different (d)iscourse patterns attached to each knowledge domain. The example of parent identity vs. work identity comes from Wenger (1998) who provides it as an example of multi-membership in different communities. Wenger's position does not unequivocally fit either the constructionist or the cognitivist camp, thereby demonstrating the fuzzy boundaries of the cognitivist–constructionist continuum set up by Benwell and Stokoe (2006). I'll return to Wenger's arguments for a social concept of identity later. For now, I will turn to the role of identity categorisation in discourse analysis approaches to identity research.

The constructionist identity theory of identity

That the constructionist perspective also impacts on the type of knowledge which can be deduced from analysing (D)iscourse (known as 'epistemology') of research can be seen in Benwell and Stokoe's (2006) focus on categorisation of identities (such as 'male', 'mother' or 'worker') as not being considered objective categories but 'discourse phenomena' (p. 3). From this perspective, there is no inner self beneath or beyond discourse, even if we talk as if there is: 'it is the very *idea* of an inner self and its outward expression which is a construction' (Benwell & Stokoe, 2006, p. 4. Italics in original). Despite this radical disregard for identity categories, Benwell and Stokoe (2006) argue that discourse analysis approaches often reproduce the categories they are trying to reject.

The constructionist perspective also tends to emphasise the impact of context on the construction of identity. Different researchers attach different vocabularies to this impact, but often build on Michel Foucault's theories of discourse. Fairclough (2003) uses Foucault's term 'orders of discourse' to emphasise the power struggle resulting in a shifting hierarchy as discourses compete for power. As mentioned in Chapter 1, I use Gee's (2011, 2014) term 'Conversation' as synonymous with 'orders of discourse'. Although Conversations influence individual and collective (d)iscourses and practices, they do not determine them, as argued by Van Dijk (2005), if they did it would mean that individuals within the same context would say and do the same, which clearly they do not. It would seem more accurate to say that Conversations and the order between them come about through a constant, mutually constitutive process between Conversation, and the (d)iscourses which invoke, shift or oppose them. Thus, the order of discourse is moulded and transformed over time (Fairclough, 1992).

The constructionist approach to identity emphasises the social aspect of identity construction, and from the description presented in the previous paragraph, it leaves little room for the notion of inner, personal identity which was emphasised in the cognitivist perspective. Indeed, Billett (2007) goes as far as arguing that through the research trajectory shifting towards the constructionist perspective in the late 20th century, 'individual' 'has seemingly become an unfashionable and tainted term' (p. 56). The focus on a collectivist and constructionist perspective can also be seen in Benwell and Stokoe's (2006) definition of identity as 'who people are to each other' (p. 6). By excluding 'who people are to themselves',

Benwell and Stokoe (2006) avoid a definition which could be interpreted as essentialist.

Cognitive and constructionist perspectives combined

In accordance with the reflexive epistemology of David (2005) and the reflexive methodology of Alvesson and Sköldberg (2009), I do not see the cognitivist and the constructionist positions in the identity debate as mutually exclusive, but rather as two perspectives which, if combined, provide a richer description of reality.

To outline a perspective combining these two seemingly dichotomous perspectives on identity, I need to argue by way of analogy. I see the 'inner self' of cognitivism as the sediment at the bottom of a river. At the top, this sediment is constantly shifting around, moved by the currents in the river. These currents in the analogy stand for forces of the Conversations at play in any given social situation, constantly shaping inner meanings and their expressions in (d)iscourse. However, while the surface level of the sediment shifts quickly, the bottom of the sediment remains fairly stable, and this stability helps regulate the flow of currents in the river. If, as argued by Weick (1995, 2001), the inner core of 'retention' (including identity) is fairly stable, then the individual remains in power over whether and how to enact or oppose Conversations.

Benwell and Stokoe (2006) express a similar standpoint when explaining their purpose for writing a book on identity and discourse. They state their purpose as reconciling the dualisms in identity research by explicating the 'processes by which people orient to consistency in their accounts of themselves and other people (underpinning the view of identity as 'fixed'), whilst simultaneously showing that identity is contingent on the local conditions of the interactional context' (Benwell & Stokoe, 2006, p. 17).

This integrating perspective on identity can be seen as aligned with Weick's (1995) argument for the need to maintain a coherent identity across social contexts. Weick's identity perspective furthermore emphasises identity as a Sensemaking process from which situations and actions are selectively interpreted, and which forms the basis for how this interpretation is enacted upon the situation.

Identity configurations and the role of identity prototypes

The duality of identity as simultaneously social and cognitive can be seen in the need for individuals to build a social basis for their cognitive identity constructs. Therefore, patterns of 'identity configurations' may be seen when examining people within a specific situation. 'Identity configuration' is adopted in the book to signify a broad span in behaviours, and identities. The boundaries of such a span can be seen as being set by the members. Jansen and Roodt (2014) describe this boundary setting through the notion of social cognition about the boundaries between 'ingroup' and 'outgroup' behaviours and beliefs. A similar argument can be found in Ybema et al. (2009).

'Prototypes', on the other hand, can be seen as representing the 'stereotypical attributes of the group as a whole by being most like ingroup members and simultaneously most different from outgroup members' (Jansen & Roodt, 2014, p. 118). While this definition seems to refer to prototypicality as behaviours, Jansen and Roodt (2014) also include a cognitive element in their definition: 'The prototype is the interrelated set of perceptions, attitudes, feelings, and behaviour that captures similarities among ingroup members and differences between ingroup members and outgroup members' (pp. 118–119).

This definition mentions, but does not separate, 'behaviours' and cognitive aspects ('perception, attitudes, feelings'). The cognitive aspects, however, can be seen both as reflected by, and as the Sensemaking basis for, those behaviours. However, the definition seems to neglect the role of communication in negotiating the boundaries of ingroup and outgroup behaviours.

The link between communication theory and social identity theory is emphasised by Hogg and Reid (2006), however. They emphasise this link first because the construction of social identities requires considerable communication of norms and practices; and second because social identity configurations can help explain communication patterns among larger populations. They see social identity theory as a means for integrating identity theory and communication theory to explain group norms.

Social identity theory

Social identity theory emphasises not only the importance of belonging to social groups, but also 'intergroup competition over status and prestige' (Hogg & Reid, 2006, p. 9). They define 'norms' as 'shared cognitive representations that, within a particular context, characterise the behaviour of members of relevant out-groups and describe and prescribe the behaviour of in-group members including ourselves' (p. 10).

Hogg and Reid (2006) argue that social identity configurations and identity prototypes can be seen as sets of norms defining members of a group in opposition to outsiders. Thereby identity prototypes can be seen as examples of individuals who seem to be 'most like ingroup members and simultaneously most different from outgroup members' (Burke & Stets, 2009, p. 119).

As a consequence of the need for defining identity in opposition to other identities, the analysis of the identity prototypes at HR Consult later in the chapter will necessarily involve the identification of other identity prototypes which are defined in opposition to an individual's preferred prototype.

Consequently, the analysis of perceptions of professional identity should be undertaken with the knowledge that interview participants will represent their practices in the light of their mental model of the social identity prototype with which they identify. This does not mean that the descriptions of their practices in the interview situation does not reflect their actual practice in the situation being described, merely that the values underlying the prototype will be accentuated in the interview. Similarly, the future practices of interview participants will be influenced by the values of the social identity prototypes with which the individuals associate themselves, even if this influence does not result in a 1:1 relation between values, identity and behaviour.

The negotiation of personal and social identity in CoP theory

I return to Etienne Wenger's (1998) Communities of Practice (CoP) theory in this chapter, because it integrates knowledge, identity, relationships and knowledge communication, which is the main research aim of the book. For a full explanation of the CoP theory, see Chapter 7.

Although Wenger (1998) does not link his CoP perspective on identity to the debate between cognitive and social constructionist perspectives on identity presented earlier in this chapter, Wenger (1998) seems to argue for a social perspective on identity by placing identity as one of the processes and outcomes of participation in CoPs. Wenger (1998) even has identity in his book's subtitle: *Learning, Meaning and Identity*. Because he sees identities as social and as situated in CoPs, Wenger argues that individuals perform different identities in the different communities in which they participate. In a footnote, Wenger (1998) states that his notion of identity rests on the notion of the mutual constitution of individuals and groups.

This perspective on personal and social identity, which has its origin in Lave and Wenger (1991), has been taken up by sociolinguistics as an argument for challenging essentialist identity categories (Benwell & Stokoe, 2006), thereby reorienting the understanding of identity as situated in 'social practice and talk, rather than pre-given, essential identities' (p. 27). Handley et al. (2006) argue that in Wenger's book on Communities of Practice (1998), Wenger shifts from identity as both individual and social towards arguing for 'the capacity of individuals to compartmentalise identities within different communities' (Handley et al., 2006, p. 650).

Billett (2013), however, opposes this reading, which he cites as popular, and instead argues, mainly based on Lave and Wenger (1991), for the emphasis on a personal identity construct in their theory.

Billett argues that Lave and Wenger's (1991) theory stands in contrast to more constructionist perspectives, such as Harré (2005), where the individual tends to be seen as a product of the social. But Billet also recognises the shift in focus towards the social emphasis in Wenger (1998). Lave and Wenger (1991) are aware of the problems of overemphasising the social, which can be seen in their caution that 'to insist on starting with social practice, or taking participation to be the crucial process, and including the social world as the core of the analysis only seems to eclipse the person' (Lave & Wenger 1991, p. 60). So, the identity concept in CoP theory seems to shift towards a more social constructionist perspective in Wenger (1998) although the roots of CoP theory rest on a balance between social and personal identity.

The next section offers a discussion of the identity theory presented in the light of Weick's Sensemaking theory. The theory part of the chapter finishes with a discussion of the implications of identity research for virtual teams, before I move to the interview analyses.

Discussion of identity theory in the light of Weick's theories of Sensemaking

The combination of Essentialist and Constructionist identity perspectives can be seen as aligned with Weick's (1995, 2001) perspective on identity (for an explanation of Weick's Sensemaking theory see Chapter 2). The retained memory layers and the values attached to past action in the course of Retrospection can be seen as the basis of a more stable core of personal identity. But retention also has a social dimension because Sensemaking is influenced by the relationships and communities in which we are embedded (Weick, 1995, 2001). It is on the basis of this retention, or 'sedimentation', that individuals negotiate the social and public identity roles which they belong to. Thereby, social calls for specific identity roles can be seen as balanced by the individual need to fulfil the role in accordance with the values of the more stable personal identity.

More specifically related to the process of Sensemaking, retained identity can be seen as shaping both how we interpret and understand situations, and how we react to situations. In the words of Weick (1995):

> Depending on who I am, my definition of what is 'out there' will also change [...] But the direction of causality flows just as often from the situation to a definition of the self as it does the other way.
>
> (p. 20)

Implications for virtual teams

The implication for virtual knowledge communication seems to be that global organisations cannot expect employees who do not have previous experience working together to form effective virtual teams. The ability to maintain a coherent sense of identity across multiple virtual teams and projects can thus be seen as a challenge. This challenge may emerge as interpersonal conflicts if team members are not aware of the different professional identities and the different knowledge communication practices associated with these identities.

In the light of the present book's focuses on the intersection of identity and knowledge communication, idiosyncratic perceptions of knowledge can be seen as a core aspect of identity in professional contexts. Different perceptions of knowledge can be seen as preferences for different aspects of the knowledge communication process. For example, an employee may find a sense of professional identity in the transformation of knowledge through Socialisation and Combination (see Chapter 6), while another may find professional pride in Internalising and externalising organisational knowledge with an aim to retain and communicate knowledge without transforming it.

The social aspect of identity, and the sense of meaning provided through the identification with like-minded individuals in a CoP, suggests that employees may seek to build communities with employees sharing their perception of knowledge, thereby building a shared, social identity founded on the perception of knowledge.

The recognition of the sense of meaning provided by participating and contributing to the practices of different communities can also be seen as an important argument for including relationship theory as well as identity theory in the present multidisciplinary approach in order to gain an understanding of how employees make sense of and communicate knowledge in global organisations.

The next chapter extends the relationship focus in Communities of Practice theory by relating it to the theories of the 'strength of weak ties', trust theory, and Transactive Memory Systems (TMS). The remainder of this chapter will provide analyses of the identity constructions of the three knowledge communication prototypes at HR Consult.

Case study: The professional identity of the Knowledge Transfer Prototype

This section analyses the perception of professional identity of the Knowledge Transfer Prototype as an operationalisation of the three identity theories presented in the chapter, i.e. the cognitivist, the social, and the CoP theory. I did not use the time and space consuming step 6 and 7 of the Discursive Sensemaking Analysis method in the analysis of the Knowledge Transfer Prototype, but the analysis is based on Template Analysis (King, 2012) and extensive analysis memos during the coding process.

Throughout the interview with Dorthe, her stories about projects and practices kept emphasising the value of highly Externalised knowledge. In constructing her professional identity in the interview, she emphasised the value of timing Power Point slides and workshop exercises to ensure as little deviance as possible in the delivery of a presentation to a client. Her professional identity seemed to be centred on this Practice. This can be seen in her descriptions of a project which she did not see as successful. In this project, she ascribes the lack of success to the failure of colleagues to deliver the learning programme as agreed. Instead, these colleagues improvised in interaction with the client audience.

Dorthe, and other consultants who seem to represent the Knowledge Transfer Identity Configuration, expressed a high respect for the HR Consult brand and the products associated with it, and built a professional identity based on the value of this knowledge of their products.

This respect emerges in the Shared Repertoire (Wenger, 1998, see Chapter 7) between employees and managers in the organisation. This Shared Repertoire builds on the vocabulary of the personality profiling system for describing personality types, which is HR Consult's primary product. In all the meetings I have participated in and in most of the interviews I have conducted, consultants and managers used this Shared Repertoire to describe not only personality types, but meeting styles, documents, teams and entire organisations.

For Dorthe, as an example of the Knowledge Transfer Prototype, her professional identity seems to be centred on this respect for the HR Consult brand and products. Similarly, the value of delivering standardised HR Consult learning programmes emerged as a distinct professional identity among some of the UK consultants. Their conformity to organisational expectations seems to construct them as simply dutiful employees, and this aspect does seem to be a characteristic of the Knowledge Transfer Prototype. It was through the emergence of the Knowledge Creator Prototype and the Knowledge Broker Prototype, that the more common Knowledge Transfer Prototype emerged as a distinct identity configuration. Unlike the two other prototypes, the Knowledge Transfer Prototype centre their professional identity on a respect for the HR Consult knowledge embedded in products, practices and the Conversation of the organisation.

I now shift to an analysis of how the Knowledge Transfer Identity Prototype communicates knowledge.

The perception of knowledge of the Knowledge Transfer Prototype valuing Explicit knowledge products seems to lead to knowledge communication practices focussing on transferring existing HR Consult knowledge to clients. When analysed using Nonaka and Takeuchi's (1995) SECI model (see Chapter 6) this knowledge communication practice can be seen as missing a knowledge creation step at the consultant level. From the perspective of the Knowledge Transfer Prototype, knowledge creation occurs at the central R&D department, and the task of consultants becomes a transmission of this Explicit knowledge to the client through learning development programmes built from the modules constructed by the R&D department. The Knowledge Transfer Prototype can be seen as first Internalising HR Consult knowledge and then externalising it in the client organisation.

Through this internalisation of the products, consultants at HR Consult become able to Combine the training modules designed by R&D into training programmes adapted to the needs of a client organisation. Consultants with a Knowledge Transfer Prototype then Externalise this knowledge within different client contexts to ensure a new process of internalisation within the client organisation. Ideally, the client is then able to apply the knowledge to solve the challenges which brought them to HR Consult in the first place. Because the Externalisation of HR consult knowledge in the client organisation builds on existing knowledge, new HR Consult knowledge does not seem to be created in this process. The main criterion for success in their role as consultants thus seems to be the extent to which existing HR Consult knowledge is Internalised and applied within the client organisation.

The main difference between the Knowledge Transfer Prototypes in Denmark and in the UK seems to arise from the larger scale of the UK organisation which entails a higher specialisation of consultants. For Dorthe at HR Consult Denmark, most of her projects with Danish organisations involve both combining explicit learning modules to address client needs for training and development and teaching the programme within the client organisation. The UK Knowledge Transfer Prototypes, on the other hand are mainly responsible for combining the training modules to address client needs, while the training was completed by consultants who specialised in specific training modules. Either way, the approach is radically different from Henrik's and Linda's approaches.

Case study: Henrik's professional identity – the characteristics of a Knowledge Creator Prototype

Through a close analysis of Henrik's professional identity as an example of a Knowledge Creator Prototype, I examine how professional identities are constructed around perceptions of knowledge, and how such identities impact on how the employee engages in knowledge communication practices with colleagues.

To open the analysis of Henrik's professional identity, the following paragraph briefly compares Henrik's first definition of his role in the organisation with the role others construct for him in the interviews and in team meetings at HR Consult. After that, I will move into a more detailed analysis of his own perception of his professional identity. A key characteristic of the Knowledge Creator is that he carries out his knowledge creating practice without involving his colleagues. This character distinguishes him from both the Knowledge Transfer Prototype, who doesn't create new knowledge, and the Knowledge Broker Prototype, who creates knowledge in close collaboration with colleagues. He only communicates the fruits of his labour with HR Consult colleagues after completing a project.

At the start of the interview, I asked Henrik to explain his role in the organisation. As his first discursive construction of his professional identity he answered, 'I'm a product manager' (Henrik, 8, 1:26, my translation). In addition to his role as a product manager, he adds his role as consultant working with five different clients and identifies himself as part of the marketing team. He is also responsible for the so-called 'Indirect Channel', i.e., consultants who have a licence to use HR Consult products, but who are not employed by HR Consult. So, Henrik's responsibilities fit the multi-team, multi-project tendency identified by Daim et al. (2012) and Suchan and Hayzak (2001). This apparently straightforward title description also became significant as an instance of Henrik's Discursive Sensemaking about his professional identity, because none of the other interviewees at HR Consult Denmark use the title 'product manager' when describing Henrik's function in the organisation, for example the Danish CEO, Birgitte, uses the title 'senior consultant' when describing Henrik's function. The title 'senior consultant' puts Henrik on the same level as several other consultants. 'Senior consultant' is also Henrik's title on the corporate website. From a linguistic level of analysis, by presenting the title as 'product manager' first and adding his other tasks in a lower intonation key, he seems to construct this role as more significant. Other interviewees construct Henrik as highly competent and willing to go the extra mile for his clients, consistent with his self-representation, which I detail in the rest of this section.

However, before moving to the analysis of his self-representation in my interview with him, I will briefly outline the perceptions others have of Henrik. The participants I interviewed at HR Consult Denmark see Henrik as not only highly competent, but also as very poor at communicating his knowledge. We got an indication of this perception in Chapter 6 in the CEO Birgitte's remark on the need to 'take knowledge out of his head'. I also observed the CEO naming Henrik as poor at communicating his knowledge to others in the organisation at a meeting where Henrik was absent. In this meeting, a new employee had been given the task by the CEO to take over a task from Henrik because he had too many. The junior employee, in diplomatic terms, described her difficulty in understanding the task and the difficulty she had getting Henrik to explain it. The CEO then commented that they all knew how difficult it was to 'get anything from Henrik'. In terms of Sensemaking, this points to a misalignment between Henrik's self-impression, or at least the impression he is trying to project in professional contexts, and the impression others have of him. This misalignment in Sensemaking suggests that Henrik sees himself as being more important than other consultants at HR Consult, thereby constructing a hierarchy between himself and others in the organisation (cf. Gee's, 2011, 2014, Building Task Politics).

Rather late in the interview, after we had just talked about Henrik's many areas of responsibility, he shifted the topic to transformation of organisational knowledge. Because he made this shift of his own volition, and not due to an interviewer question or prompt, this shift seems significant in terms of Henrik's Discursive Sensemaking about his professional identity. As Discursive Sensemaking, this shift suggests not only the value he attaches to his knowledge transformation and creating practice, but also his justification for his knowledge transformation practice as being of value to the organisation. It is important for him to emphasise the value that his knowledge transformation is bringing to HR Consult Denmark. In terms of practices, he emphasises the practice of 'developing products' which is both part of the opening (l. 1) and the conclusion (l. 6) of the quote below. But as Discursive Sensemaking, the quote below also constructs his identity as an outsider in the organisation: he deliberately points to his argument for the value of knowledge creation as 'my belief' (l. 4). So, he constructs client-centred knowledge transformation as a personal value, i.e., an aspect of his professional identity. But by shifting to his inability to convince others to follow his knowledge creating practice (l. 5–6), he focusses on a sense of isolation with his professional identity, which he considers more valuable than his colleagues' professional identities. He even laughs (Transcribed as '£', in l. 7) at the others' inability to develop products.

This Sensemaking analysis is supported by the linguistic detains in the quote: his repetition of the discourse marker 'so' preceded by a brief pause, indicates the coming Discursive Sensemaking interpretation of his Practice. Lexically, his choice of the verb 'do' (l. 2) strongly emphasises action, but immediately connects his call for action to his 'belief' (l.4), thereby building a connection between his professional values and his knowledge creating practice. The Lexical repetition of the phrase 'developing products' (l. 1and l. 6) renders it significant. This is underlined by his high key pronunciation of the intonation unit in l. 1 which renders the Practice of 'developing products' significant.

Henrik:

1 ^\So in terms of developing products
2 /there's lot's \we can still /do
3 \which will attract more customers. (..)
4 \That's my belief. (.)
5 \And it's not /necessarily
6 \A belief I can convince (.) others in the shop[1] to follow. (.)
7 \ Because they're not ^used \to developing products--because £they don't'£
8 ^It's a strange world for many of them. (.)

(Henrik, my translation, 132, 27:48)

Quote notes:

[1] 'The shop' is Henrik's colloquial term for HR Consult Denmark.

To conclude on the analysis of the quote above, Henrik connects his own Practice of developing products to the ability of the organisation to attract new clients. But the most significant part of the quote still seems to be his construction of his opposition to his colleagues, arguing as he does that his practice is a 'strange world for many of them' (l. 8).

As an example of Henrik's willingness to work hard to fulfil his value of knowledge creation, and his sense of being alone with this identity is the fact that he has taken responsibility for redesigning the corporate website, because he is dissatisfied with the one offered by HQ in the UK. He has tried to engage his colleagues in contributing stories about their successful cases thereby demonstrating their specific knowledge expertise, but Henrik explicitly states his frustration that they have not contributed. In the interview he provided a lengthy description of this work, which he showed me on his computer while describing his considerations in selecting content and designing the layout of the page. Rather than quote the passage, I instead use his description of the work on the website as a sign of Henrik's construction of himself as someone who is ready to go the extra mile, and who is ready to stand up for his professional beliefs, even if it means contradicting the opinion of the entire marketing department at the global HQ. He does not address the possibility that his colleagues did not contribute because they were happy with the existing website's alignment with the corporate brand designed by HQ.

This description of his frustration with his colleagues' lack of engagement in building the website sparked a topic shift to Henrik's desire to develop new products. Before moving to this desire to develop products, I will briefly analyse his transition from the topic of designing a new website to the topic of creating knowledge. As transition he uses two intonation units, the first of which is an admittance that, like his colleagues, he has not done much work on the website. The second intonation unit explains this with reference to a specific order from above ('I'm told I shouldn't develop so much', l. 2). So, the second intonation unit justifies his own lack of contribution by reference to a restriction of his autonomy, whereas he appears to be unforgiving of the others' lack of contribution because he considers it a sign of unwillingness to commit to the knowledge communication involved in the project. In terms of Discursive Sensemaking it's interesting that he connects his work on the website to a restriction of his autonomy. I return to his construction of autonomy as a value in the next section of the analysis. Linguistically, his use of the passive voice (I'm told, l. 2) hides agency, but leaves little doubt that he is referring to the CEO, Birgitte. In terms of Prosody, his shift from high key onset in the main clause, falling to low key with little pitch variation in the subclause signals dissatisfaction and perhaps also suggests tiredness. Immediately after the quoted sentence he contradicts it with three consecutive 'but's followed by a list of other tasks which have also taken up his time. Here is the quote of the two intonation units shifting from the topic of the website to the topic of knowledge creation:

Henrik:

1 '^I haven't done it _either (.hh)
2 _because I'm told I shouldn't develop so much'

(Henrik, my translation 124, 27:38).

To conclude on the analysis of the quote above, the transition gains significance in terms of his Discursive Sensemaking because it shifts the frustration he feels from a focus on his colleagues to a focus on management as limiting his practice of developing organisational knowledge.

In the passage following this transition, he puts full focus on the intrinsic value of creating knowledge to achieve client satisfaction. As Discursive Sensemaking, the quote below first sums up his argument that his Practice of transforming organisational knowledge is beneficial to the client (l. 1–3), and then he explicitly connects this Practice to his own sense of satisfaction ('That's an incredibly exiting process for me', l. 4). Thus, he argues for an intrinsic value in transforming knowledge and thereby constructs knowledge transformation as a key value in his professional identity. However, in the last part of the quote, he again constructs himself as a pioneer in having this identity as a Knowledge Creator (l. 6). This time, he not only constructs himself as being in opposition to his colleagues, but as being the only one 'in the world' (l. 6) with a knowledge creating focus. At the end of the quote below (with his earlier description of like-minded colleagues in his Community of Practice this is clearly an overstatement), his Discursive Sensemaking explicitly constructs his own knowledge transformation approach as being of high value to the organisation not only in Denmark but globally (l. 7–8).

At the linguistic level, his extensive use of high key pronunciation (l. 1, 2, 6 and 7) gives the impression that he is highly passionate about the topic. Thereby Henrik constructs knowledge creation as significant not only at the linguistic level but at the Discursive Sensemaking level. Thereby he gives the impression that he holds the process of knowledge creation as a strong value underlying his professional identity. The focus on the client (l. 3) is constructed as highly significant through the pauses between each syllable. Through the high key pronunciation of 'understand' (l. 7), he also constructs his own opposition to the rest of the organisation as significant. In terms of Lexical choices, his choice of the first-person singular pronoun throughout the quote suggests that he sees knowledge creation as an individual process, even though he does seem to include the client in the process.

Henrik:

1 \But that ^\who:le ^\process _which is called
2 /I ^transform \this into something
3 \which bene(.)fits (.) /the (.) client. (.)
4 That's an incredibly exciting process for me, because (.)
5 \I can see: that /there is not--/there is not,
6 (.)/apparently ^any one \doing this in the /world.
7 _and it's /I don't ^understand it,
8 \because that's where the value lies for [HR Consult]

(Henrik, my translation, 73, 12:27)

To conclude on the analysis of the quote above, it both demonstrates Henrik's Discursive Sensemaking of the intrinsic value of transforming organisational knowledge to client needs, but also his construction of his own professional identity as being in opposition to the practices of the rest of the organisation.

Henriks individual knowledge creation Practice does not seem to be reflected in the knowledge management theories presented in Chapters 6 and 7 of this book. Henrik clearly sees his practice of knowledge creation as a solitary process, whereas the SECI model emphasises socialisation as key process in knowledge creation, and CoP theory emphasises Joint Enterprise and Mutual Engagement as important aspects of how developing a knowledge domain can give meaning and identity to the participants in the knowledge creation practice of a CoP. But, as I demonstrated in the previous chapter, Henrik is not alone with his knowledge creation strategy, although there only seems to be a few others in the Community of Practice he participates in.

Henrik attaches strong values to this practice of knowledge creation. This can be seen in the following quote, where his Discursive Sensemaking builds an image of knowledge creation as a Practice which is not only 'exciting', as in the quote above, but also painful ('it might hurt a bit', l. 6) and requires that people 'are a bit hard on themselves' (l. 10). He also builds an image of knowledge creation as a practice where you go where you have not 'gone before' (l. 2). Thus, he discursively attaches a set of values to the Practice of transforming organisational knowledge. These values centre on the need to get out of your comfort zone. Although these values seem to be an important aspect of his own professional identity, he widens the scope to the entire organisation in l. 3, claiming that it is required by a knowledge organisation. This Sensemaking analysis is supported by the linguistic cues: the use of the deontic modal[1] verb 'ought to' (l. 1) highlights the passage as based on Henrik's values: there is no outside agent causing this obligation, it is Henrik's Sensemaking perspective which dictates his Practice as signalled by the choice of 'ought to'. In terms of Prosody, Henrik's passion about the professional values in the passage is signalled through his extensive use of high key onset (l. 4, l. 7 and l. 9). His devotion of an entire intonation unit to the word 'Listen' (l. 4) is not only a call to be heard, but an emphatic expression that he feels what he says is important.

Henrik:

1 /But people ought to go out (.)
2 \where they have not necessarily gone before. (.)
3 /Because it's required \in a knowledge organisation like HR Consult.
4 \^Listen.
5 /if you just \come in and do (.) what you wanna do (.)
6 /and don't go beyond \where it might hurt a bit (.)
7 ^then you _don't ^learn \anything. (..)
and a knowledge organisation (.)
9 /they ^need \people who--who \are a bit hard on themselves (.)
10 /In terms of \learning.

(Henrik, my translation, 292, 58:46)

To conclude on the analysis of the quote above, Henrik's emphasis on hard work is not only a part of his Sensemaking and his (d)iscourse but also his Practice, this linguistic construction of a Practice as being hard work can be triangulated with other interviewee statements: Other participants at HR Consult construct Henrik as hard working as well. For example, 'Morten', a senior administrative employee at HR Consult Denmark, stated that if the in-house translator, 'Rasmus' did not have time to translate an English language HR Consult product into Danish, Henrik just did it himself at night.

To sum up, the Knowledge Creator Prototype, which Henrik represents, works hard to fulfil their own expectations for what useful organisational knowledge is, regardless of how others see them. Henrik attaches strong values to the commitment to develop organisational knowledge and expects others to live up to them. This is not only Henrik's practice: a similar set of values attached to a similar knowledge transformation practice was found when analysing the interview with 'John' from HR Consult UK.

Henrik's solitude with his need to constantly transform and create organisational knowledge emerged as a theme in others' constructions of him. To one participant, whom Henrik constructs as someone he respects, Henrik's constant transformation of organisational knowledge made it difficult for him to maintain knowledge about which products the organisation was able to offer, and particularly what to charge clients for products designed by Henrik rather than R&D at HQ. So, although HR Consult was able to produce revenue on the basis of Henrik's knowledge creation, the benefit was not without challenges.

That others in the organisation do not always look favourably on his knowledge creation Practice can also be seen in the following quote from my interview with 'Morten'. Through Prosodic cues Morten constructs a sense that he is criticising rather than praising Henrik in this passage, particularly the many emphasised words and high key words construct this impression of irony. The short intonation units breaking up the grammar also suggests that he is weighing his words carefully holding back an explicit criticism which nevertheless emerges through his use of irony.

Morten:

1 '[Henrik] has
2 \a (.) burning wish to \market our, erm products in (.)
3 ^all the forums \ £he can get away with£
4 /and all the different ^forms
5 \he can manage to get ^done (.) erm (.)
6 =so he's really the primary mover within
7 \within marketing

('Morten', my translation, 35, 0:04:40)

To conclude on the analysis of the quote above, Henrik is also constructed by others as highly ambitious in his drive to transform and re-create organisational knowledge. Henrik's Discursive Sensemaking about organisational knowledge as a process thus has implications for both how he perceives his own knowledge communication Practice (as working hard to help clients with their challenges) and how his colleagues at HR Consult Denmark see him as hard working and sometimes overly ambitious. The professional identity of a Knowledge Creator seems to entail hard work leading to an identity as a knowledge leader, but also as sometimes highly ambitious in the work he undertakes to fulfil his ideals for useful knowledge as being transformed and situated within a client context.

Henrik's vision for a different organisational strategy is not limited to the website. Like Linda, representing the Knowledge Broker Prototype, he is critical of the core product line offered by HR Consult. This (d)iscourse of opposition to the Externalised organisational knowledge in the form of the core product line of HR Consult can be seen in the quote cited below. As part of his Discursive Sensemaking in this quote Henrik makes this criticism overt ('it's not cool enough', l. 4). In the quote he contrasts the organisational 'psychometric focus' (l. 3) with his own client centric focus (l. 7), thereby building a value hierarchy with his own Sensemaking perspective as the superior one. This value hierarchy seems to be performing the Building Task. The Prosody of the quote supports this Sensemaking perspective through a higher key in l. 1 and l. 4 signalling that Henrik is passionate about the topic. This passion is also signalled in the breakup of the grammar in l. 1–3: 'we have they are again they are they have' suggesting that he is so emotional about the topic that he stumbles over the words. The discourse marker 'So' in l. 5 is emphasised through its repetition signalling that a Discursive Sensemaking interpretation is coming. In presenting his own Discursive Sensemaking perspective after the discourse marker, he adopts the value-laden 'we are strong enough' (l. 7). This can be juxtaposed with the distance he signals to the organisational 'psychometric focus' (l. 3) through the use of the demonstrative pronoun 'this'. But his use of the first-person plural pronoun 'we' throughout the passage signals a sense of belonging to the organisation, and as having the organisation's best interest at heart when making the criticism. The choice of 'we' when speaking about the direction and strategy of the entire organisation can be juxtaposed with use of the first-person singular pronoun 'I' when speaking about his colleagues in the local work environment of HR Consult Denmark, quoted earlier.

Henrik:

1 '\Many of the [core product workshop materials] we
2 \they are, \again they are,
3 \they have this psychometric focus.
4 […] \it's not ^cool enough.
5 \So, so we, erm, we need to move beyond that
6 /and we need to be conscious
7 \that we are strong enough to understand the client,

(Henrik, my translation, 91, 16:16)

To conclude on the analysis of the quote above, Henrik questions the organisational Conversation as presented in the official organisational product line. This 'psychometric' focus which Henrik questions seems to favour the knowledge interests of the founder of the company who built the core product line of HR Consult on his psychometric system of personality profiling. Instead, Henrik proposes a client-centred approach, favouring the transformation of HR Consult's knowledge products to situate the knowledge communication and client learning within the client's own frame of reference.

In response to what Henrik had said about creating knowledge and about how it could benefit HR Consult globally if there were more people who transformed and created knowledge, I constructed my own subject position (or identity) as being on his side in his opposition to an organisation which, according to Henrik, did not give him due credit for his time-consuming knowledge creation. I did so in order to prompt him to reflect more explicitly on values and opinions which he had hinted at and implied in the interview until this point. To achieve this, I stated that I was surprised that HR Consult, who claim in their value statement to be a 'learning organisation', wasn't more geared towards learning about the experiences of consultants in the field, particularly in relation to how HR Consult knowledge was transformed and changed as consultant's engaged with client contexts. In terms of Discursive Sensemaking, his response shows his lack of respect for other consultants whom he does not consider to be on his own level (l. 6–9). This quote also constructs his practice of testing colleagues which he also described in other situations, not quoted in this analysis. In the quote below, the test he refers to does not seem to refer to a specific episode, but as an example of his Practice in a number of situations. The Practice he describes gives an insight into how he makes sense of what he sees as his colleagues' lack of effort.

The Sensemaking analysis above is supported by the Prosodic cues in the quote: the high key onset and considerable pitch shift in the short, three syllable intonation unit beginning the quote (l. 1) constructs an impression of his complete agreement with my statement that important knowledge construction happens at the consultant level. Combined with his increased pace (l. 3–14), these Prosodic details give the impression of his passion for this topic. His ability to stay coherent and not stumble on words or hesitate despite the fast pace indicates familiarity with the argument, suggesting that the argument is part of his ongoing Sensemaking about his work environment.

Henrik:

1 ^Yes \It /does.
2 \that's absolutely right because
3 [faster pace] \one of the challenges we /have
4 also more on the product side
5 /that is \that (.h)
6 \well the consultants who do not
7 /(..) already \have the head for
8 \or the interest in
9 \having to do with things down at the /substantial level
10 [normal pace] _y'know (.) ^make (..) [faster pace]
11 \you have to make ten PowerPoints for this ^group,
12 /you have three ^hours--
13 --\what are they going to look like.--
14 --\You cannot use any /you've used \before. (..)
15 [normal pace] \Then people are up the creek. (.) erm (.)
16 /But they don't ^have \to be
17 \if they dared to (.) to think for themselves.

(Henrik, my translation, 82, 0:13:12)

To conclude on the analysis of the quote above, Henrik expects his colleagues to create new knowledge, and he only invests his trust in their competence if they are able to do so. What he expects here can be related directly to the SECI cycle (see Chapter 6): he sees his colleagues as not working hard enough to achieve the deep Internalisation of HR Consult knowledge to be able to produce new knowledge situated within the client context. Instead, he sees them as combining the existing knowledge products and applying them within the client context.

I also interviewed some of the consultants who Henrik describes as being 'up the creek' (l. 18 in the quote above), and they seem to be just as value-based in their professional identity which, as Henrik correctly but derogatively describes above, does not include creating new knowledge, but rests on a practice of communicating existing HR Consult learning programmes to clients.

I term this other professional identity prototype the Knowledge Transfer Prototype because it is centred on a belief that the highly Externalised training modules designed by HR Consult R&D should be delivered as intact and as unchanged as possible to the client, because considerations for retention and application have been built into the design of the training modules. Therefore, they find no reason to re-invent something that works. Thus, Henrik seems justified in characterising their knowledge communication practice as he does, although from his Discursive Sensemaking perspective he does not see the value in the approach.

Earlier we saw how Henrik attached value to deep internalisation of organisational knowledge to achieve a level of understanding allowing the consultant to improvise, thereby combining explicit and tacit, complex knowledge and externalising the knowledge creation into PowerPoint slides and course materials, which can be used to engage others in the internalisation of the new knowledge. This analysis suggests a rather more complex Combination step co-occurring with Socialisation and Externalisation, rather than the rigid step-by-step process implied by the SECI model. In short, Henrik's Socialisation step is performed in interaction with his client rather than with his colleagues.

Henrik's client-centred knowledge creation approach to situate his knowledge communication within the client context is evident in the quote below. In the quote, his Discursive Sensemaking centres on the notion of 'making things valuable to the client' (l. 3). He explicitly dissociates this from the practice of adopting the existing codified learning solutions produced by the R&D department in the UK (l.5). Dissociation of the two concepts which were not combined until brought to the foreground in a (d)iscourse is also a way of building a connection. Henrik even argues that the client will have to 'commit violence' to themselves to be able to use the existing HR Consult learning modules. The colloquialism of l. 9 expresses his dissatisfaction with the conventional knowledge communication practice in the organisation. As a final note on his Discursive Sensemaking he explicitly uses the 'product manager' title again (l. 2), thereby positioning himself and his knowledge communication approach at a higher level than his colleagues. At the linguistic level, Henrik uses

Prosody to signal the significance he attaches to the value of transforming and situating knowledge within the client context: he uses high key onset to make the intonation unit in l. 3 stand out, and by separating the individual words in that intonation unit with pauses, he puts strong emphasis on each word. Thereby, he signals that 'making things valuable to the client' (l. 3) is a strongly held professional value. His strong feelings about his client-centred approach are also signalled in the elaborate repetition in l. 6–8 of the same content that was presented in the intonation unit in l. 5. Through the repetition and particularly through the strongly value-laden Lexical choices in the repetition ('commit violence to yourselves' l. 7), Henrik constructs a deep gap between the implied value of his own approach and what he constructs as its opposite: the use of existing learning modules designed by HR Consult R&D to be combined at the Explicit level to adapt to all client training needs.

Henrik:

1 _So, \so it's about, --
2 --/so in ^my \role as product manager it's about, (.)
3 ^making (.) things (.) \valuable to the client. (.)
4 \And not just, (.)
5 \here's something from England which might fit you.
6 _Or \here's a learning guide which, (.)
7 \I think if you (.) if you commit violence to yourselves,
8 \then this is what you should follow. (.) \Fuck that

(Henrik, my translation, 91, 0:15:59)

To conclude on the analysis of the quote above, Henrik's focus on the value of a client-centred knowledge transformation in this quote and elsewhere in the interview can be understood as an intuitive realisation of Lave and Wenger's (1991) concept of situated learning. Wenger would argue that the client will only be able to benefit from HR Consult knowledge if it is situated within, i.e., transformed to the clients' situation and context. Only then will they be able to Internalise and reapply the learning to improve the challenges, which led them to buy HR Consult's services in the first place.

Henrik can be understood as a Knowledge Creator because he builds an identity of opposition to the existing organisational Conversation and criticises employees who are not willing to commit to the level of work effort required to undertake his own level of knowledge transformation.

In his opposition to organisational Conversation his criticism goes wider than his circle of colleagues in Denmark. He builds on a (d)iscourse valuing client satisfaction through tailored and customised solutions and uses this (d)iscourse to distance himself from the psychometric focus in the core products of HR Consult.

Case study: Linda's professional identity – the characteristics of Knowledge Broker Prototype

Through a close analysis of Linda's professional identity as a Knowledge Broker Prototype in the following section, I examine how she constructs a professional identity on the basis of her perception of knowledge.

A professional self-identity based on a client-centred knowledge communication practice emerges as a consequence of the opposition between Linda's own perspective on organisational knowledge and the perspective which seems to be an aspect of the organisational Conversation in the form of, amongst others, blogs on the intranet, corporate meetings and global conferences hosted by HR Consult HQ. Linda distances herself from this Conversation and doesn't quite bring it into the foreground, except through vague references like 'people are saying' (Linda, my translation, 205, 27:10). Through her descriptions of her knowledge communication practice presented in the last chapter, Linda starts to build a set of values underlying her professional identity as Knowledge Broker Prototype. These values centre on the focus of helping the client by building a learning solution tailored to their needs.

This professional identity can be seen in the quote presented in Chapter 5 (Linda, my translation, 205, 27:10) where Linda attached significance to the phrase 'I just spend that time because I think it's fun', thereby signalling that her time-consuming knowledge transformation practice is not just a matter of obligation towards her own or the client's organisations, but a personally held value underlying her professional identity. Linguistically, she constructed this significance through two Prosodic cues: first, she shifted to high key onset, thereby making the statement stand out from the surrounding (d)iscourse, and second, she added emphasis to 'fun'. Semantically, 'fun' is an interesting choice here because time-consuming work could be seen as dreary and difficult. By selecting 'fun' and placing it at the salient end-of-phrase position, she constructs a professional identity based on passion for knowledge creation, rather than being based on satisfaction in fulfilling organisational requirements to be cost effective and utilise tried and tested pre-designed learning programmes.

This misalignment between Linda's knowledge communication Practice and the organisational expectations can be interpreted in terms of Weick's (1995, 2001) theories of Sensemaking (see Chapter 2). The misalignment arises between, on the one hand, the organisational Conversation, or 'changing ecology' (Weick, 1995), and the values and professional identity which is part of Linda's retention on the other hand. As predicted by Weick's Sensemaking theory, this misalignment leads to a Sensemaking process to justify her Enactment. Although this Sensemaking is made explicit in the interview, and thereby fixed in time, this does not mean that it has not been an ongoing process, or that it has not been verbalised in other contexts with like-minded colleagues. But because the interview is a snapshot, and I haven't observed her Sensemaking process per se, I refer to it as Discursive Sensemaking.

In the following quote, Linda raises the importance of autonomy even further by building a connection between her autonomy and her continued willingness to stay in the organisation. As part of her Discursive Sensemaking about the autonomy she is granted, she builds a connection between her close personal relationship with the founder of the company and the autonomy she is granted to pursue her knowledge creating strategy. Thereby she creates further distance between herself and the middle managers, who she constructed as not understanding her approach. The most significant aspect of her Discursive Sensemaking in the quote below nevertheless seems to be her comment on the autonomy she has been granted ('I've been allowed to' l. 2).

Linda's conscious or unconscious linguistic choices underline the Sensemaking analysis above and makes her argument for staying in the organisation stand out. The quote stands out from the rest of the interview, because of the abrupt shift in Prosody from fast pace, high key enunciation (l. 2) to slow pace, low key and low volume enunciation (l. 4). The shift seems significant because Linda generally speaks in a higher pace than other participants in my study, and rarely hesitates or uses low key intonation. Therefore, the slow pace and low volume when building the connection to her continued existence in the organisation (l. 4) gives the impression that she is speaking as much to herself as to the interviewer. Her volume in the rest of the interview is fairly high, maybe due to her experience as a professional presenter, so the low volume here stands out, thereby strengthening the impression that she is talking to herself. Furthermore, the three pauses and empty fill-in sounds at the end of l. 4 suggest that she briefly needs to collect herself before proceeding, thereby giving the impression that she attaches strong emotion to the argument about finding her motivation to stay in the organisation mainly in her ability to pursue her own knowledge creating strategy:

Linda:

1 So erm (.)
2 [faster pace]^\but, well, as I said--I've /been allowed to--
3 --\And so that's also why
4 [slow pace, low volume] _I am still here (.) erm (.) and (.) erm
5 [faster pace and normal volume] and then it helps if you know the family [i.e. the owners] 6 then-
6 -then you're also kind of (.) [slow pace] _left alone a bit.

(Linda, my translation, 370, 57:13)

To summarise the analysis of the quote above, Linda is making sense of her existence within the organisation with reference to her professional identity centred on the autonomous approach to network building and knowledge transformation. But in the quote above she also builds Politics by suggesting that it is not organisational policy or culture which grants her the autonomy here, but her personal connection with the founder.

Regardless of whether she interprets the origin of her autonomy correctly or not, she explicitly connects the autonomy to pursue her knowledge creating strategy to her willingness to stay in the organisation. Because a similar argument was made by Henrik, the implication seems to be that employees with professional identities centred on the intrinsic and organisational value of creating knowledge should be granted a high level of autonomy to do so. Because both Henrik and Linda do put in extra hours to transform and re-create organisational knowledge (both in their own and others' description of them), there seems to be no reason for organisations not to grant them the autonomy they need to perform their particular knowledge communication practice.

The lack of understanding for Linda's approach, which she expressed in another quote (Linda, my translation, 278, 39:06, see Chapter 5, is also evident in Linda's statements about a decision to hold monthly face-to-face meetings with the virtual team of eight Client Relations Managers of which Linda is one. In the quote below, Linda shows awareness that her project does not quite follow corporate strategy; in her Discursive Sensemaking about the decision to conduct face-to-face meetings she seems to imply that her immediate managers lack knowledge about the Practices of the Client Relations Management Team. Linda states that she doesn't know why the two managers made the decision, but then offers her own interpretation: the decision to hold monthly, co-located meetings seem to her to be an attempt to regain leadership ('rally the troops', l. 5). This interpretation implies that Linda considers the two middle managers to be disconnected from what she does. She almost constructs her own project as being opposed to their focus on 'how much money we make' (l. 6), although as mentioned, an important part of her justification for her approach is precisely the longer-term Return On Investment (ROI) of her project. In the context of her Discursive Sensemaking about the future ROI, her statement here should be seen more as a criticism of the organisational Conversation focussing on short-term revenue. The focus on short-term revenue seems to be an implication of an organisational Practice of evaluating managers on the basis of how much revenue their employees generate. As pointed out by Gee (2011, 2014) what is not said can sometimes be as significant as what is said; in this quote Linda refrains from expressing any need for the meetings on the part of her or the other team members; from her Discursive Sensemaking perspective the decision seems to have been made based on the middle managers' own need.

This Sensemaking analysis of the quote is supported by the linguistic analysis: Linda's use of the demonstrative pronoun 'those' (l. 3) suggests that she constructs a sense of distance between herself and the managers. The validity of this interpretation seems to be strengthened by her referring to the same managers by their names: because they were already part of the discourse in the interview there seems to be no reason for the demonstrative pronoun here except to signal a sense of distance to the middle managers.

1 Petersen: What were the arguments behind that decision?
2 Linda: /it was a bit difficult \to find out if the argument,
3 \was simply for those managers, [provides names of the two managers of the Client Relations Management Team]
5 =/to rally the \troops, y'know.
6 \They are being evaluated based on how much money we make.

(Linda, my translation, 236, 32:59)

To summarise the analysis of the quote above, Linda herself does not express any need for monthly face-to-face meetings. Instead, her Discursive Sensemaking about the decision constructs an image of the two middle managers as disconnected from the Practices of the Client Relations Management Team, and as trying to regain control. She thereby also underlines that it is not of their own volition that the two middle managers grant Linda the autonomy she requires to pursue her knowledge transformation practice.

Linda's autonomy and client-centred approach does not mean that she does not care about the success of HR Consult, though. On the contrary, like Henrik, she shows concern for leveraging learning outcomes and knowledge created for her client to an organisational level. But Linda does not feel she has the support of the middle managers, and due to the organisational practice of evaluating managers 'based on how much money we [the consultants] make' (Linda, my translation, 236, 32:59, quoted earlier) she may not be able to lift it herself. In contrast to the middle managers, she refers to her close relation with the founder of the company. But to challenge her fondness of this relationship, which she also cited as the reason why the middle managers left her alone (Linda, my translation, 370, 57:13, analysed earlier), I chose to question the quality of the relationship. I therefore summarised her argument about the future value of transforming knowledge. Because my comment below summarises opinions she has herself voiced earlier in the interview, I quote my comment below.

Petersen:

1 /But they[1] are not quite\ interested enough
2 \in your experiences with
3 /transforming \this to Adobe[2]
4 and running it virtually, and, well,
5 _potentially (.)
6 ^\I can see that the first couple of times it's a lot of work to transform it.
7 \Transforming knowledge is time consuming.

8 ^But, but in the long run, well
9 (.) if they start a more erm,
10 it's a bit more of a bottom-up innovation of the product.

(Linda, my translation, 382, 57:30).

Quote notes:

[1] 'They' refers back, termed 'anaphoric reference' (Halliday & Hasaan, 1976/2014), to the organisation in general. Linda has just stated that she has a strong relation with the founder of the organisation and with other people at the very top of the organisation.

[2] Linda introduced Adobe Meeting as the ICT used to facilitate the online learning in her project for Soft Tech.

Although the phrase 'I can see…' (l. 3) suggests that this is my observation, it summarises views which Linda expressed earlier in the interview. However, the phrase 'I can see…' served the purpose of building rapport with Linda, suggesting that I understood her perspective. My summary and the reflection did serve its purpose by sparking the Discursive Sensemaking in the response cited below where Linda expresses frustration that HR Consult seems to have a culture where no one will help her lift the experience and knowledge gained from the Soft Tech project to a wider organisational level. The project for her client Soft Tech is the one she states that she spends the most time on (see Chapter 5). The quote below can thus be seen as her Discursive Sensemaking about the organisation as being rather unwilling to support and invest in innovation from front line consultants.

In the quote below, she again constructs her self-identity as being in opposition to the organisational Conversation and strategy. She argues that the success of her knowledge transformation process for the Soft Tech project can be leveraged to an organisational level and applied to other clients, thereby providing HR Consult with the ability to deliver their products on a virtual platform for any dispersed client organisation. She emphasises her own concern for the organisation by arguing that her own sense of success (l. 8) is premised on her project being used more widely in the organisation (l. 9). She explicitly constructs the connection between the organisational focus on making money (l. 13) and the inability of the organisation to learn from her project until it has lived up to this organisational criterion for success.

The Prosody of the quote supports this interpretation: she constructs her own efforts to communicate the experiences from the Soft Tech project as significant through her high key onset in l. 7 and 8. By doing so, she builds up to the 'conflict' (l. 11). In l. 11 she does not specify who the conflict concerns, but the Prosodic cues just mentioned indicate that she is talking about a conflict between what she sees as a short-sighted organisational focus on making money as opposed to her commitment to develop and transform organisational knowledge to apply and situate it within new client contexts.

Linda:

1 Yes. Well erm with regard to what I've seen, well (.)
2 \too much of these individual ways of running it
3 /for there to be a group to \sort of say
4 \hey, why don't we /help out \here,
5 \and why don't we try to--to--to
6 \take this to a new customer'.
7 ^Well that's obviously what I'm doing.
8 ^\I definitely want for my /own \success--
9 -=it's only a success if this is used somewhere else as well. (.)
10 So I'm out talking about it a lot.
11 (lower key, slower pace) Erm but, well there's /definitely \a conflict
12 y'know with '^it's very interesting \what you're doing [Linda], but, erm,
13 \we need to see whether it makes money first--\and then we need to see
14 whether it--/whether you can handle \it--
15 -and we're not quite sure we have the resources to do something like that.'

(Linda, my translation, 388, 58:07)

To summarise the analysis of the quote above, Linda shows awareness of the situated nature of her client-centred knowledge approach, and awareness that it will need to go through a new knowledge creation SECI loop to shift it to an organisational level from which it can be applied in other organisational settings. Nonetheless, the incomprehension of her managers seems the most salient aspect of this quote. She does not seem to feel she has the organisational support to undertake the knowledge creating and communicate it to the wider organisation, and due to the organisational focus on making money, she may not be able to lift it herself.

Gee's notion of (D)iscourse is relevant to the performance of being a good HR Consult consultant. The strategy documents, speeches, intranet videos and documents lay down how to be a good HR Consult consultant, thus shaping a corporate Conversation. But Linda resists this identity call; she carves out her own (D)iscourse and identity with a set of values and practices attached to it. This may not be an easy or cost-free endeavour, however. This can be seen in Linda's refusal to live up to the corporate strategy of selling standardised, modular HR development training, as we shall see in the following analysis.

Linda's Knowledge Broker prototypical identity goes beyond strategy and revenue to deeper values centred on helping the client solve the challenges they face. In other words, making money for her organisation is not motivation in itself for Linda; she seeks a deeper meaning in what she does. She makes this professional identity value explicit in her Discursive Sensemaking in the quote below. She constructs what she sees as meaningful work by contrasting it to the knowledge communication approach of the Knowledge Transfer Prototype. From the linguistic perspective, Prosodic cues in the quote below indicate agitation and strong emotion through the audible exhalation at the beginning of l. 1, and through the onomatopoetic 'argh' at the end of l. 1. Underlining her agitation, her pace increases during the passage, finally leading to a breakup in the grammar as she stumbles over the words. Combined, these cues suggest agitation over a strongly felt issue, i.e., her Sensemaking criticism of the HR Consult business strategy. In terms of Lexis, her use of the deontic modal 'can't' (l. 9 and l. 11), is again an example of her justifying action through reference to obligation, in this case being obliged not to follow the knowledge communication practice common among her colleagues and encouraged by the middle managers. Her use of epistemic modality hides agency here: by using the modal to express obligation, she avoids or neglects to point to whom or what causes that obligation. However, as we've seen earlier, it seems to be her own value system which obliges her to adopt a client-centred knowledge communication approach emphasising transformation of the organisational knowledge. These Prosodic and linguistic cues add up to an impression of a deeply seated opposition to the Conversation of her organisation resulting in a somewhat heated defence of her own strategy emphasising a need for her work to make 'sense' (l. 5), a word which is given significance through its high key enunciation:

Linda:

1 (.h)\But I have some kind of--argh
2 ^\that's not the way I kind of
3 _\think is very ^exciting
4 _now we're back to =\what makes ^sense.
5 erm so e:rm (..)
6 [faster pace]
7 /so I've simply \stopped-- (faster pace)
8 --\I can't se:ll that--I can'--I don't even at all--think--myself--myself
9 \if I dont' believe in it then erm
10 \then--then I can't sell it.

(Linda, my translation, 369, 56:00)

To conclude on the analysis of the quote above, Linda explicitly shows the importance of the values underlying her professional identity. Finding meaning in what she does and aligning her practice, or in Weick's (1995, 2001) term 'Enactment', with the values underlying her professional identity seems to be more important to her than the organisational Conversation encouraging a different knowledge communication strategy.

Linda is very aware of how the middle manager would react if she heard this Sensemaking about the organisational knowledge communication Practice, as we shall see in the quote below. She thereby shows awareness that she is resisting a larger organisational Conversation by adopting a different Virtual Knowledge Communication practice. In terms of Discursive Sensemaking in the quote below, Linda re-introduces her immediate middle manager into the Conversation as if she was just an example to support her point. The middle manager was named and identified as Linda's manager earlier in the interview, so the distance signalled by the premodifier 'someone like' (l. 1) followed by the middle manager's full name is also used to position the middle manager as an outsider, distanced from Linda's own practice. As another effect of introducing the middle manager into the (d)iscourse, she shifts her argument about different perspectives on strategy from the Client Relations Management Team to middle management level. Linda underlines the importance of her manager's alleged opposition to her own Sensemaking by repeating the phrase 'she would definitely frown if she heard I said that' at the end of the quote. In terms of Prosody, she quickens her pace when repeating the phrase, and there is no time spent on reflecting on which words to choose or how to present this, suggesting that this is an important part of her Sensemaking, and/or that she is agitated because she feels strongly about the issue.

Linda:

1 Someone like [name of middle manager]
2 \she would –
3 (faster pace)--/she would definitely _fro:wn
4 \if she heard I said that.--
5 --\she would.
6 /she would definitely \frown if she heard I said that. (..)

(Linda, my translation, 370, 56:15)

To sum up on the analysis of the quote above, Linda uses the middle manager, who is above her in the organisational hierarchy, as an example of someone who would be opposed to the professional values which Linda attaches to her opposition to the knowledge communication practice of the more mainstream Knowledge Transfer Prototype. By doing so, Linda shifts the difference in knowledge communication practices between her own and her colleagues' practices, to a higher level in the organisation, suggesting that the strategy of the Knowledge Transfer Prototype can be seen as endorsed by the organisational culture and management practice. Three months after the interview, Linda choose to leave HR Consult to join a small HR consultancy started up by another disgruntled HR Consult employee. Linda stated that she was frustrated both about the lack of support for her knowledge communication practice and the restriction of her autonomy as the key reasons.

A consequence of the division between prototypes at HR Consult seems to be that CoPs emerge as divisions within the Client Relations Management Team. This division is the topic of the next section, which also signals a shift from analysing the characteristics of Linda's professional identity, towards focussing more on what the configurations of professional identity prototypes mean for the communication of knowledge at HR Consult.

In the quote below, Linda constructs this difference in practices and Identities as having been an Explicit topic within the team. Central to her Discursive Sensemaking in this quote is the focus on the 'need' (l. 1) for a social basis for her identity among 'sparring partners who are a bit similar to ourselves' (l. 1–2). She uses this identification with some of the team members as her justification for not knowing much about the other team members ('therefore I know less about what the others are doing', l. 5–6). In terms of grammar, she renders the division significant by using the discourse marker 'so' to signal that a conclusion or Sensemaking interpretation is coming. In terms of Prosody, this conclusion is given further emphasis by the high key onset on 'So':

Linda:

/We all need \to have some (.) sparring partners
/who are a bit similar \to ourselves. ^So there's clearly a e:rm (.)
division in--in the team at that level— ¨
[fast pace]--/and therefore I know less \about
[slow pace] \what the others are doing

(Linda, my translation, 363, 53:23)

To conclude on the analysis of the quote above, Linda constructs an image of a shared professional identity within each of the two smaller communities of 'sparring partners' (l. 1).

She states that the three she identified by name are the ones who share her approach to the work, and that they are the ones she calls first, 'if there are any issues', while she attaches the predicate 'more old school sales people' to the others.

Although Linda states that the two CoPs in the Client Relations Management Team respect each other, the quote below shows that Linda experiences no sense of a shared understanding. From the linguistic perspective the distance between the two CoPs within the team is highlighted in the quote below through the opposition between the third-person plural pronoun, 'they', and the first-person singular pronoun, 'I', (l. 1 and 2). By using high key onset when enunciating the pronouns, she puts emphasis on this sense of opposition.

Linda:

1 \^They don't really get what I'm doing,
2 and ^I \don't really get what ^they're doing,
3 (.)\and that's just fine.

(Linda, my translation, 254, 0:35:55)

Therefore, the analysis of the quote above shows how Linda explicitly constructs an opposition between the two CoPs in the Client Relations Management Team by centring on a lack of understanding for what the others are doing.

Notes

1 Deontic modality is used to express obligation or permission (Hjulmand, 2012).

References

Alvesson, M., & Sköldberg, K. (2009). *Reflexive methodology* (2nd ed.). Los Angeles, CA: Sage.
Benwell, B., & Stokoe, E. (2006). *Discourse and identity.* Edinburgh: Edinburgh University Press.
Billett, S. (2007). Work, subjectivity and learning. In *Work, subjectivity and learning* (pp. 1–20). Dordrecht: Springer.
Billett, S. (2013). Including the missing subject: Placing the personal within the community. In *Communities of practice: Critical perspectives* (pp. 65–77). London: Routledge.
Burke, P. J., & Stets, J. E. (2009). *Identity theory.* Oxford: Oxford University Press.
Daim, T. U., Ha, A., Reutiman, S., Hughes, B., Pathak, U., Bynum, W., & Bhatla, A. (2012). Exploring the communication breakdown in global virtual teams. *International Journal of Project Management, 30*(2), 199–212. doi: 10.1016/j.ijproman.2011.06.004
David, M. (2005). *Science in society.* New York: Palgrave Macmillan.
Fairclough, N. (1992). *Discourse and social change.* Cambridge: Polity Press.
Fairclough, N. (2003). *Analysing discourse: Textual analysis for social research.* London: Routledge.
Gee, J. P. (2011). *An introduction to discourse analysis.* London: Routledge.
Gee, J. P. (2014). *How to do discourse analysis: A toolkit.* London: Routledge.
Halliday, M. A. K., & Hasan, R. (1976/2014). *Cohesion in English.* London: Routledge.
Handley, K., Sturdy, A., Fincham, R., & Clark, T. (2006). Within and beyond communities of practice: Making sense of learning through participation, identity and practice. *Journal of Management Studies, 43*(3), 641–653. doi: 10.1111/j.1467-6486.2006.00605.x
Harré, R. (2005). Positioning and the discursive construction of categories. *Psychopathology, 38*(4), 185–188. doi: 10.1159/000086088

Hogg, M. A., & Reid, S. A. (2006). Social identity, self-categorization, and the communication of group norms. *Communication Theory, 16*(1), 7–30. doi: 10.1111/j.1468-2885.2006.00003.x

Jansen, P. G., & Roodt, G. (2014). Conceptualising and measuring work identity. Retrieved from: http://link.springer.com/book/10.1007/978-94-017-9242-4

King, N. (2012). Doing template analysis. *Qualitative Organizational Research: Core Methods and Current Challenges, 426*, 77–101.

Lave, J., & Wenger, E. (1991). *Situated learning: Legitimate peripheral participation.* Cambridge: Cambridge University Press.

Nonaka, I., & Takeuchi, H. (1995). *Knowledge-creating company: How Japanese companies create the dynamics of innovation.* Oxford: Oxford University Press.

Suchan, J., & Hayzak, G. (2001). The communication characteristics of virtual teams: A case study. *IEEE Transactions on Professional Communication, 44*(3) 174–186. doi: 10.1109/47.946463

Van Dijk, T. A. (2005). Contextual knowledge management in discourse production. In R. Wodak, P. Chilton (Eds.). *A new agenda in (critical) discourse analysis* (pp. 71–100). Amsterdam: John Benjamins.

Weick, K. E. (1995). *Sensemaking in organizations.* London: Sage

Weick, K. E. (2001). *Making sense of the organization.* Oxford: Blackwell.

Wenger, E. (1998). *Communities of practice: Learning, meaning, and identity.* New York: Cambridge University Press.

Ybema, S., Keenoy, T., Oswick, C., Beverungen, A., Ellis, N., & Sabelis, I. (2009). Articulating identities. *Human Relations, 62*(3), 299–322. doi: 10.1177%2F0018726708101904

9 Relationships supporting virtual knowledge communication

Chapter Contents

This chapter presents three theories important for virtual knowledge communication. Firstly, trust is both an antecedent and an outcome of virtual knowledge communication, but it can be difficult to build and maintain a trust- based relationship when you rarely meet in-person. Secondly, knowledge of who-knows-what in the organisation (a so-called Transaction Memory System) enables you to find the novel knowledge needed to complete a project. Finally, studies of weak and strong ties (i.e., weak and strong relationships) show that novel knowledge is often found outside your normal network of relationships, among weak ties, because your strong ties tend to know what you already know. These three theories allow analysis of virtual knowledge communication at HR Consult where Linda and her Knowledge Broker Prototype exhibit the ability to trust weak ties quickly (so-called 'swift trust'), and to build on a variety of knowledge sources in their virtual team allowing them to achieve client satisfaction in a complex virtual project.

The impact of relationships on virtual knowledge communication

Relationships can both be seen as antecedents and outcomes of virtual knowledge communication. As an antecedent, a strong relationship can

DOI: 10.4324/9781003015925-11

be seen as founded on trust and mutual understanding which in turn are prerequisites for communicating complex knowledge effectively; in short, professional relationships can be seen as a prerequisite for virtual knowledge communication. As an outcome of knowledge communication, relationships can be seen as strengthened if both parties feel they gained useful knowledge by engaging in communication with the other party.

Before we take a deeper look at these three theories of effective professional relationships, let me briefly summarise the core arguments in the previous two chapters. First, Chapter 7 presented Wenger's Communities of Practice (CoP) theory where the relationships among practitioners sharing the same knowledge domain were seen as essential both for creating a sense of meaning and Identity for the individual and for developing the knowledge domain of the community (Lave & Wenger, 1991; Wenger, 1998; Wenger et al., 2002). All capitalised words, such as 'Communities of Practice', are defined in the glossary at the back of the book). Second, Chapter 8 presented Identity theories emphasising the social basis for Identity formations thereby demonstrating the importance of relationships for supporting the individual's sense of Identity.

This chapter can thus be seen as adding to both knowledge theories and Identity theories by presenting three theories which deepen the understanding of how relationships support knowledge communication be it virtual or face-to-face. Thereby this chapter also deepens the understanding of the challenging virtual work environment (see Chapter 5).

Trust as antecedent and outcome of knowledge communication

Nonaka's knowledge creation spiral (see Chapter 6) necessitates an ongoing exchange between the individual and the social dimension, and between the Tacit and the Explicit dimensions of knowledge. Trust is mentioned briefly in later articles by Nonaka and his associates as a so-called *knowledge asset* making knowledge creation between individuals more effective (Nonaka & Toyama, 2005; Nonaka & von Krogh, 2009). However, those articles do not elaborate on how trust can be defined or analysed, nor do they theorise on how and why trust can function as mediator for effective knowledge communication.

In relation to CoP theory (see Chapter 7), trust can be seen as arising through Participation and Reification in a CoP. But trust is not treated theoretically as a separate construct by neither Lave and Wenger (1991), Wenger (1998) nor Wenger et al. (2002). This chapter tries to fill those gaps by integrating theories on trust from applied psychology. The trust concepts are presented in this chapter.

Trust in this book refers mainly to interpersonal trust, or what is sometimes termed 'horizontal trust' (Fage-Butler, 2011). However, trust may also be vertical in the sense that we can trust institutions, and in that sense the organisational context of individual team members may also affect levels of trust in a virtual team at a more abstract level.

As an antecedent of virtual knowledge communication, high team trust could thus be argued, supported by the findings of Baskerville and Nandhakumar (2007), to increase the individual propensity to attempt communication of tacit knowledge. Conversely, trust is important for the communication of knowledge because it functions as an inbound filter between the individual level and the social level; if I trust a source of knowledge, regardless of whether it is a person, an organisation or a website, then I have a propensity to quickly accept knowledge from that source as valid. This could be why the studies by De Jong and Elfring (2010), Costa (2003), Dirks (1999), Rispens et al. (2007) and Spreitzer and Mishra (1999) have all indicated a positive relationship between high levels of trust and high team performance. The correlation between trust and knowledge communication has also been found in quantitative studies such as Chowdhury (2005) and Staples and Webster (2008). This correlation follows logically from the seminal, though not exhaustive, definition of trust proposed by Mayer et al. (1995), which has been cited more than 20.000 times according to Google Scholar, and used by e.g. Abrams et al. 2003; De Jong and Elfring 2010; Palanski et al. (2011):

> [Trust is] the willingness of a party to be vulnerable to the actions of another party based on the expectation that the other will perform a particular action important to the trustor, irrespective of the ability to monitor or control that other party.
>
> (Mayer et al. 1995, p. 712)

There are countless other definitions of interpersonal trust, but there is a tendency towards consensus on viewing trust as the willing exposure to vulnerability or risk based on beliefs about another party. Mayer et al. (1995) also address risk specifically:

> There is no risk taken in the willingness to be vulnerable (i.e., to trust), but risk is inherent in the behavioural manifestation of the willingness to be vulnerable. One does not need to risk anything in order to trust; however, one must take a risk in order to engage in trusting action. The fundamental difference between trust and trusting behaviour is between a "willingness" to assume risk and actually "assuming" risk.
>
> (p. 712)

Let's dig a little deeper into these two quotes. In the first, Mayer et al. (1995) construct a distinction between trust as belief, i.e., an aspect of cognition, and trust as actions and practices founded on these beliefs, which they term 'trusting behaviours'. A similar emphasis on the distinction between trust belief and trust behaviour can be found in Nooteboom (2011) in his book on trust.

Linking this to the discussion of knowledge communication theory in Chapters 6 and 7, knowledge communication can be seen as a form of trust behaviour because we open ourselves to criticism from others by attempting to voice to our Tacit ideas and reflections. These reflections may, if considered valid, or useful to the interlocutor(s), evolve into new knowledge, or alternatively just be ignored. Attempting to voice more tacit aspects of our knowledge can thus be seen as taking a risk.

My model of interpersonal trust in Figure 9.1 is based on a systematic search for case studies examining the interplay of dispersed teams, knowledge communication and trust in organisational contexts. I identified the trust concepts cited in the studies, then went back to the original articles presenting the concepts and constructed the model in Figure 9.1 on the basis of those concepts.

Figure 9.1 can be seen as an idealised system which should be considered as an open system influenced by other social factors omitted for the sake of clarity. It should also be considered as a dynamic system, where trust beliefs in the relation between individuals evolve based on the behaviour (actions) of the other but is also affected by the corporate context in which they are embedded. This is reflected by the double arrows between all levels of the model. The societal and cultural levels were excluded from the model for the sake of clarity, not because they are unimportant. The corporate context is included, both because it is a more immediate concern in this research project than the cultural, and because Mayer et al. (1995)

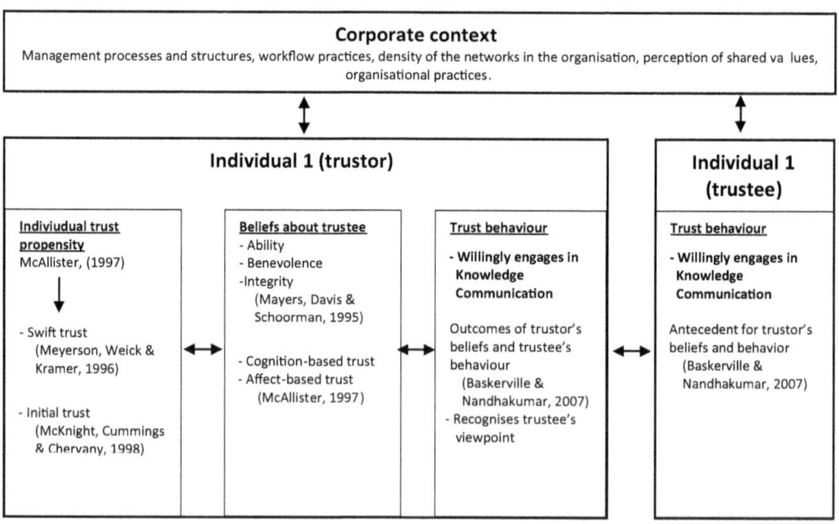

Figure 9.1 Model of interpersonal trust combining theories of trust from applied psychology

argue for the impact of contextual factors on interpersonal trust. The model does not reflect the impact of relationships on propensity to trust. For example, participation in a strong CoP may lead to a propensity to trust other members of the Community of Practice even if there has been no previous interaction between the parties. A limitation of the model can thus be seen in its singular focus on trust theories.

The perspective of the individual is adopted in the trust model (the 'trustor' in Figure 9.1), therefore the beliefs and trust propensity are omitted for the trustee, since these cannot be perceived by the trustor. The relation between the two individuals is a dynamic and reciprocal one as indicated by the double arrows. The terms 'trustor' and 'trustee' are only rhetorical means to emphasise where the perspective is put, and to separate the two individuals in the following argumentation: in practice, an individual could be trustor and trustee simultaneously, because of the reciprocal nature of the relationship. It should be noted that relationships never exist in the dyadic vacuum indicated by the model; they are embedded a complex interplay of social relations each involving different levels of trust beliefs and behaviours. Also, it should be noted that beliefs about the abilities of a person within one knowledge domain does not necessarily mean that similar beliefs will be held with regard to the person's abilities within another knowledge domain. After these general comments on the figure, the specific trust concepts will be described in the following.

Based on behavioural research findings, McAllister (1997) argues that individuals have different levels of 'propensity to trust', influenced primarily by upbringing and culture. This is supported by Mayer et al. (1995). 'Propensity to trust' is included here only to indicate that trust beliefs are not influenced solely by the trust behaviour of the trustee or organisational context, but also by the personal history and upbringing of the individual. Trust propensity, like other aspects of the model, should not be seen as static: the propensity of an individual to trust others may change if trust beliefs are consistently confirmed or let down by the behaviour of others.

Related to 'propensity to trust', are the concepts of 'swift trust' and 'initial trust'. 'Swift trust' was introduced by Meyerson et al. (1996) as a concept to explain findings that teams who have never met may still exhibit trust behaviours. 'Initial trust', was introduced by McKnight et al. (1998) to explain a similar finding. The only explanation for the different terminology seems to be that the scholars were not aware of each other's findings. Although Swift trust is fragile and temporary, studies have indicated that high levels of Swift trust do provide performance advantages for virtual project teams (Jarvenpaa & Leidner, 1999; Kanawattanachai & Yoo, 2002; Robert et al., 2009; Zolin et al., 2004). However, these researchers have not examined how levels of Swift trust can be increased. Nor do they offer solutions to overcome the temporal and fragile nature of Swift trust in short-term teams. It seems logically sound to assume that individual propensity has a high impact on swift trust, since this trust does not originate from knowledge about the trustee, but the correlation does not seem to have been examined empirically.

Both McAllister (1995) and Mayer et al. (1995) argue that trust is based on beliefs about the other, but they use different though complementary concepts to explain the basis of those beliefs. I'll go over McAllister's concepts first and then explain Mayer et al.'s concepts in subsequent paragraphs.

McAllister's (1995) concepts describe the origin of trust within the trustor as being either affect-based (emotional) or cognition-based (rational, knowledge-based). Affect-based trust seems to cover the familiar notion often described as 'clicking' with someone or 'having good chemistry'. This notion is not directly associated with the three trust concepts proposed by Mayer et al. (1995), however, trust beliefs about the Benevolence or Integrity of a trustee may be partly based on a sense of affection towards the person. But Benevolence trust and Integrity trust may also be founded on knowledge about the trustee's previous actions, in which case they could be seen as arising from what McAllister (1995) terms Cognition-based trust. 'Cognition-based trust' describes trust based on knowledge about the other person's previous behaviour; a person's 'track record' of abilities, competencies and dependability leading to well-founded expectations about future behaviour from that person, regardless of whether one has an emotional ('Affect-based') tie with that person. Affect-based trust can also be seen as a sense of identification with the trustee.

Mayer et al. (1995) propose the concepts Ability, Integrity and Benevolence trust, based on a review of trust literature at the time of publication. They argue that the three concepts 'appear to explain a major portion of trustworthiness' (p. 717). 'Ability Trust' refers to trust in another person's competence within a given context; an individual may have high abilities in some areas while being incompetent in others. 'Integrity trust' refers to the trustor's perception of the trustee's tendency to 'walk the talk'. Mayer et al. (1995) emphasise that Integrity beliefs are high when trustor and trustee share value systems. Thus, perception of Integrity can be seen as closely linked to a sense of identification, because Integrity can be seen as evaluated on the basis of personal values underlying the Identity of the trustor. Finally, 'Benevolence trust' is the perception of: 'the extent to which a trustee is believed to want to do good to the trustor, aside from an egocentric profit motive.' (Mayer et al., 1995, p. 718). Of Mayer et al.'s (1995) trust concepts, Benevolence seems to be the one of which is closest related to McAllister's affect-based trust, because it rests on a feeling of a close connection: 'Benevolence suggests that the trustee has some specific attachment to the trustor. [...] Benevolence is the perception of a positive orientation of the trustee toward the trustor.' (Mayer et al., 1995, p. 719).

Mayer et al. (1995) emphasise the connection between trusting behaviour and trusting beliefs. They argue that the behaviours of the trustee are the basis for how the trustor builds trusting beliefs about the trustee. Reciprocally, the trustor's beliefs have a high impact on whether the trustor engages in trusting behaviour towards the trustee. For example, if the trustor believes in (trusts) the trustee's ability, the trustor is likely to exhibit trusting behaviour, such as asking for advice or giving certain responsibilities to the trustee. In practice, all five trust beliefs (Cognition-based, Affect-based, Ability, Integrity, and Benevolence) will interact to support split-second decisions about whether to engage in trusting behaviour.

To sum up, McAllister's (1995) trust concepts seem to emphasise the basis of trust as founded on either knowledge or emotion, whereas Mayer et al. (1995) focus more on how the trustee's behaviour leads to different types of trust beliefs.

This notion of 'trust beliefs' can be seen, in the light of Weick's (1995, 2001) Sensemaking theory (see Chapter 2), as an aspect of the Selection and Retention of the trustor arising from the behaviour ('Enactment') of the trustor to change the shared context.

Through a selective interpretation of the trustee's behaviour, the trustor then forms beliefs which are retained and used as a basis for future enactments, for example as a basis for deciding future engagement in the form of, first, sharing knowledge with the trustee, either in the hope that the trustee can help evaluate or develop that knowledge based on their competence (i.e., Ability Trust). Or, second, ask a question based on the belief that asking the trustee will yield useful knowledge. This behaviour could be seen as a sign of Ability Trust, based on the belief that the trustee will be competent in the specific knowledge domain. Asking for help can also be a sign of Integrity trust, because it can be a sign that the trustor believes the trustee will not violate confidentiality and that trustor believes that asking will not be seen as weakness which could jeopardise the trustor's position.

From the perspective of Weick's Sensemaking, this notion of belief is based on previous behaviour. The trustee's behaviour can be seen as an Enactment changing the shared Ecology, of trustor/trustee. Through a Selective interpretation of the trustee's behaviour, the trustor then forms beliefs which are Retained and used as a basis for future enactments, for example as a basis for deciding future trust behaviour.

I now turn to case study examples to operationalise these trust concepts

Case study: A sense of belonging in Henrik's virtual community

As the quote below demonstrates, the selection of members of the Henrik's virtual community has been a strong factor in building Ability Trust (Mayer et al., 1995) between the members. This Ability Trust is based on the mutual knowledge that each member was selected for the community based on his or her track record of knowledge creation. In this case, the ability to transform organisational knowledge and build learning programmes which achieve both client satisfaction and generates revenue for the organisation. Based on this selection process, Henrik's Discursive Sensemaking about the CoP constructs them as highly competent consultants ('the selected few', l. 1–2). He constructs his own ability by referring to his recollection of the invitation to be in the community: 'we see you as a talent [...] you're welcome here' (l. 5–6). He feels a sense of pride in being invited into the community of consultants who are all Knowledge Creator Prototypes: 'it's also a feather in my cap' (l. 9). It seems to be this Sensemaking about the community as having reciprocal trust in each other's abilities which is the basis for Henrik's Sensemaking about the CoP as a site for communication of the situated and transformed knowledge which each of the members has produced for their clients.

This interpretation is supported by the linguistic cues: the repetition of the Lexical choice 'few' in l. 2 and l. 7 underlines the importance Henrik attaches to the notion of standing out as one of only a handful of knowledge creators in the organisation. In terms of prosody, his drawing out of the vowel sound at the end of l. 1 draws attention to the following intonation unit, which he devotes to the noun phrase 'the selected few' (l. 2), thereby emphasising the honour of being invited into the community. He ends l. 2 with an end-of-sentence-intonation contour, even though the sentence continues in the next intonation unit; by breaking off in mid-clause in l. 3 and shifting to the voice of the community inviting him in (l. 4–8), Henrik seems to be avoiding praising himself directly. But that the invitation is important for his Sensemaking about his own ability is signalled in the use of high key onset four times when stating that 'it's a feather in my hat' (l. 9).

Henrik:

1 'Here, \here I'm definitely in a group o:f \the selected _few.
2 which is a,
3 _well ^\[Henrik], you:,
4 \we see \you as a talent (.) \you're allowed to be--
5 \you're welcome here. (.)
6 \We are, we are these few people from Europe who,
7 \who are here and,
8 \^well--^it's \also a ^feather in my
9 ^ cap _\in some sense.

(Henrik, my translation, 156, 0:32:15)

To conclude on the analysis of the quote above, the Head of Development, who instigated the community, has built a notion of reciprocal swift trust between the community members through the deliberate selection of people with specific abilities. They all know that the others were selected because they share a similar professional Identity which builds on a knowledge communication approach of transforming HR Consult knowledge to specific client contexts and needs. This sense of reciprocal Ability Trust, which Henrik expresses in the quote, is used as his justification for why he is able to share his complex and situated knowledge with the community.

Having explained the importance of trust for virtual knowledge communication, I now return to a theory of knowledge about who-knows-what in the organisation.

Linking knowledge theory to Transactive Memory Systems (TMS) theory

In Chapter 5, the theory of Transactive Memory Systems (TMS) was introduced in relation to the virtual work environment. The present section returns to TMS to review it in the light of the knowledge theories from Chapters 6 and 7. The integration of these theories contributes to the advancement of both Nonaka's knowledge creation theories and Wenger's Communities of Practice theories by introducing a different type of knowledge, namely knowledge about where expertise is located within the organisation. By using others in the network or team as 'memories' for knowledge and skills not held by the individual, a team can thus become more than the sum of the parts, as illustrated by Hollingshead and Brandon's (2003) research: They demonstrated that individuals were better able to activate their own knowledge domain if they knew they were solely responsible for that domain, while others in the team had their own areas of expertise which could be activated by them as needed. Thus, dividing and conquering knowledge domains seems to allow each team member to focus on their own area of expertise.

Wegner (1986) uses the dyadic relation of a couple whereas Wenger has larger CoPs as his level of analysis. But despite this difference there are noteworthy similarities between the theories. Like Wenger, Wegner's TMS theory (1986, 1995) uses the concept 'domain' to describe a Situated, evolving body of knowledge, but in opposition to Wenger (1998), Wegner (1986, 1995) argues that couples build separate, rather than shared knowledge domains. Wegner (1995) found evidence of couples where one party would be offended if the other intruded on their knowledge domain. By each being in charge of their own domain of knowledge, a couple can build on the different Tacit expertise of each person, thereby collectively becoming more adept at solving challenges than if they had shared responsibility for all aspects of the domain.

TMS theory can also be linked to Nonaka and Takeuchi's (1995) notion of 'knowledge redundancy', which emphasises that there must be some overlap between the knowledge domains of employees of they to engage in mutual knowledge creation. It could be argued that knowing who-knows-what, rather than acquiring the knowledge others have, should be the focus for organisations when building virtual knowledge communication processes. Similarly, in working with organisational CoPs, awareness of subdomains within the community may contribute to efficient knowledge creation and communication within the community, precisely because of the differences rather than the similarities in the community.

Conversely, the inability to build on domain differences may prevent people sharing a domain when building a CoP. Knowledge hoarding provides an example of this where the individual perception of the value of personally held knowledge prevents that individual from communicating it with others. Presumably, a network sharing a domain without a practice of communicating (or Reifying) their knowledge domain would still find Identity and meaning in what they do; they would make sense of the network by building an Identity of opposition, rather than a sense of community. Wenger (1998) does include non-participation in a CoP as a form of Identity formation, but this is realised as adjunct to his main theory of Identity as situated in CoPs, whereas in Wegner's TMS theory, the difference between subdomains and the division of labour between them are central to the maintenance and evolution of knowledge.

The importance of different knowledge domains can also be seen in the Strength of Weak ties theory presented in the next section.

The role of weak and strong ties in communicating knowledge

Like TMS theory, but unlike Communities of Practice theory, findings from studies using Social Network Analysis (SNA) seem to contradict the value of a mutual, shared knowledge domain. Shared knowledge domains can be seen as based on so-called strong ties. But counter intuitively, weak ties can sometimes prove to be stronger.

In SNA theory, the strong knowledge relations, similar to the relations within a CoP, are termed 'strong ties'. Granovetter (1973) argues that the knowledge redundancy in a group with strong ties means that to gain novel knowledge, people need to go outside the strong tie network or community, because the weak ties at the edge of or outside the strong tie network have access to different knowledge networks; hence the title of Granovetter's (1973) article, 'The strength of weak ties'. The difference between a 'strong tie' and a 'weak tie' is broadly defined as frequency of communication (Granovetter, 1973), but has been re-defined within specific SNA studies with emphasis on particular types of strong ties. For example, a 'strong knowledge tie' could be one where two parties reciprocally identify the other as someone they communicate knowledge with on a weekly basis and have done so for some time. Granovetter's (1973) findings on the importance of weak ties builds on a study of how people found their current job. Most often information about new job openings came from weak ties.

These findings challenge the importance of strong CoP relations because they suggest that, although you need strong ties to communicate knowledge effectively, the stronger the tie, the less likely it is that the tie will lead to novel knowledge. This can be seen in Hansen's (1999) study of cross-boundary product development in an electronics company where he found that weak ties were most effective in simple projects where they facilitated cross-unit knowledge access. However, Hansen (1999) also found that weak ties tend to slow down the communication of complex knowledge. 'Complex knowledge' would in Nonaka's terminology be knowledge with a lot of Tacit presuppositions.

The different knowledge communication qualities of weak and strong ties have also been examined in a study focussing on the mediating effect of trust on the receipt of 'useful knowledge' (Levin & Cross, 2004). 'Useful knowledge' in the study is defined as the respondent's perception of the usefulness of knowledge received. The study found that strong ties only seem to be more effective in providing useful knowledge, because they are more trusted than weak ties. When controlling for perceived trustworthiness, weak ties were more effective than strong ties in providing useful knowledge (Levin & Cross, 2004), i.e., if the (self-reported) level of trust in a weak tie and a strong tie is the same, the weak tie will be more effective in providing knowledge perceived as 'useful' to the recipient. Like Hansen (1999), Levin and Cross (2004) found that strong ties were more effective at providing complex knowledge, but only if there was a high level of trust in the other party's ability. Two points of interest to this research project emerge from Levin and Cross' study:

1 Trust seems to facilitate more effective communication of knowledge regardless of tie strength.
2 The knowledge perceived as most useful seems to be received from trusted weak ties.

With regard to the first proposition, the same interrelation between trust and knowledge has been found in the review of the literature on virtual teams (see Chapter 5) leading to the conclusion that trust is an antecedent and an outcome of knowledge sharing.

With regards to the second proposition, the ability to build swift trust seems to be highly valuable in the current virtual work environment characterised by participation in multiple teams and projects simultaneously. I now turn to a practice perspective to see how the three Prototypes build the relationships constituting their TMS.

Discussion of relationship theory in the light of Weick's theories of Sensemaking

This section rounds off the theory part of the chapter with a discussion of 'the strength of weak ties', trust theory and TMS theory in the light of Weick's (1995, 2001) Sensemaking theory (see Chapter 2).

Reliance on strong or weak ties to find new knowledge can be seen as a preference depending on the Sensemaking perspective of the knowledge seeker; some people may have a preference, based on their Identity and previous experiences (i.e., their Retention) for seeking knowledge mainly within their network of strong ties, or to be bolder and go beyond the strong ties to seek new knowledge among weaker ties.

These weaker ties could be someone with whom the person seeking new knowledge has had little previous relations, or it could be someone in the wider network of a known strong tie, such as Linda's use of other colleagues' strong tie network, which I'll analyse in the next section. There may also be differences in preference for building strong ties with people who are seen as sharing the professional Identity of the person seeking knowledge, or for building strong ties with people with a different Identity because they may provide a different perspective. Regardless of these preferences, employees may benefit from awareness of the strengths of building on both types of ties. Specifically for virtual work environments, the Sensemaking belief in the value of trusting in weaker ties may influence the effectiveness of virtual teams.

However, trust beliefs can be seen as based on knowledge of the other; without knowledge of another's track record, it can be difficult to know whether to trust those abilities in the future. In the light of Sensemaking theory, trust beliefs and the knowledge on which those beliefs are founded can be seen as an aspect of Retention formed through the Enactment of others. In cross-domain virtual teams there may be a stronger need to focus on communicating knowledge of other team members' competencies in order to build Ability Trust beliefs about other team members. Trust beliefs, seen as part Retention, can then form a basis for deciding how to act in a given context, e.g., whether to attempt to communicate more tacit, complex knowledge or not. This reflects Nandhakumar and Baskerville's (2006) argument that trust can be seen as both antecedent and outcome of knowledge communication.

Communicating knowledge about each other's competencies can, aside from building trust beliefs, also be seen as a way to build a TMS (Transactive Memory System; Wegner, 1986). Particularly if a virtual team has different knowledge domains, it seems important for team members to know the strengths of different perspectives in order to be able to build on these differences as a strength rather than as a hindrance. This can be seen as one of the key characteristics of the 'Knowledge Teams' presented in Chapter 5. As demonstrated by Hollingshead and Brandon (2003), each team member may perform better within their own knowledge domain, if they are aware of which knowledge domains others in the team are responsible for. This was also the case for Linda's Knowledge Broker. A strong TMS can thus be seen as way to make sense of the knowledge strengths of different relations, both within a team and in the wider networks among employees in an organisation.

In the remainder of this chapter, I will turn to the case study analysis of how the three prototypes use professional relationships to ground their perceptions of HR Consult knowledge and as a social booster for their prototypical identities.

Case study: Relationships supporting the knowledge transfer identity

This section analyses how the Knowledge Transfer Prototypes use relationships to support their perception of knowledge and the virtual knowledge communication practices attached to it. The analysis builds on the coding and memoing on the data set, but due to space constraints the fifth and sixth steps of the Discursive Sensemaking Analysis method (see Chapter 4) have been reserved for the Knowledge Creator and the Knowledge Broker Prototype.

The relationships which Dorthe, a Knowledge Transfer Prototype from HR Consult Denmark, constructs as most important to her work at HR Consult are built on more personal, Affect-based connections. When asked for examples of how these relations supported her in her work as a consultant, she gave examples of sharing leads for potential clients, and the fundamental feeling of connecting on a personal level with someone.

The latter seems to represent Affect-based trust, while the former, i.e., exchange of client leads, seems to suggest that it is not the communication of complex, Tacit knowledge which she values in her professional relationships. For Dorthe, the relationships she constructed as the most important to her was a co-located consultant and a member of staff at HR Consult Denmark. When I interviewed Dorthe, this consultant had just left the organisation due to dissatisfaction with the CEO. A few months later, Dorthe left too.

For the UK members of a virtual team of HR Consult employees, half the team seemed to represent some form of the Knowledge Transfer Prototypes, while the others, including the two members interviewed for this study, represented the Knowledge Creator or the Knowledge Broker Prototype. The Knowledge Transfer Prototypes communicated mainly with each other and didn't engage in knowledge communication with the other half of the team.

For Dorthe at HR Consult Denmark, knowledge communication in her global project for training sales staff for duty-free shops in European airports consisted mainly of communication with the project coordinator. Asked directly, Dorthe stated that there was little need to communicate with the other consultants because they were all implementing the same training programme, and any issues in the individual countries should, and were, solved by the project coordinator and her supervisor, the project manager.

An effect of the high focus on transferring explicit knowledge from the R&D department to front line consultants and on top clients seems to be that communication in the internationally dispersed project team occurs mainly between the individual consultant and the project manager, rather than between the consultants who share experience of interaction with the client. This practice means that the TMS, i.e., knowledge of each other's different abilities, is not developed between the consultants on the project. In other words, despite having worked on the same project, the consultants have not really worked together.

The Knowledge Transfer Prototype represents a strong contrast to the Knowledge Creator analysed in the next section.

Case study: CoPs dividing a virtual team at HR Consult UK

In Chapter 7, I looked at how Linda saw herself as unique in HR Consult UK. But despite this self-image, she is not alone with her client-centred professional Identity in the Client Relations Management Team (the virtual team under which HR Consult has organised her). But the difference in prototypical identities seems to emerge as a division within the virtual team of HR Consult consultants she participates in. In the quote below, Linda's Discursive Sensemaking centres on the division in the team between those adopting her client-centred Knowledge Broker approach and those who seem to be more Knowledge Transfer Prototypes. Linda signals the opposition between the two CoPs within the team through her construction of how much she knows about what the others are doing, which can be seen as a description of the strength of her personalised TMS, i.e., knowledge of who-knows-what in the team. Linda's case demonstrates both the power of strong relationships and the potential danger when opposing identities result in divisions within virtual teams who do not acknowledge the value of other approaches to the job.

The division she constructs is realised at the linguistic level through a number of prosodic cues. She starts the passage with 'well' which signals that she does not have an answer ready at hand, and it may function as a discourse marker signalling that a reflection is coming. This interpretation is underlined by her interruption of herself with the subclause, 'the thing is' (l. 2), suggesting that she considers her answer to be problematic. The emphasis on 'everyone' (l. 2) constructs a listener expectation of an answer which opposes the interviewer's call for information about her relations with the whole team. She then shifts the topic of her answer from the indefinite 'everyone' to the definite 'Ed' and 'John'. By naming them she also attaches more Significance to these two than to the indefinite 'everyone' in the rest of the team. L

Linda:

Well I know--
--\the thing is I don't know what *everyone* is--
--^I know what /*Ed* and ^*John* are doing (.)

(Linda, my translation, 361, 53:05)

To sum up on the analysis of this quote, Linda explicitly constructs a division in the Client Relations Management Team. The division seems to emerge as a lack of mutual knowledge about the practices of other team members. This division can be analysed as emerging in a strong TMS, i.e., mutual knowledge about each other's different abilities and knowledge, between the members with which Linda identifies and a weak TMS with regard to members she does not identify with.

As an argument for her closer relation with Ed and John, Linda explicitly points to their shared professional Identity in the quote below. Based on her elaborate description of her approach to the knowledge transformation of HR Consult's products and new knowledge production to tailor the products to an online platform, I asked her whether it was their approach to 'being creative with the products which they shared' (Linda, my translation, 363, 0:57;40). After answering this question affirmatively, she elaborates on the differences between the two communities within the team. In her answer, quoted below, the first-person plural pronoun 'we' (l. 1) is an Anaphoric Reference to herself and the three others in the team whom she named as the ones sharing her approach. At the Discursive Sensemaking level, she identifies their time-consuming knowledge communication approach as centred on spending most of their time on one client, even though all the consultants in the team have a portfolio of other clients to maintain. Her Discursive Sensemaking about the team demonstrates that even though the team members have the same job title and job description, their approach to the tasks differ, strongly signalled by her juxtaposition of 'we' (l. 1), and 'the others' (l. 8). She also seems to point to this different approach as a source of identification between members of her in-group: 'We have [...] a better understanding of what we're doing' (l. 1–2).

This interpretation is supported at the linguistic level. 'So' (l. 1) functions as a discourse marker signalling not only a conclusion, but a Discursive Sensemaking interpretation and justification for her choice of strong ties in the virtual team. In terms of prosody, she emphasises 'understanding' (l. 1) thereby rendering this as Significant and implying that there is little understanding across the division in the team. The emphasis on 'one' (l. 4) implies that the others have more than one client, thereby rendering the opposition in the team Significant again. To underline the effect of these grammatical and prosodic cues to render the opposition Significant, she finishes the quote by repeating that the others do it 'in a different way' (l. 16), the second time amplified by the adverbial 'completely', which is spoken with emphasis (l. 17).

Linda:

1 ^/So we have kind of a better *understand\ding,*
2 \of what we're doing—we've told (.)
3 erm—*quite* a lot.
4 /and we all have kind of (.) *one* \client which we like (.)
5 _erm
6 \maintain
7 /and who is our \our big project. (.)
8 ^\The others e:rm have--
9 /a wider base of clients and and run smaller stuff—or--erm--
10 --/but faster.
11 _And--and
12 /they actually charge,
13 /if not as \much money as we do
14 \and sometimes even more than we _do--
15 --/They do it in a different way.—
16 --^*completely* different way.

(Linda, my translation, 363, 53:15)

To conclude on the analysis of the quote above, Linda explicitly constructs a divide in Practices of the team members, but at the same time shows that she is not alone in her approach to client-centred knowledge transformation. The sense of mutual knowledge and identification between members seems to emerge as CoPs which divide the team despite the team's shared knowledge domain as HR Consult employees with identical job titles. This shows the complex interplay of personal and social identities, because the identities of the community members are not a characteristic of the CoP, as argued by Wenger (1998), rather it is as much the professional identities of the individuals in the Client Relations Management Team which define the CoP. The quote above also highlights the different prototypical solutions to the multi-project problem of a lack of identification in virtual teams (Daim et al., 2012; Suchan & Hayzak, 2001). Linda and the ones she identifies with in the HR Consult Virtual Team solve this by doing a bare minimum for the majority of their projects, and focus most of their energy on a single, high-profile client at a time. While this approach may not be in the best interest of HR Consult, it shows how employee mental models adapt to the demands of a multi-project virtual work environment.

In the quote below, Linda constructs this difference in practices and identities as having been an explicit topic within the team. Central to her Discursive Sensemaking in this quote is the focus on the 'need' (l. 1) for a social basis for her Identity among 'sparring partners who are a bit similar to ourselves' (l. 1–2). She uses this identification with some of the team members as her justification for not knowing much about the other team members, 'therefore I know less about what the others are doing', (l. 5–6). In terms of grammar, she renders the division Significant by using the discourse marker 'so' to signal that a conclusion or sensemaking interpretation is coming. In terms of prosody, this conclusion is given further emphasis by the high key onset on 'So':

Linda:

/We all need \to have some (.) sparring partners
/who are a bit similar \to ourselves.
^So there's clearly a e:rm (.)
division in--in the team at that level— ¨
[fast pace]--/and therefore I know less \about
[slow pace] \what the others are doing

(Linda, my translation, 363, 53:23)

To conclude on the analysis of the quote above, Linda constructs an image of a shared professional Identity within each of the two smaller CoPs of 'sparring partners' (l. 1). Through her identification of the three other team members as sharing her client-centred knowledge communication practice, she also constructs Ability Trust towards them.

This Ability Trust is also signalled elsewhere in the interview where Linda identifies the same three employees as the ones she goes to if she needs a different perspective on a presentation or workshop she is working on, and with whom she shares her successes and failures. This Ability Trust seems to be based on shared values underlying that Identity as important for their incentive to share knowledge with each other. She states that those three are the ones who share her approach to the work, and that they are the ones she calls first, 'If there are any issues', while she attaches the predicate 'more old school sales people' to the others.

The quote below can be analysed as an example of her sense of identification with a colleague, Ed from the Client Relations Management Team. Linda's inclusion of him on her high-profile team can be described as a trust behaviour. She constructs trust in his abilities and Integrity. This trust seems to be founded on her knowledge of his track record in the HR Consult Virtual Team (the Client Relations Management Team). She trusts his ability enough to have him as part of her team. Linguistically, the adverbial 'even' (l. 1) has the effect of constructing the sentence as more than just information about Ed being on the team, but rather presenting this fact as being out of the ordinary. In other words, it constructs her taking him on-board the Virtual Team for the Soft Tech project as an unusual action, justified by the trust she places in him:

Linda:

1 Ed, I even use on (.) \on my project.
2 Erm (,) so he is one of my coaches.

(Linda, my translation 363, 54:50).

To conclude on the analysis of the quote above, Linda not only seems to share the knowledge transformation aspect of her Identity with three of the members of the HR Consult consultant team, but she also trusts one of them, Ed, as a relationship characterised by Ability and Integrity trust enough to include him on the Soft Tech project. Thereby she exhibits one of the key characteristics which I identified as an aspect of the Knowledge Broker Prototype in Chapter 5: that the Situated knowledge creations for clients are not done through interactions only with the client, but also with colleagues.

Although Linda states that the two CoPs in the Client Relations Management virtual team respect each other, the quote below shows that Linda experiences no sense of a shared understanding. From the linguistic perspective the distance between the two CoPs within the team is highlighted in the quote below through the opposition between the third person plural pronoun, 'they', and the first-person singular pronoun, 'I', (l. 1 and 2). By using high key onset when enunciating the pronouns, she puts emphasis on this sense of opposition.

Linda:

1 \^They don't really get what *I'm* doing,
2 and ^*I* don't really get what they're doing, (.)\and that's just fine.

(Linda, my translation, 254, 0:35:55)

Therefore, the analysis of the quote above shows how Linda explicitly constructs an opposition between the two CoPs in the HR Consult Virtual Team of consultants by centring on a lack of understanding for what the others are doing. This can be described as a typical example of in-group/out-group construction.

Linda's sense of ownership over her project does not mean that she does not value relationships within the team she has put together for the Soft Tech project. On the contrary as the analyses in the following section will show, the high level of trust in the Soft Tech virtual project team and the shared Identity as Knowledge Brokers allows the team, first, to build on the strengths of the different knowledge domains in the team; and second, to build on competencies in the wider networks of each member through referred trust. Referred trust can be seen as the ability of each member to place their trust in colleagues outside their network, simply because they are members of another trusted team member's network. For this to work and for trust to be maintained in the team, a prerequisite seems to be that the trust so invested is not violated. But for Linda's Virtual

Team for the Soft Tech project this does not seem to be the case. These two key abilities of Linda's Soft Tech project team, and therefore of each virtual team member, are what I characterise as the core of the Knowledge Broker Prototype: first, the ability to utilise a strong TMS in the virtual team to allow complex knowledge creation occurs mainly where the specific expertise is located in the virtual team and using ICT (Information and Communication Technology) to Combine and coordinate the more explicit outcomes of this knowledge creation. Second, the ability to use Trusted Weak Ties and referred trust to find the necessary abilities and knowledge not possessed by the team members.

Even though the Knowledge Creator Prototype and the Knowledge Broker Prototype share the focus on transforming and situating knowledge within its context of application, the Knowledge Broker Prototype differs by relying on the skills and abilities of others to complete their own projects. Thereby the Knowledge Broker Prototype exhibits a strong Transactive Memory System, i.e., strong networking skills. The Knowledge Broker Prototypes can thus be seen as strong networkers, who to a large extent utilise their network to complete their tasks and projects. That this network is maintained and supported by ICT does not seem to be problematic to the Knowledge Broker Prototype. The Knowledge Broker Prototype can thus be seen as a mental model highly adapted to virtual work in global organisations. The flip side of the coin is that they don't take orders from above too seriously; their strongly held opinion about how to achieve client satisfaction outrank management attempts to cut man-hour expenses on each project.

The following section analyses how Linda's statements about how she put together the Knowledge Broker for the Soft Tech project can be seen as exemplifying the core characteristics of a Knowledge Broker (see Chapter 5). It seems she utilises her network of trusted weak ties to find the necessary competencies and abilities for transforming HR Consult's knowledge to an online platform to communicate and situate the knowledge within Soft Tech's contexts and challenges. But her building this Knowledge Broker, also shows the importance of identification based on similar perceptions of organisational knowledge as a process of knowledge creation.

The excerpt quoted below shows Linda's Discursive Sensemaking about her approach to building the Knowledge Broker to solve the challenge of building an online learning solution for Soft Tech. It was a requirement from Soft Tech that the solution was designed for an online platform in which the employees from Soft Tech's global organisation could engage in interpersonal interaction despite being geographically dispersed. As part of her Discursive Sensemaking, Linda constructs the team she was looking for as risk-takers willing to 'dare' get involved in her project (l. 13). By attaching significance to risk-taking, she simultaneously constructs herself as a risk-taker willing to dare 'something new' (l. 4). By implication, her construction of her and her team as daring, constructs the colleagues who were unwilling to participate as the opposite, thereby signalling a lack of identification with those employees. Despite difficulties getting a team together (signalled by the 'many', 1.6, consultants unwilling to participate), she argues for an imperative need to find the right people ('I simply had to', l. 12), spoken with emphasis after breaking off a sentence (in l. 11) which didn't show the potential to convey the imperative she needed to communicate. It is also noteworthy that she insists on this need to find the right people despite the middle managers' efforts to dissuade her ('they have really tried to run it more locally', l. 1), even if it means finding the right people outside the organisation.

From a linguistic perspective, the 'had to' (l. 12) is a modal construction signalling a strong obligation, so-called 'deontic modality'. But the use of the modal verb hides the grammatical agent (i.e., source) of this obligation. However, there seems to be no other agent than herself and her strong value system obliging her to undertake the time-consuming project. Furthermore, the emphasis she adds to 'had' (l. 12) suggests that she is finding it difficult to find a reason and simply emphasises obligation in place of the arguments she failed to deliver in the two sentence fragments of l. 2 and l. 3). This again underlines her professional Identity as highly autonomous and as feeling a strong need to fulfil client needs despite the work effort and despite the challenges of finding the right competencies at HR Consult UK. However, the obligation she expresses also underlines her determination to utilise her network to find the competencies she requires for the project.

This Sensemaking interpretation is supported by the linguistic details of the quote: In terms of prosody the high key onset (l. 4) puts emphasis on 'something new', which in the following line is identified as being the requirement for delivering the project virtually (l. 5). In the quote, 'they' (l. 1) functions as an Anaphoric Reference to Linda's middle managers at HR Consult UK:

Linda:

1 ^/They have really tried \to run it more locally,
2 \but (.) /well, I simply couldn't find the resources for, --
3 _/which I thought \were, (..)
4 ^\well, I was into something new, /you know? (.)
5 \delivering [HR development consulting] virtually.
6 \And the project didn't suit many of the [consultants] we've got,
7 _\the virtual didn't suit them.
8 \They weren't used to it, a:nd
9 ^\'ooh that's a lot /of work' [..]
10 \and I couldn't get them on-board the project. (.)
11 /So that's why I \simply was (.)
12 /I simply had to use the ones \who can do it.
13 _\And, well, dare and that sort of thing.

(Linda, my translation, 189, 25:21)

To conclude on the quote above, Linda describes her project as new and innovative, and, by describing the other consultants as seeing the project as time consuming, she builds an image of herself and her team members as daring, and willing to put in the effort to transform HR Consult knowledge to an online platform. By contrasting her global virtual team with the more local colleagues (l. 1) she also implies that her team is more effective. In short, Linda glorifies her virtual knowledge team and her own position as a strong networker and Knowledge Broker.

In the next quote Linda elaborates more on just how dispersed her Soft Tech project team is, and how she used her network to build a Knowledge team based on a shared Identity as Knowledge Broker Prototypes, an enthusiasm for their Joint Enterprise (Wenger, 1998), and an ability to build on referred trust to expand the capabilities of the team through the Transactive Memory System of each team member. In terms of Discursive Sensemaking, Linda constructs herself as a strong networker in the quote below, but she is also showing passion and excitement about the breadth of the team. Prosodic cues add to the impression of her excitement about the network. These cues include slightly higher key and faster pace in this passage than typical for rest of the interview, combined with the two high key emphasised words.

Linda:

/and so it's \simply been. for ^me _y'know
/because I'm pretty strong \as networker, \well e:rm
_/where I've brought in ^\different people--a:nd
/if it worked,
[..]
/Well if it worked \and they had an erm
/enthusiasm \for what I /was doing,
\well then we moved on with /them.
/then when ^they knew someone,
\well, we pulled them in.--
--\And it didn't matter as much,
/if it was people who worked /fo:r HR Consu:lt
/or they were someone \out in our /wider netwo:rk.
\That didn't--
--We've simply ended up with a team who--,
--\in spite of this being an English project,
/my main consultant
\she's from ^Canada and £that£ (hh) is simply because
/she happened to be in \England at the time where I started.

Linda 153 (18:30)

At no point in the interview does she problematise the geographical distance, the time difference, or the mediation of technology in the team communication. What matters seems to be the shared Identity and the enthusiasm for the Mutual Engagement and Joint Enterprise of the team (Wenger, 1998). It should be noted, however, that there are fewer intercultural challenges than if it had included Indian or Asian members on the team.

By using vocabulary from Wenger's (1998) theories of Communities of Practice, I suggest that Knowledge Broker Prototypes in Linda's team exhibit characteristics of a voluntary Community of Practice, which serves as a source of shared Identity and meaning for the team members. Simultaneously, they are able to perform as an organisational team with a pre-set goal and a time frame for the completion of that goal.

In terms of relationship theory, Linda's team shows the effectiveness of trusted weak ties and referred trust. The Canadian consultant, whom Linda names elsewhere in the interview and whom I call 'Susan', was referred to Linda by someone in HR Consult headquarters as a substitute. The reference seems to have built swift trust for Linda. But although they started as trusted weak ties, their interactions on the project have evolved the relation into a strong tie, and the collaboration has fostered their mutual trust in each other's Ability, Integrity and Benevolence. As mentioned in this chapter, Ability Trust can be seen as being a form of Cognition-Based Trust (McAllister, 1995), but Linda also describes the people she brings on-board as having an 'enthusiasm', which might best be described as a sign of Affect-based trust. This trust was built through a few face-to-face interactions in the UK, but mainly through their frequent communication through Skype. Linda stated that Skype was used not because of the visual cues, but because of the low cost of the calls.

Due to her trust in Susan's abilities and passion, Linda seems to have no problem building on Susan's network to find the necessary competencies for the team. In the following quote she shows this by describing how Susan brought more people on to the project. Considering the sense of ownership Linda exhibited over the project in one of the quotes analysed earlier, Linda's inclusion of Susan in core decisions such as team memberships seems to exhibit a considerable level of reciprocal trust between them. As Discursive Sensemaking, Linda's description of the growth of the team seems to show pride in the efficiency of her global virtual team. But although she emphasises the network ('people know someone who know someone', l. 6), she also emphasises that they work well together. Partly, it seems that their ability for collaboration and Mutual Engagement is based on their selection of people they already had a good working relationship with, and second their selection of people with whom they shared a professional Identity as risk-takers and knowledge brokers. From the linguistic perspective, Linda's prosody underlines the breadth of the network by enunciating 'Canada' (l. 2) and 'Australia' (l. 3) in high key. By drawing out the vowel sounds of the two place names, Linda seems to suggest that these are just two examples. In fact, these two are the main members of the team, although they also have a so-called 'technical host' based in Austin, TX, who designs all the technical aspects of the project work. For example, this technical host has helped them build so-called 'break-out rooms' where a smaller subset of the course participants can discuss a topic or exercise online without the interference from the rest of the group.

Linda:

/And then she \has brought in more people. (.)
/And that's both people from
^Canada: _a:nd /I have one from ^Australia:
/and stuff like that, /y'know?
\who work on an English project--^Simply (.)
[faster pace]\because people know someone who knows someone.
\And work well together.

(Linda, my translation, 153, 19:10)

To conclude on the analysis of the quote above, Linda has been able to build her team using weak trusted ties in the form of colleagues recommending other colleagues with the particular set of skills required for the Soft Tech project, but who also exhibited an ability to work together.

But although the team seems to be built from weak trusted ties, the Mutual Engagement and Joint Enterprise (Wenger, 1998) of the team has evolved their relationships into strong ties. This can be seen specifically in the contrast Linda constructs between her immediate managers, on the one hand, and Susan on the other hand. This occurred immediately after Linda had stated that her managers aren't able to challenge her. In contrast to the inability of her managers to understand what she was doing, Linda stated that Susan was able to challenge her on 'what does the client want to tell us, and what is it we are going to do' (Linda, my translation, 279, 38:35). In other words, Linda attaches Significance to the shared professional Identity of fulfilling client needs, and the Mutual Engagement which she and Susan commit themselves to as part of their Joint Enterprise for Soft Tech.

Commenting on the Australian member of the team, who was an 'old friend' of Susan's (Linda, my translation, 189, 24:43), Linda elaborates on her use of her dispersed network of weak ties. In terms of Discursive Sensemaking Linda constructs HR Consult in opposition to the previous organisation she worked in by centring on the notion of a network approach at HR Consult. The previous organisation, one of the leading European suppliers of telecommunication services, is named by Linda in the interview. I have given it the pseudonym European Phone. Thereby Linda again attaches significance to her network as a value. By contrasting her work at HR Consult with her work for European Phone where her network did not play an important role and where employee autonomy was low, Linda suggests that her network approach is an aspect of a

Conversation, or organisational culture, at HR Consult. But as neither the UK managers I interviewed, nor 'John', the other UK consultant I've interviewed, emphasise network as an important aspect of work culture at HR Consult UK, the emphasis on the network seems to be Linda's Discursive Sensemaking interpretation. This interpretation is supported by her construction of her immediate middle managers as trying limit her extensive use of her network in the quote analysed earlier: 'They [i.e. Linda's immediate middle managers] have really tried to run it more locally' (Linda, my translation, 189, 25:21).

From the linguistic perspective, prosodic details, such as several phrases with high key onset (l. 2, l.5 l. 7, l. 9 and l. 15) and a generally higher pitch range (level of tonal variation within each intonation unit), signal enthusiasm, but also construct the network approach Linda has adopted as unusual. Her enthusiasm also seems to be the cause of her stuttering pronunciation of the word 'in' (l. 8), after which she quickly interrupts the prepositional phrase (signalled by the prepositional head 'in', l. 8) and starts a new phrase:

Linda:

1 Yes.
2 ^Very \old (.) old,
3 Yes (.) ^old \friends. (.)
4 ^So ^that's \kind of what I mean about those networks. (.)
5 (faster pace)_I mean /I've never had it ^that \networked before.
6 (normal pace]_I mean \where you actually, (.) erm,
7 [faster pace] /there is ^no \reason why [name of Australian team member]
8 should be--in--in--in--
9 ^/she doesn't work \for [HR Consult]. Erm
10 [normal pace] _/she definitely \has a good understanding of [HR Consult product line]
11 and--and \she's accredited
12 \but it definitely wouldn't have happened at [European Phone]
13 \that you had gone so far out.
14 You know erm erm.
15 ^But you do here.

(Linda, my translation, 189, 24:43).

As a final comment on Linda's use of relationships for the Soft Tech project, she seems aware of her own network value, even arguing that her network extends to the highest management levels of the organisation. Linda constructs the founder of the organisation as a very close relation and stated at one point in the interview that her relationship with him goes deeper than the work relation, thereby building on Affect-based trust. So, although she attaches significant intrinsic value and sense of shared

Identity to her relationship constructions in the quotes above, she does not have a naïve notion of the relations she has built within her team as purely based on Shared Identity and Mutual Engagement. To paraphrase Linda's argument, she sees the others as having their own agendas, including using Linda to get a closer relation with the top of the UK headquarters, and becoming part of the potential future work which they, too, see for the Soft Tech project. To Linda it seems to be fine that they may have these ulterior motives. As mentioned previously she herself uses the close relations within the Client Relations Management Team to fulfil her needs in her project.

To conclude on how relationships are used to support the Knowledge Broker Prototype, Linda uses both the dispersed relations in a subset of the Client Relations Management Team, and a much wider network transcending both geographical and organisational boundaries to find colleagues sharing her focus on creating Situated Learning solutions. But unlike the Knowledge Creator Prototype, Linda engages other members of these CoPs directly in her project thereby building a Knowledge Broker team characterised by the ability to use their dispersed network to find the necessary abilities or knowledge domains. Furthermore, they are able to use the trust and TMS within the team to build on the diversity of knowledge domains in the team similar to the Knowledge Teams, which I argued for in Chapter 5.

References

Abrams, L. C., Cross, R., Lesser, E., & Levin, D. Z. (2003). Nurturing interpersonal trust in knowledge-sharing networks. *The Academy of Management Executive (1993–2005), 17*(4), 64–77. doi: 10.5465/ame.2003.11851845

Baskerville, R., & Nandhakumar, J. (2007). Activating and perpetuating virtual teams: Now that we're mobile, where do we go? *IEEE Transactions on Professional Communication, 50*(1), 17–34. doi: 10.1109/TPC.2006.890849

Chowdhury, S. (2005). The role of affect- and cognition-based trust in complex knowledge sharing. *Journal of Managerial Issues, 17*(3), 310–326. http://www.jstor.org/stable/40604504

Costa, A. (2003), Work team trust and effectiveness, *Personnel Review, 32*(5), 605–622. doi: 10.1108/00483480310488360

Daim, T. U., Ha, A., Reutiman, S., Hughes, B., Pathak, U., Bynum, W., & Bhatla, A. (2012). Exploring the communication breakdown in global virtual teams. *International Journal of Project Management, 30*(2), 199–212. doi: 10.1016/j.ijproman.2011.06.004

De Jong, B. A., & Elfring, T. (2010). How does trust affect the performance of ongoing teams? The mediating role of reflexivity, monitoring, and effort. *Academy of Management Journal, 53*(3), 535–549. doi: 10.5465/amj.2010.51468649

Dirks, K. T. (1999). The effects of interpersonal trust on work group performance. *Journal of Applied Psychology, 84*(3), 445.

Fage-Butler, A. M. (2011). *Towards a new kind of patient information leaflet?: Risk, trust and the new value of patient-centred communication*. Aarhus: Aarhus University.

Granovetter, M. (1973). The strength of weak ties. *American Journal of Sociology, 78*(6), 1360–1380.

Hansen M. T. (1999). The search-transfer problem: The role of weak ties in sharing knowledge across organization subunits. *Administrative Science Quarterly 44*(1):82–111. doi: 10.2307/2667032

Hollingshead, A. B., & Brandon, D. P. (2003). Potential benefits of communication in transactive memory systems. *Human Communication Research, 29(*4), 607–615. doi: 10.1111/j.1468–2958.2003.tb00859

Jarvenpaa, S. L., & Leidner, D. E. (1999). Communication and trust in global virtual teams. *Organization Science, 10*(6), 791–815. doi: 10.1287/orsc.10.6.791

Kanawattanachai, P., & Yoo, Y. (2002). Dynamic nature of trust in virtual teams. *Journal of Strategic Information Systems, 11*(3–4), 187–213. doi: 10.1016/S0963-8687(02)00019-7

Lave, J., & Wenger, E. (1991). *Situated learning: Legitimate peripheral participation.* Cambridge: Cambridge University Press.

Levin, D. Z., & Cross, R. (2004). The strength of weak ties you can trust: The mediating role of trust in effective knowledge transfer. *Management Science, 50*(11), 1477–1490. doi: 10.1287/mnsc.1030.0136

Mayer, R. C., Davis, J. H., & Schoorman, F. D. (1995). An integrative model of organizational trust. *Academy of Management Review, 20*(3), 709–734. doi: 10.5465/amr.1995.9508080335

McAllister, D. J. (1995). Affect-based and cognition-based trust as foundations for interpersonal cooperation in organizations. *Academy of Management Journal, 38*(1), 24–59. doi: 10.5465/256727

McAllister, D. J. (1997). The second face of trust: Reflections on the dark side of interpersonal trust in organizations. *Research on Negotiation in Organizations, 6*, 87–111. https://web2-bschool.nus.edu.sg/wp-content/uploads/media_rp/publications/Rr27C1423033661.pdf

McKnight D. H., Cummings, L. L., & Chervany, N. L. (1998). Initial trust formation in new organizational relationships. *Academy of Management Review, 23*(3), 473–490. doi: 10.5465/amr.1998.926622

Meyerson, D., Weick, K. E., & Kramer, R. M. (1996). Swift trust and temporary groups. *Trust in Organizations: Frontiers of Theory and Research, 166*, 195.

Nandhakumar, J., & Baskerville, R. (2006). Durability of online teamworking: Patterns of trust. *Information Technology and People, 19*(4), 371–389. ISSN: 0959–3845

Nonaka, I., & Takeuchi, H. (1995). *Knowledge-creating company: How Japanese companies create the dynamics of innovation.* Oxford: Oxford University.

Nonaka, I., & Toyama, R. (2005). The theory of the knowledge-creating firm: Subjectivity, objectivity and synthesis. *Industrial and Corporate Change, 14*(3), 419–436. doi: 10.1093/icc/dth058

Nonaka, I., & von Krogh, G. (2009). Tacit knowledge and knowledge conversion: Controversy and advancement in organizational knowledge creation theory. *Organization Science, 20*(3), 635–652. doi: 10.1287/orsc.1080.0412

Nooteboom, B. (2011). *Trust - Forms, foundations, functions, failures, figures.* Cheltenham: Edward Elgar.

Palanski, M. E., Kahai, S. S., & Yammarino, F. J. (2011). Team virtues and performance: An examination of transparency, behavioral integrity, and trust.

Journal of Business Ethics, 99(2), 201–216. https://link.springer.com/content/pdf/10.1007/s10551-010-0650-7.pdf
Rispens, S., Greer, L. L., & Jehn, K. A. (2007). It could be worse. *International Journal of Conflict Management, 18*(4) 325–344. doi: 10.1108/10444060710833450
Robert Jr, L., Denis, A., & Hung, Y. T. (2009). Individual swift trust and knowledge-based trust in face-to-face and virtual team members. *Journal of Management Information Systems, 26*(2), 241–279. doi: 10.2753/MIS0742-1222260210
Spreitzer, G. M., & Mishra, A. K. (1999). Giving up control without losing control: Trust and its substitutes' effects on managers' involving employees in decision making. *Group & Organization Management, 24*(2), 155–187. doi: 10.1177%2F1059601199242003
Staples, D. S., & Webster, J. (2008). Exploring the effects of trust, task interdependence and virtualness on knowledge sharing in teams. *Information Systems Journal, 18*(6), 617–640. doi: 10.1111/j.1365-2575.2007.00244.x
Suchan, J., & Hayzak, G. (2001). The communication characteristics of virtual teams: A case study. *IEEE Transactions on Professional Communication, 44*(3), 174–186. doi: 10.1109/47.946463
Wegner, D. M. (1986). Transactive memory systems. In B. Mullen & G. R. Goethal (Eds.), *Theories of group behavior* (pp. 185–208). New York: Springer-Verlag.
Wegner, D. M. (1995). A computer network model of human transactive memory. *Social Cognition, 13*(3), 319–339.
Weick, K. E. (1995). *Sensemaking in organizations.* London: Sage.
Weick, K. E. (2001). *Making sense of the organization.* Oxford: Blackwell.
Wenger, E. (1998). *Communities of practice: Learning, meaning, and Identity.* New York: Cambridge University Press.
Wenger, E., McDermott, R., & Snyder, W. M. (2002). *Cultivating communities of practice: A guide to managing knowledge.* Boston, MA: Harvard Business School Press.
Zolin, R., Hinds, P. J., Fruchter, R., & Levitt, R. E. (2004). Interpersonal trust in cross-functional, geographically distributed work: A longitudinal study. *Information and Organization*, 14(1), 1–26. doi: 10.1016/j.infoandorg.2003.09.002

10 Conclusion and discussion of theory and findings

Chapter Contents

> The main argument in this book has been that Virtual Knowledge Communication in global organisations is affected by three interrelated aspects: perceptions of knowledge, identity and relationships. Understanding these three aspects of how employees build virtual knowledge communication practises, increases the ability organisation to build effective virtual teams because we can address the strengths and weaknesses of each of the prototype, while solving any interpersonal issues before they escalate.

This chapter discusses and integrates the multidisciplinary literature review presented in Part 2 of the book. I'll start the chapter with a summary of the theoretical framework of the book. Then I devote three sections to a discussion of what each of the knowledge communication aspects (perception of knowledge, Identity and relationships mean for virtual knowledge communication in a global organisation, HR Consult.

DOI: 10.4324/9781003015925-12

The chapter is rounded off with suggestions for implications of the study, and suggestions for future research directions.

Sensemaking theory as theoretical framework

The book has adopted Weick's (1995, 2001, see Chapter 2) theories of Sensemaking as a framework for integrating the theories on the virtual work environment, and the three aspects impacting on knowledge communication in global organisations: perception of knowledge, identity and relationships.

The book proposes Discursive Sensemaking Analysis (DSA) as a method to combine this Sensemaking perspective with a Discourse Analysis method to analyse interviews and interview participants' creation of meaning, i.e., 'Sensemaking', in interview statements and (d)iscourse within the specific context of a research interview. The book collectively describes the analytical tools used to analyse this (d)iscourse as Discursive Sensemaking Analysis or DSA.

Combining Weick's (1995, 2001) Sensemaking perspective and Van Dijk's (2005) similar socio-cognitive perspective in a Discursive Sensemaking framework encompassing and diffusing the theoretical perspectives on knowledge, identity and relationships has implications for how those theories are used in the analytical apparatus of the book. This will be explored in the following.

The book proses that in telling stories about their practices, interviewees engage in a form of Retrospective Sensemaking (Weick, 1995, 2001) through which identities of self and other are constructed and aligned with the content and morale of the story. In this sense, participant stories reflect cognitive processes as well as social identity constructions. These identity constructions are considered to be similar though not identical to the identities they perform in other professional contexts. This assumption can be seen as grounded in Weick's argument about how identity impacts on how we make sense of the situations and contexts in which we are embedded. Weick argues that we have a deep-seated human need to maintain a coherent identity across different social contexts, and that this need for a coherent identity impacts on how we perform the different social roles which are called for by different social contexts; we don't act and speak the same way when we are with our children, our colleagues, our parents or our spouses, but this does not mean that we do not have a coherent and deep-seated sense of self across these contexts, or that a researcher examining how twenty people perform each of these roles will not be able to find (d)iscursive and behavioural patterns which characterise each person across these social contexts.

To sum up, the book considers identity to be simultaneously 'essentialist' and 'socially constructed'. Identity should be seen from an 'essentialist' perspective in the sense that most people experience having an identity which is part of their sense of self; they use this identity as a lens for making sense of their experience of the social contexts in which they are embedded, and retrospectively rationalise their own behaviours to fit this self-image. Simultaneously, identity should be seen as socially constructed in the sense that we always try to adapt our (d)iscourse and our behaviours to the social contexts we are embedded in. I do not see these two perspectives as mutually exclusive, but rather as co-dependent and co-constitutive.

Perceptions of knowledge

Chapters 6 and 7 on perceptions of knowledge refrained from employing the definition of knowledge which is often adopted in knowledge management literature. This definition builds on versions of the knowledge definition from antiquity, defining knowledge as 'justified true belief' (e.g., Nonaka & Takeuchi, 1995, p. 58). Instead, Van Dijk's (2005) definition was adopted, because knowledge from his perspective is not justified as 'true', but is believed to be true by a specific '(epistemic) community' at a specific point in time:

> [Knowledge is] shared beliefs satisfying the specific (epistemic) criteria of an (epistemic) community. … Each community, or historical moment of a community, has its own criteria that allow members to establish that some beliefs are treated and shared as knowledge, whereas others are not.
>
> (Van Dijk, 2005, p. 73)

I adopted Van Dijk's definition of knowledge, because it shares Weick's insight that human beings do not perceive the world as it is, only through the filter of our simultaneously individual and social identities, and our past experiences. This definition also implies that knowledge is only communicated within an (epistemic) community if that community considers the knowledge to be both true in the light of the epistemic criteria of the community, and if the knowledge is perceived as useful within the practices of the community.

This theorisation of knowledge as depending on the Sensemaking of specific (epistemic) communities should not be seen as categorical or as necessarily inhibiting communication of knowledge between different (epistemic) communities. But employees and organisations may not necessarily be aware of these communities; in the case of HR Consult there was a tendency in the global organisation to assume that employees in the R&D are necessarily the Knowledge Creators, while sales staff and consultants necessarily live up to management expectations to deliver knowledge products as they are without changing or transforming products to client contexts. This may not present a problem in an organisation selling a tangible product, such as tractors, but in the service sector, products may be intangible knowledge, and the notion of situated knowledge may lead sales staff and consultants to adapt and transform knowledge products to address client challenges.

When employees make sense of their virtual work environment, no single approach can be seen as 'correct'. From a Sensemaking perspective, employees can have different perceptions of which aspects of organisational knowledge they perceive as useful. Thus, the perception of knowledge can be seen as grounded in the particular Sensemaking perspective of the employee. In the terminology of Van Dijk (2005) this can be seen as a 'Mental Model' which is used as a basis for deciding how, why and with whom to engage in knowledge communication practices. Because the perception of knowledge can be seen as a value-set underlying the practices an employee engages in, these knowledge perceptions can be seen as the basis for professional identity formations.

Like technologies, knowledge is perceived as useful or not by a given community at a given point in time. Perceptions of knowledge can also be seen as dependent on the Sensemaking of the individual and the groups the individual identifies with, i.e., the 'epistemic community'. This perception of knowledge as perspectives can be seen as an extension of Nonaka and Takeuchi's (1995) SECI model. Within the same knowledge domain, knowers and the epistemic communities in which they are embedded, can be seen as having preferences for different aspects of knowledge and for different knowledge conversion processes; for example, some employees may have a preference for knowledge with a higher emphasis of the explicit over the tacit, while others find meaning in creating and communicating knowledge with a high level of tacit presuppositions. This can be seen as an aspect of the professional identity of an individual and may lead to knowledge communication practices reflecting such a professional identity, as we see clearly in the cases of Henrik (Knowledge Creator) and Linda (Knowledge Broker). On the other hand, Dorte (Knowledge Transfer Prototype) emphasises compliance with the existing, highly explicit knowledge when communicating with colleagues. She emphasises the Internalisation and Externalisation steps of Nonaka and Takeuchi's (1995) SECI model (Chapter 6).

Linda, with her preference for perceiving knowledge as a process (demonstrated through a preference for Socialisation and Combination steps of Nonaka and Takeuchi's, 1995, SECI model), might find a higher level of perceived usefulness when knowledge is transformed, adapted and thereby 'situated' to use Lave and Wenger's (p. 191) term within a specific context and purpose of application.

If organisations are aware that knowledge creation may occur at all levels and departments, there could be a considerable learning opportunity which could benefit the entire organisation. On the other hand, if employees do not recognise and respect each other's different perceptions of knowledge and the knowledge communication practices associated with these, it could lead to miscommunication and misunderstanding, and could potentially exacerbate the divide between members of a virtual team.

Identity prototypes as both cognitive and social

With regard to identities, interview participants can be seen as making sense of contexts and practices through their mental models of the identity prototypes with which they associate themselves. Jansen and Roodt (2014) describe prototypes as socially constructed archetypes. These archetypes seem similar to Van Dijk's 'mental models' as both are continuously (re) produced through interaction between social actors within a specific context. Because prototypes are social as well as cognitive, employees can analytically be seen as part of what this book has described as 'Identity Configurations'.

Such Identity Configurations should not be seen as either rigid categories or as communities in which everyone communicates and engages in practices with each other. Rather, 'identity configurations' are an analytical construct used to group employees who, through an analysis of the stories they tell in the interview, can be seen as sharing similar identities. Because identity prototypes can be seen as mental models through which participants retrospectively make sense of their practices, they may emerge more clearly in retrospective interviews than if observing the daily practices in the organisation. If prototypes, as argued by Jansen and Roodt (2014), can be seen as mental models accentuating both inter-group differences and intra-group similarity, then we might expect, in the light of Weick's theory of Sensemaking as Retrospective, that participants in research interviews will describe their practices with a high emphasis on establishing a fit between, on one hand, the actions and situations they describe, and on the other hand the identity prototypes with which they associate themselves. Thus, I do not assume that there can be any universal truth to be discovered in the interviews, but rather that the interviews should be seen as a series of Sensemaking perspectives on a shared reality. As Rhodes and Brown so eloquently put it: 'Ours is not a quest for scientific truth, but a quest for meaning' (2005, p. 167). Each of these participant perspectives can be seen reflecting a prototypical identity of a specific identity configuration.

These prototypes and the Sensemaking perspectives associated with them can be seen as Enacted in patterns of knowledge communication practices. This theoretical perspective implies that to find solutions to the challenges identified in virtual work environments (see Chapter 5), we need an understanding of not only the patterns of knowledge communication practices, but the Sensemaking perspectives underlying these practices.

Linking this discussion of identity to discourse theory, the negotiation of identity can be seen as an interaction between, on the one hand, social and institutional discourse practices forming a contextual landscape, which James Gee (2011) terms 'big "C" Conversations' while Fairclough (2003) uses the term 'orders of discourse'. But as I argued in the chapter on Discourse Analysis (Chapter 3) these (D)iscourses shape but, from my perspective, do not determine the discursive choices of the individual. Similarly, the need to maintain a coherent sense of identity limits the influence of (D)iscourses as these pass through a filter of Sensemaking. This filter consists of previous experiences and the need to maintain a plausible identity across contexts. In a similar vein, Billett (2007) argues for the 'potent mediating role being exercised in these negotiations [of identity] by the individual' (p. 57).

This perspective on identity as both having a personal and interpersonal dimension can be seen as grounded in Benwell and Stokoe's (2006) theories of identity (see Chapter 8). Both Weick (1995) and Benwell and Stokoe (2006) argue for the individual need to have a coherent sense of identity across social contexts, but identity formation in both theoretical perspectives can be seen as evolutionary in the sense that identity is adapted to the requirements of different social contexts. Yet despite this adaption, most of the core identity and the values and experiences on which it is based remains intact.

The next section will shift this discussion of identity towards the social and relational aspect, and how relationships impact on both the cognitive and social aspects of identity, as well as virtual Knowledge Communicating practices.

Relationships supporting virtual knowledge communication practices

Using terminology from Wenger (1998), the specific forms of 'Participation' and 'Reification' in the practices of different Communities of Practice (CoP) can be seen as influenced by the perception of knowledge in the community and the identity prototypes associated with this perception of knowledge. This book shares Wenger's (1998) argument that identity is grounded in Participation and Reification centred around the practices associated with specific knowledge domain of the CoP. But Wenger argues that it is the sense of community which gives rise to the social identity of the CoP members. This book, on the other hand, proposes that the Sensemaking process leading to specific perceptions of knowledge can also form a foundation for a sense of professional identity which the individual seeks to support through the CoP relationships in which the individual engages. Extending Wenger's theory, organisational CoPs can thus be seen as arising through the sense of identification between professionals sharing similar perceptions of knowledge.

The knowledge communication practices, as a form of Reification, can be seen as the basis for building both TMS, i.e., a knowledge of who-knows-what in the community, and for building mutual trust. The formation of a TMS can aid in the ability of a community or team to build on the different knowledge expertise within the community. The notion of different areas of knowledge expertise within a CoP reflect Wenger's (1998) notion of boundary brokers, who have the ability to bridge the gaps between administrative, social and geographic boundaries. In this capacity, Knowledge Brokers are highly important for a healthy communication of knowledge in a global organisation.

The research interview as context for Discursive Sensemaking

The perception of identity as sedimentary with a slowly changing core and an ever-changing surface, as argued in Chapter 8 has a number of implications for how research interviews can be used as data. First, interview statements, as (d)iscourse, can be seen as influenced by several social contexts which are rarely brought into focus in the (d)iscourse, but which can be seen as present in the Retention of the participant's Context Models. In this sense, Van Dijk's term 'Context Model' can be seen as similar to Gee's notion of 'big "C" Conversations', which also consists of the unstated background of (d)iscourse, i.e., a specific utterance. These contexts include, first, the semi-dispersed organisational context, second, the professional communities with which the participants associate themselves or, just as importantly, dissociate themselves from. Third they include national cultures, and the immediate context of the interview situation calling for self-representation in the best possible light.

I use Discourse Analysis as a means to untangle some of this web of discourses and individual perceptions and beliefs, knowing that my interpretations are only interpretations. Nevertheless, I build my interpretations on the assumption that although we all construct and reconstruct our identities in the social relations we engage in, we do so with a need for that construction to fit with our sense of self and fit the social contexts. This argument is supported by Weick's theories of Sensemaking (Weick, 1995, 2001). This sense of self may be a construction we build, repair, and reconstruct throughout our lives, but it still remains stable enough for us to construct a coherent account of our lives and actions, and it is this need for coherence across the communities and the interactions we engage in which make it possible to do studies based on interview data in which the stories told in research interviews are seen (however problematically) as reflecting participants' (cognitive) Sensemaking process and the (social) practices which they engage in. This includes the identity prototypes with which they associate themselves. This implies that the analyses in this book have not taken the interview statements as 1:1 representations of the inner states of participants (i.e., the cognitive level) or of the organisational contexts they describe (i.e., the context/social level). The interviews have rather be seen as expressions of how individuals make sense of their virtual knowledge communication practices and the virtual work environment in which those practices are undertaken.

Impact of findings on virtual knowledge communication

The findings indicate two main tendencies in perceptions of knowledge at HR Consult: a Knowledge Transfer approach, a knowledge creation approach and a Knowledge Broker. At HR Consult the three perceptions of knowledge tended to be polarised, and therefore seemed to have considerable implications for knowledge communication practices at HR Consult.

The Discursive Sensemaking of employees sharing the Knowledge Transfer perception of knowledge tended to have a high respect for HR Consult knowledge strategies and corporate vision. They perceived organisational knowledge as encoded into the tried and tested organisational knowledge products, such as PowerPoints, exercises and workshop materials. For these employees, the main role of the consultant in communicating organisational knowledge was to make sure that client understood and applied the knowledge as intended by HR Consult. For some consultants, such as Dorthe at HR Consult Denmark, this still meant considerable interaction with the client organisation to follow-up and make sure that the development programme was applied. But to others in the Knowledge Transfer Identity Configuration, such as the ones at HR Consult UK, this perception of knowledge meant a high focus on selling standardised HR Consult licences (known as accreditations) to clients combined with selling standardised, computer-generated personality profiles to all client staff, thereby ensuring maximum profit at little expense to HR Consult UK. Client practitioners with such licences would then be left with the responsibility for applying HR Consult training and development within their own company.

The perception of knowledge adopted by Henrik, exemplifying the Knowledge Creator, and by Linda, exemplifying the Knowledge Broker Prototype, differs from the Knowledge Transfer Prototype by seeing organisational knowledge as a process in ongoing transformation. This perception of knowledge means that organisational knowledge is used as ideas which form the basis for their time-consuming work to understand client challenges and to integrate client knowledge with HR Consult knowledge. However, the Knowledge Broker perception of knowledge differs from the Knowledge Creator in their use of their large network knowledge (i.e. What Wegner calls a Transacting Memory System (TMS, see Chapter 8). The Knowledge Broker uses this TMmS t differento find skills needed to solve a virtual team project.

This difference in perceptions of knowledge has two implications for knowledge communication at HR Consult. First, employees with different perceptions of the same knowledge products seem to have no incentive to communicate knowledge with each other. In fact, both Henrik and Linda express frustration that their colleagues and managers do not understand what they are doing, nor are they willing to commit to similar time-consuming knowledge creation activities. Using the vocabulary from Nonaka and Takeuchi's (1995) SECI model, the Knowledge Transfer Prototype can thus be seen as mainly Internalising and Externalising existing knowledge with few tacit presuppositions while the Knowledge Creator and the Knowledge Broker Prototype engage in completing a full SECI spiral of knowledge creation - i.e., Socialising with. The Knowledge Creator does not involve colleagues in this work, while the Knowledge Broker Prototype uses his/her dispersed global network within and beyond the organisation to build Knowledge Broker Teams with the ability to leverage the diversity of knowledge expertise within and beyond the team.

Implications of professional identity prototypes for virtual knowledge communication practices

Professional identities emerged as grounded in the different perceptions of organisational knowledge. This may not seem surprising given that, in a service sector context, the product is intangible knowledge products. This is also true for HR Consult who sell individual, team, sales and leadership development and training. What surprised me was how strongly values-based the consultants seemed to be in their very different perceptions of organisational knowledge. These differences emerged mainly between the Knowledge Transfer Prototype on one hand, and the Knowledge Creator and the Knowledge Broker on the other.

The Knowledge Transfer Prototype, Dorthe, at HR Consult Denmark, built her professional identity on respect for HR Consult knowledge products and the highly detailed instructions on how to implement them. This meant that knowledge communication centred on exchanging detailed information about how to implement a solution. In international projects this approach meant that project communication was limited to communication between the project coordinator and the individual consultants. Therefore, the consultants in Dorthe's project did not experience working together and did not build a sense of the different competencies within the team (i.e., a Transactive Memory System, TMS).

The Knowledge Creator, exemplified by Henrik, was a rare professional identity at HR Consult. Another participant in the UK, John, constructed a professional identity based on similar values, and both Henrik and John identified a few colleagues who shared a similar professional identity. Henrik centred his identity on the value of a time-consuming process of transforming HR Consult knowledge in interaction with the client, thereby building what Lave and Wenger (1991) describe as 'Situated learning'. He worked with a high level of autonomy, granted to him because of his ability to generate extra revenue when satisfied clients returned for more. Looking down on his local colleagues, such as Dorthe, due to their unwillingness to engage in the knowledge creation, Henrik preferred to perform his knowledge transformation without involving colleagues. The Knowledge Creator thus seems to find it difficult to communicate knowledge with the Knowledge Transfer Prototype because they disagree on the nature of useful knowledge, and Henrik's preference for working alone means that the value of his knowledge creation becomes difficult to leverage at an organisational level without support from colleagues and managers recognising the potential value of knowledge creation at all levels of the organisation.

The Knowledge Broker Prototype, exemplified by Linda, also engaged in transforming HR Consult's knowledge to apply and situate it within different client contexts. Like Henrik, she justifies her client-centred approach with reference to further revenue generated when satisfied clients return for more. But unlike the Knowledge Creator, Linda recognises the limits of her own expertise, and engages in interaction with colleagues to undertake this knowledge transformation collaboratively as a Knowledge Broker. Due to the lack of Knowledge Creators in her local environment, Linda used her abilities as a networker to identify consultants within and beyond HR Consult with the abilities needed for the project. She thereby builds a Knowledge Broker team characterised by its ability to build on reciprocal trust and on a deep knowledge of the different abilities within the team, i.e., a strong TMS.

Relationships and their impact on virtual knowledge communication practices

Like identities, relationships constitute one of the seven building tasks of language identified by Gee (2011, 2014). Wenger's *Communities of Practice* (CoP) theory (1998) also emphasises the importance of relationships and communication. But where Gee focuses on relationships as a discursive construction, Wenger emphasises relationships within Communities of Practice (CoP) as the core of human Sensemaking and sense of identity.

Similarly, in the analyses of interview data, relationships were, on one hand, a linguistic or discursive construction of the participants' perception of self and other. These discursive constructions were used as a foundation on which to construct professional identity. But on the other hand, the relationships constructed were used to justify the participants' Discursive

Sensemaking about their virtual knowledge communication practices, and as a source of finding meaning in their work as consultants at HR Consult.

Because knowledge was already constructed by HR Consult R&D, Dorthe as an example of a Knowledge Transfer Prototype, seemed to find little meaning in building relationships around creating and communication of knowledge built through her work as consultant. For the Knowledge Transfer Prototype, emphasis was put on relationships where they felt a level of emotional connection, which can best be described using McAllister's (1995) concept Affect-based trust. The effect of this approach on relationships can be seen in the division in the UK Client Relations Management Team, where the Knowledge Transfer prototypes did not seem to engage in relationships with consultants such as Linda and John, who do find meaning in building relationships based on communication of their knowledge creations and in exchanging ideas and new applications of HR Consult knowledge.

In the interview with Henrik in particular, the polarisation of professional identities into separate CoPs in the organisation emerged as a significant finding. Henrik argues that his participation in a globally dispersed CoP of consultants who share his identity as Knowledge Creators provides meaning for him to the extent that he states that the CoP is the reason he stays at HR Consult Denmark. At HR Consult Denmark he does not feel that his time-consuming knowledge transformation is acknowledged and leveraged by either colleagues or managers.

Linda, as an example of a Knowledge Broker Prototype, expresses a similar frustration that neither her colleagues nor her managers seem interested in lifting the knowledge she has created with her globally dispersed Knowledge Broker team. Her construction of the team shows how trusted weak ties and chance meetings can be used to establish strong virtual knowledge communication relations between colleagues with similar professional identities. Despite being dispersed across three continents, the team demonstrates an ability to use a strong knowledge of the different areas of expertise, i.e., a strong TMS, to leverage the different strengths of each team member, thereby collectively creating a solution tailored to the client's needs.

To sum up, the findings demonstrate the interconnection of perceptions of knowledge and configurations of professional identities which were supported in configurations of relationships in more or less siloed CoPs at HR Consult. The case is not necessarily representative in this respect, but as a critical case, it demonstrates that despite an organisational culture building a (D)iscourse which seems to value a Knowledge Transfer approach to knowledge communication, professional identities emerge resisting this approach. These identities seem to be centred on different perceptions of what useful knowledge is in their work as a consultant. Because of the availability of ICT (Information and Communication Technology), employees with professional identities resisting organisational (D)iscourse show the ability to build dispersed networks and CoPs which may even, as in Linda's case, transcend organisational boundaries.

Implications for the book's readers

The findings presented in this book have implications which reach beyond HR Consult. The research shows how perceptions of knowledge, professional identities, and the relationships used to support those identities are intertwined and have considerable impact on knowledge communication practices in a global organisation, HR Consult. Although the specific findings of how the three knowledge communication aspects affect knowledge communication within the HR Consult may not be generalisable, their nature as co-constitutive and intertwined and their impact on knowledge communication practices may well be generalisable to other organisations and sectors.

This possibility for generalisability despite the limitations presented in the previous section also arises from the status of HR Consult as a critical case exemplifying an organisation in which knowledge creation occurred mainly in the R&D department, and where local offices were largely independent organisations, although partly owned by the main organisation. By centring the study on the consultant level, the case might lead to expectations that employee professional identities centred on how to best use the detailed HR Consult knowledge products to address client challenges, i.e., that consultant's exhibited knowledge communication behaviour similar to the Knowledge Transfer Prototype. Instead, the study shows first how employees can form identities and knowledge communication practices which call organisational (D)iscourses, practices and strategies into question. And second, how these employees, despite being marginalised in their local work environments, are able to build global relationships with like-minded colleagues across and beyond the global organisation to support this resistance to an organismal discourse.

This use of ICT to find a social basis for identities which may be marginalised in local departments or organisations seems likely to apply to other organisations and other sectors. Furthermore, the two marginalised identities at the consultant level of HR Consult seem to be potential knowledge leaders with the potential to innovate and transform organisational strategies and products.

Implications for organisations

The findings suggest that organisations might benefit from an increased awareness of the configurations of professional identities and how they affect knowledge communication practices within the global organisation. By understanding the knowledge communities formed informally by employees to support similar professional identities, organisations can become better at intentionally supporting and leading these communities. One strategy to explore could be building bridges between configurations of professional identities by building (D)iscourses around the strengths and challenges of different professional identities in their approaches to organisational knowledge.

Implications for project managers

Key challenges for project managers described in virtual team literature include selecting team members and guiding team practices, especially with regard to communicating knowledge in the project. By raising awareness of the influence of perceptions of knowledge on the professional identities and relationships which employees engage in, project managers gain a tool for improving this process.

Linda's case in particular, and the division among consultants in the Client Relations Management Team of which she is a part, points to the need for project managers to increase awareness of the configurations of different professional identities. They could benefit from the findings of the study by increasing awareness of the strengths and challenges of different professional identities and their perceptions of knowledge. This increased awareness seems to have two implications. First, in selecting team members for the project, awareness of potential team members' hypothetically different perceptions of knowledge could help guide the selection of team members for particular roles and tasks within the project. Second, the book provides project managers with a vocabulary for helping team members reflect on their identities in relation to knowledge communication practices within and beyond the project. This vocabulary can help make the team explicitly aware of different perceptions of organisational knowledge and how it can affect practices and their understanding of their roles in the project. Thereby, the vocabulary, addresses not only different areas of expertise, but also relationships to support team knowledge communication practices.

Perceptions of knowledge, professional identity and relationships can therefore be used by project managers as discussion points early in the team life cycle to acknowledge and leverage the diversity of the team, and to build an effective TMS in the team.

Implications for virtual teams

Virtual teams might benefit from the book by specifically addressing team differences in perceptions of organisational knowledge, such as seen in the Knowledge Transfer Prototype, the Knowledge Creator Prototype and the Knowledge Broker Prototype at HR Consult. This might help the team de-personalise interpersonal conflicts and differences in practice thereby decreasing the challenges in the division of the Client Relations Management Team at HR Consult, for example.

Future research directions

Future research might examine how perceptions of knowledge, identities and relationships affect knowledge communication within other organisations and other sectors. Further research might approach this from several angles including but not limited to research on intrapreneurship, action research and project management. After presenting these three possible research directions, I suggest how Discursive Sensemaking Analysis might be applied in other studies.

One possible direction for future research could be using the three key knowledge communication aspects identified in the project (perception of knowledge, professional identity and relationships), to explore the potential for knowledge creating within global organisations. The findings from the analysis of the interviews with Linda and Henrik show how organisational culture and middle management practice can risk strangling the innovative knowledge creating spirit. The book shows how a focus on the intersections of perception of knowledge, professional identity and relationships can reveal intrapreneurial communities within an organisation. At HR Consult, these intrapreneurial prototypes, the Knowledge Creator and the Knowledge Broker Prototype, were seen by middle managers as difficult to manage and difficult to understand. The three knowledge communication aspects identified in this book could be used to explore entrepreneurship in other organisations and other sectors. Thus, future research might fruitfully explore how and whether organisational intrapreneurship is identified, recognised and leveraged in other organisations.

Action research might also fruitfully examine whether an intentional focus on the intersections between perceptions of knowledge, professional identities and relationships can help team members and project managers to build and manage more effective semi-dispersed teams. Action research is an interactive inquiry process that balances problem solving actions implemented in a collaborative context with data-driven collaborative analysis or research to understand underlying causes enabling future predictions about personal and organisational change (Reason & Bradbury, 2002).

Within research on project management, this project also offers opportunities for further research on how the three intertwined knowledge communication aspects can be used to understand and improve the selection process and the teamwork for semi-dispersed projects.

The method developed for the study, Discursive Sensemaking Analysis, was built on a multidisciplinary theoretical foundation. No single scholar can review sufficiently each of the fields covered by this multidisciplinary approach, but the field of Discourse Analysis has arguably suffered the most, and Discursive Sensemaking Analysis will therefore need further integration within this field. Particularly, further work needs to be carried out to integrate it with Van Dijk's (2014) socio-cognitive approach to knowledge, which seems to be aligned with Weick's Sensemaking theory, although Van Dijk (2014) does not cite Weick. Despite these limitations, the combination the three knowledge communication aspects with, on one hand, Sensemaking as (social) cognition of both identity and context, and, on the other hand, (d)iscourses as a linguistic representation of this (social) cognition may fruitfully be adopted by future research. The wider applicability of the Discursive Sensemaking Analysis method developed for the project arises from the detailed description of each step of the project from design of the interview guide and initial coding stages to development of a feasible transcription system for prosodic details through to considerations for structuring the writing up of findings. Within business and management studies, DA approaches rarely seem to be described with this level of transparency. Although I recognise that the method does not live up to the level of detail expected in DA approaches within Linguistics and Applied Linguistics, DA approaches within Business Studies and the Social Sciences rarely provide the more detailed linguistic analysis undertaken by this book through Discursive Sensemaking Analysis.

References

Benwell, B., & Stokoe, E. (2006). *Discourse and identity*. Edinburgh: Edinburgh University Press.

Billett, S. (2007). Work, subjectivity and learning. In *Work, subjectivity and learning* (pp. 1–20). Dordrecht: Springer.

Gee, J. P. (2011). *An introduction to discourse analysis*. London: Routledge.

Gee, J. P. (2014). *How to do discourse analysis: A toolkit*. London: Routledge.

Fairclough, N. (2003). *Analyzing discourse. Textual analysis for social research*. London: Routledge.

Jansen, P. G., & Roodt, G. (2014). Conceptualising and measuring work identity. Retrieved from: http://link.springer.com/book/10.1007/978-94-017-9242-4

Lave, J., & Wenger, E. (1991). *Situated learning: Legitimate peripheral participation*. Cambridge: Cambridge University Press.

McAllister, D. J. (1995). Affect-based and cognition-based trust as foundations for interpersonal cooperation in organizations. *Academy of Management Journal, 38*(1), 24–59. doi: 10.5465/256727

Nonaka, I., & Takeuchi, H. (1995). *Knowledge-creating company: How Japanese companies create the dynamics of innovation*. Oxford: Oxford University.

Reason, P., & Bradbury, H. (2002). Action research: An opportunity for revitalizing research purpose and practices. *Qualitative Social Work, 2*(2), 155–175.

Rhodes, C., & Brown, A. D. (2005). Narrative, organizations and research. *International Journal of Management Reviews*, 7(3), 167–188. doi: 10.1111/j.1468-2370.2005.00112.x

Van Dijk, T. A. (2005). Contextual knowledge management in discourse production. In R. Wodak & P. Chilton (Eds.). *A new agenda in (critical) discourse analysis* (pp. 71–100). Amsterdam: John Benjamins. doi: 10.1007/0-387-36921-X_12

Van Dijk, T. A. (2014). *Discourse and knowledge: A sociocognitive approach.* Cambridge: Cambridge University Press.

Weick, K. E. (1995). *Sensemaking in organizations.* London: Sage

Weick, K. E. (2001). *Making sense of the organization.* Oxford: Blackwell.

Wenger, E. (1998). *Communities of practice: Learning, meaning, and identity.* New York: Cambridge University Press.

Glossary

Definitions tend to oversimplify concepts, but can nevertheless be a useful point of reference and departure. This glossary provides short definitions of all capitalised words in the book.

Ability trust To what extent we believe that a colleague embodies the competencies needed to perform their tasks.

Affect-based trust Trust belief based on positive feelings towards an employee. Typically, people might say that they have a good chemistry, or 'we just clicked'.

Ba An intangible mental space, which is the foundation for knowledge creation. Ba can be both physical, mental and/or virtual.

Benevolence Trust The intentions and motivations of an employee and whether these go beyond egocentric profit making. This component of trust blossoms when the employee feels appreciated in a win-win relationship, where the value is created and distributed in a fair manner.

Building Tasks The seven things we construct in language are (refer to the relevant glossary terms for definitions): significance, practices (activities), identities, relationships, politics (distribution of social goods), connections, and sign systems and knowledge.

Changing Ecology A social situation which is dynamic and changing thereby requiring ongoing Sensemaking processes.

Cognition based trust Trust belief based on knowledge about another employee.

Combination The process of creating new knowledge by combining existing Explicit knowledge.

Community of practice A group of people who interact on a regular basis to learn and develop a shared knowledge domain and the practices attached to it.

Connections Through (D)iscourse, we build connections between concepts, e.g. through metaphors, between sentences, e.g. by using pronouns and adverbs such as 'nevertheless', and between discourses, e.g. through repetition of aspects of past conversations.

Context Context is not 'just out there'; it is something people actively construe, negotiate over, and change their minds about. Thus context is simultaneously a cognitive mental model, and a socially constructed phenomenon.

Conversations Also known as 'grand' or 'mega' discourse or 'orders of discourse'. Refers to the larger social discussions such as the importance of staying healthy or the culture of an organisation. They remain as a background which is occasionally brought to the foreground to be supported or resisted in discourse.

Critical Discourse Analysis Discourse Analysis in a critical vein analyses how hegemonic power structures are inforced through politics, mass media and education thereby marginalising voices and enforcing inequality in gender, race or religion.

Deontic modality When a modal verb, such as 'may' or 'must', is used to affect a situation by giving permission or assigning obligation, this is deontic modality.

Discourse This concept is essentially fuzzy, but can be broadly defined as language in use within specific situations for specific purposes. It can also be defined as the process of sensemaking through text and talk. A common ground in the disparate approaches is the perception of language as active, processual and outcome orientated. Discourses can be divided into little 'd' discourse, which is a specific text or utterance gaining specific meaning in a specific context, and big 'D' Discourse, which includes other semiotic elements such as specific clothing and gestures used to pull off being, for example, a father, a judge or businessman. See also Conversations.

Discourse Analysis A qualitative approach to the analysis of social phenomena, often with an emphasis on how (d)iscourse is used to invoke or resist larger social Conversations, and how (D)isourse is used to perform specific social identities.

Ecological Change A change in the normal practise or in the social situation.

Enact/Enactment When deciding how to react to a situation, we chose our actions based on what worked in the past, and what can plausibly support our sense of identity.

Equivocal/Equivocality The term is used to describe situations in which there is no single 'correct' interpretation or enactment, and in which the current Retention does not necessarily provide an answer.

Explicit Knowledge This is the aspect of knowledge which has been articulated in words or documents. Explicit knowledge always has a Tacit dimension which is presupposed and left unsaid.

Externalisation The process of transforming Tacit knowledge into a more Explicit form.

Extracted Cues The elements and perspectives which are selected for storing in Retention or used as a basis for Enactment.

Generalisability In quantitative studies, the size of the population determines the possibility for generalising findings to larger populations. In qualitative research, findings cannot be generalised unproblematically. However, theories built on qualitative data can be tested in other settings to increase generalisabilty.

Identity In this book identity can be defined as a mental model which consists of both a deeper sense of self and a more surface level where several social identities are performed, or socially through participation, negotiated in response to demands of specific social situations.

Identity Configuration Describes employees with similar perceptions of knowledge, a similar professional identity and a similar use of relationships to support their practices and identities.

Identity Prototype A mental model of the idealised identity, which an employee tries to live up to in the Sensemaking process. They represent identities which are most like in group and least like out group. This book identifies three Identity Prototypes, the Knowledge Creator, the Knowledge Broker and the Knowledge Transfer Prototypes, see separate entries for a definition of each prototype. see also the entry for 'Identity Configurations'.

Information and Communication Technology Collective term for technologies such as mobile phones and computers.

Integrity trust To what extent we believe that a colleague adheres to acceptable principles and keeps the promises he/she makes.

Internalisation The process of transforming Explicit knowledge into a more Tacit form through learning.

Intonation Unit A stretch of language consideration of one Intonation contour, typically marked a brief pause or Pitch change.

Joint Enterprise A sense of community based on a shared practise.

Knowledge Broker Prototype Thrives on using their networking skills to build virtual teams equipped to build new Knowledge tailored to client needs. Doesn't miss challenging organisational strategies and practices.

Knowledge Creator Prototype Thrives on a work environment where they can satisfy their intellectual need for creating complex knowledge solutions. Finds motivation in participating in a Community of Practise with like-minded colleagues. Doesn't miss challenging organisational strategies and practices.

Knowledge Management The collection of methods relating to creating, sharing, using and managing the knowledge and information of an organisation. It refers to a multidisciplinary approach to achieve organisational objectives by making the best use of knowledge. (Wikipedia)

Knowledge Transfer Prototype Thrives on delivering predesigned solutions as intact as possible. Finds motivation in Affect-based relationships and in living up to cooperate strategies.

Knowledge Team A high-performing virtual team building on weak trusted ties to communicate complex knowledge thereby solving projects to high customer satisfaction.

Lexical choice We build significance through the words we select. For example, by choosing 'cordial' over 'heartily' to increase formality.

Mental Model To reduce complexity, we build simplified mental models of contexts, knowledge, identities and relationships.

Modal verb Verb expressing obligation or permission, for example, 'must' or 'can'.

Pace The speed with which an intonation unit is pronounced.

Phenomenology/Phenomenological A philosophy of science position. Its main point is that consciousness and object are not separate but co-constitutive; consciousness is always consciousness about something, and an object is always an object for someone.

Pitch range The difference between a speaker's highest and lowest pitch over a stretch of time.

Post-structuralism Post-structuralism rejects the structuralist notion that the dominant word in a pair (e.g. 'good' versus 'evil') is dependent on its counterpart and instead argues that founding knowledge either on pure experience (phenomenology) or on systematic structures (structuralism) is impossible.

Practices Through (D)iscourse, we build institutionally and culturally recognised ways of doing things.

Pragmatic A stand of Linguistics concerned with the intersection of context (social situation) and language, examining the way the context, Intonation and stress can create situated meaning beyond the literal, constative function. Phrases, sentences and texts are considered as speech acts, with specific purposes and effects.

Prosody, prososdic cues Collective term for five characteristics of how we say things. Consists of Stress, Intonation, Pitch, volume and Pace.

Reification Making something abstract real, for example, by writing a text or producing a picture. In Community of Practise theory such knowledge objects can be seen as the physical outcome of participation in a community.

Replication, replicability of research The ability to repeat a scientific inquiry within a different setting getting the same results.

Retention Consists of past experiences, mental models and the identities we have built over time.

Retrospective/retrospection We make sense of the world through our past experiences and the identities we have built over time. We also build on past experiences and identities when deciding how to act in response to complex situations.

Sensemaking Describes the mental and social process of making sense of a changing environment or social situation. Sensemaking is guided by past experiences and current identity.

Significance One of the seven Building tasks of language in use. We constantly make Prosodic, Syntactic and Lexical choices to render some meanings, phrases or words more important than others.

Situated knowledge Learning (or knowing) which is adapted to specific contexts and practices, rather than being general and abstract.

Social Good Typically defined as an action that provides some sort of benefit to the others. Examples include trust, cooperation, clean air, water, education.

Socialisation Through a master/apprentice like interaction, tacit knowledge can be communicated to others.

Sociology of Knowledge Approach to Discourse Interested in the social production, circulation and transformation of knowledge.

Stress Stress can be used rhetorically to add significance to a word or phrase.

Syntax, syntactic choice The word order and phrases in a sentence, such as noun phrases and verb phrases. Syntax can be used rhetorically to add significance to certain phrases or to hide who is performing an action as in the phrase 'I'm told' which doesn't say who is doing the telling.

Tacit knowledge Unspoken aspect of knowledge which can be difficult to communicate to others due to its embodied or ingrained nature. It is always an aspect of explicit knowledge.

Transactive Memory System Knowledge of who knows what in the organisation. This knowledge may be formalised in an online database or intranet, or be an aspect of personally held knowledge.

Validity In quantitative studies, validity refers to a measure of how reliable a result is. In qualitative studies, validity cannot be measured and this book suggests considering quality of craftsmanship instead.

Virtual Team Aka 'distributed', 'dispersed' or 'hybrid' team. Virtual teams work together primarily, but rarely exclusively, using Information and Communication Technology often across vocational, geographical, temporal and/or oganisational boundaries.

Virtual Knowledge Communication All teams constantly communicate knowledge to solve tasks. But communication of knowledge goes beyond mere transfer of bodies of knowledge. The choice of 'communication' rather than 'transfer' or 'sharing' indicates that communication of professional knowledge is challenging and requires knowledge not only of one's own knowledge domain, but also knowledge about what others in the team know (see also Transactive Memory System).

Volume Refers to how loud a phrase or word is spoken.

Appendix A

Transcription conventions

Sign	*Description*
/	Rising intonation in the following part of the intonation unit – If this persists throughout the intonation unit it typically indicates a question.
\	Falling intonation in the following words – if the sign precedes the last syllables of an intonation unit, it typically constitutes the verbal equivalent of a full stop.
Word	Italicised word is emphasised through higher volume.
^	Indicates that the following is spoken in high pitch. This is often used to add emphasis or create a contrast to the previous discourse.
_word	Indicates that the intonation unit is spoken in low pitch. This is often used to indicate a foregone conclusion or information which the speaker seems is obvious or a self-evident piece of information. But depending on the context, it may also indicate tiredness or frustration on the part of the speaker.
=	Indicates that the following is spoken in mid-pitch. The code is only used if the pitch shifts from high to mid-pitch within an intonation unit. If the entire intonation unit is spoken in mid-pitch, this is not noted in the transcription.
.	Final contour – the verbal equivalent of a full stop at the end of an intonation unit. Can end a sentence fragment in oral discourse to add emphasis to the preceding constituent as in the following example where emphasis is added to 'guys', who are given the predicate 'good people' in the next intonation unit: '/So ^these \guys. (.) /They're good ^people.' ('Henrik', my translation, 303, 1:00:37).
,	Continuing contour – the verbal equivalent of a comma at the end of an intonation unit. This can occur in mid-sentence to emphasise certain grammatical elements. For example, the continuing contour is used in the following (Combined with fronting the adverbial to sentence initial position) to add emphasis to the location where the speaker feels at home: '/and there, (.) \I feel at home there.' ('Henrik', my translation, 303, 1:00:37).

(.)	Pause, less than a second.
(..)	Pause, more than a second.
--	Utterance cut off – interruption by self or another speaker. If the utterance is cut off by another intonation unit (i.e., a new line), the new intonation unit will be started by "--" to indicate that it follows immediately on from the previous intonation unit.
[faster pace]	Pace of enunciation, which can also be described as a faster rhythm has not been assigned a shorthand but will be indicated in square brackets on a separate line before the passage to indicate that it pertains to all following lines until a new square bracket with e.g.: '[normal pace]'. If the faster pace pertains only to one intonation unit, '[faster pace]' will be inserted at the beginning of that intonation unit and will be assumed to return to normal in the next intonation unit.
£word£	Words between £-symbols are spoken while laughing.

Index

Note: **Bold** page numbers refer to tables; *italic* page numbers refer to figures and page numbers followed by "n" denote endnotes.

For Product Safety Concerns and Information please contact our EU
representative GPSR@taylorandfrancis.com
Taylor & Francis Verlag GmbH, Kaufingerstraße 24, 80331 München, Germany

www.ingramcontent.com/pod-product-compliance
Ingram Content Group UK Ltd.
Pitfield, Milton Keynes, MK11 3LW, UK
UKHW021306260926
475702UK00048B/745
* 9 7 8 0 3 6 7 8 5 7 9 5 0 *